African Synodal Theology

African Synodal Theology

♦

A Tall Tree Is as Strong as Its Roots

Edited by
AGBONKHIANMEGHE E. OROBATOR

ORBIS BOOKS
Maryknoll, New York 10545

Founded in 1970, Orbis Books endeavors to publish works that enlighten the mind, nourish the spirit, and challenge the conscience. The publishing arm of the Maryknoll Fathers and Brothers, Orbis seeks to explore the global dimensions of the Christian faith and mission, to invite dialogue with diverse cultures and religious traditions, and to serve the cause of reconciliation and peace. The books published reflect the views of their authors and do not represent the official position of the Maryknoll Society. To learn more about Maryknoll and Orbis Books, please visit our website at www.orbisbooks.com.

Copyright © 2025 by Agbonkhianmeghe E. Orobator

Published by Orbis Books, Box 302, Maryknoll, NY 10545-0302.

All rights reserved.

No part of this publication may be reproduced or transmitted in any form or by any means, electronic or mechanical, including photocopying, recording, or any information storage or retrieval system, without prior permission in writing from the publisher.

All Vatican documents can be found at www.vatican.va.

Queries regarding rights and permissions should be addressed to: Orbis Books, P.O. Box 302, Maryknoll, NY 10545-0302.

Manufactured in the United States of America

Library of Congress Cataloging-in-Publication Data

Names: Orobator, A. E. editor
Title: African synodal theology : a tall tree is as strong as its roots / edited by Agbonkhianmeghe E. Orobator.
Description: Maryknoll, NY : Orbis Books, [2025] | Includes bibliographical references and index. | Summary: "African theologians reflect on synodality showing how African culture can contribute to the synodal path of the universal church"— Provided by publisher.
Identifiers: LCCN 2025021523 (print) | LCCN 2025021524 (ebook) | ISBN 9781626986442 trade paperback | ISBN 9798888660980 epub
Subjects: LCSH: Church renewal—Catholic Church | Councils and synods | Church—Catholicity | Christianity and culture—Africa | Theology, Doctrinal—Africa | Catholic Church—Doctrines
Classification: LCC BX1746 .A58 2025 (print) | LCC BX1746 (ebook)
LC record available at https://lccn.loc.gov/2025021523
LC ebook record available at https://lccn.loc.gov/2025021524

Contents

Acknowledgments vii

Introduction: Of Roots and Trees ix
     Agbonkhianmeghe E. Orobator

1. A Spirituality of Synodality:
   Drawing from the Wells of African Spirituality 1
       Anne Arabome

2. Theological Foundations of Synodality 23
       Marcel Uwineza

3. Communication and the Synodal Church:
   Ngiga as an African Symbol of Synodality 45
       Chijioke Azuawusiefe

4. Scriptural Foundations of a Synodal Church 65
       Josée Ngalula

5. Synodality or the "Remodeling" of the Church 83
       José Minaku Lukoli

6. Dialogue, Discernment, and Trust—
   An Ethic for Synodality in a Global, Divided Church 100
       Anthony Egan

7. Religious Women Teachers of Synodality:
   The "Abundant Catch" of the Peripheries 121
       Léocadie Lushombo

8. The Gift of Authority in a Synodal Church 143
       Ludovic Lado

9. Consecrated Women Religious Journeying Together
   for a Missionary Synodal Church in Africa 163
   Veronica Jemanyur Rop

10. Theological Foundations of Co-Responsibility 183
    David Kaulemu

11. A Synodal Church of the Young and the Young at Heart . . . 201
    Sheila Leocádia Pires

Afterword: Ubuntu, Dance, and Poetry of Synodality 221
    William O'Neill

Contributors 225
Index 231

Acknowledgments

The African Synodality Initiative (ASI) operates under the auspices of the Jesuit Conference of Africa and Madagascar (JCAM). ASI's goal is to develop creative ideas and resources to support local churches in Africa, enabling them to engage fruitfully and constructively in the synodal process as the pilgrim and missionary People of God. We are deeply grateful to the European Family Foundation that generously provided the resources to make this publication possible. Special thanks go to all the partners and collaborators of ASI, including the president, staff, and personnel of JCAM.

Orbis publisher Robert Ellsberg was, as always, a wonderful colleague to work with. Sincere thanks to the students, faculty, and staff of the Jesuit School of Theology of Santa Clara University. I am deeply grateful for the companionship, friendship, and love of Oghomwen n'Oghomwen Anne Arabome, SSS, and Chuks Afiawari, SJ. Their unwavering support sustains me, and I consider it a true privilege to have them in my life.

At the time of writing and editing this volume, Pope Francis was still alive. In honor of his passing and in gratitude for his legacy of synodality, these essays have not been edited to mark his death. We have opted to maintain the language in which they were originally written, fully aware that they will be published during the pontificate of Pope Leo XIV.

Introduction

Of Roots and Trees

Agbonkhianmeghe E. Orobator

> The time has come to take a courageous step forward and to develop a theology of synodality, a theological reflection that can help, encourage and accompany the synodal process, for a new, more creative and daring missionary phase, inspired by the *kerygma* and involving every component of the Church's life.[1]

Synodality is an ecclesiology in need of a theology. From the International Theological Commission (ITC) to Pope Francis and the Synod on Synodality (2021–2024), intense efforts abound to construct a theology for synodality. Pope Francis recognizes this necessity in his critical articulation of the shape of a fundamentally contextual theology and declares that a "synodal, missionary, and 'outgoing' Church" needs a corresponding "outgoing" theology.[2] Far from being an acquired asset, synodality presents a theological task to articulate a synodal way of being Church (Final Document of the Synod on Synodality [FD] 30, 87).

---

[1] Address of the Holy Father to Participants in the Plenary Session of the International Theological Commission, November 28, 2024.

[2] Pope Francis, *Ad theologiam promovendam*, November 1, 2023.

The nature of theology and the role of the theologian in this enterprise of synodal construction have been variously identified, emphasized, and underscored. The ministry of theologians is "a service to the People of God," and theologians "are called to foster an encounter with Christ and to attain a deeper understanding of his mystery, so that we can better appreciate 'what is the breadth and length and height and depth, and to know the love of Christ that surpasses all knowledge' (Eph 3:18–19)."[3] To accomplish this task, theology assumes the nature of light precisely because it makes visible hidden contours and emerging features of a synodal Church.[4]

Between Inspiration and Aspiration

The term *synodality* may seem a novel idea, but as an ecclesial tradition and episcopal practice, it has a long and venerable history.[5] Quiet clearly, Pope Francis did not invent the notion of synodality, nor does he hold a personal patent on it. However, more than any of his predecessors, Francis has elevated the profile of synodality, created a compelling vision of synodality, and positioned the Church firmly on the synodal path, believing that "the journey of synodality is the journey that God wants from his Church in the third millennium."[6]

The documents of the Synod on Synodality repeatedly reference Vatican II as the inspiration for synodality. Theologians, experts, and the International Theological Commission routinely

---

[3] Pope Francis, *Ad theologiam promovendam*, November 1, 2023.
[4] See Address of the Holy Father to Participants in the International Congress on the Future of Theology Organized by the Dicastery for Culture and Education, December 9, 2024.
[5] ITC, Synodality in the Life and Mission of the Church, March 2, 2018, 3.
[6] Pope Francis, address commemorating the fiftieth anniversary of the institution of the Synod of Bishops, October 17, 2015.

draw the link, suggesting that synodality is the coming to fruition of the council or its maturation. The Final Document is explicit and categorical on this point.

> Rooted in the Tradition of the Church, the entire synodal journey took place in the light of the conciliar magisterium. The Second Vatican Council was indeed like a seed thrown onto the field of the world and the Church.... The Synod 2021–2024 continues to draw upon the energy of that seed and develop its potential. The synodal journey is indeed putting into practice what the Council taught about the Church as Mystery and Church as People of God, called to holiness through continual conversion that comes from listening to the Gospel. In this sense, the synodal journey constitutes an authentic further act of reception of the Council, thus deepening its inspiration and reinvigorating its prophetic force for today's world. (5)

Undeniably, the resonances between Vatican II and the Synod on Synodality are strong with regard to basic understandings such as the primacy of baptism, the Church as the People of God, and other such ideas as papal primacy and episcopal collegiality. Besides, the Synod of Bishops owes its origins directly to Vatican II.

Beyond being an act of reception and implementation of Vatican II, the synodal process constitutes a further development of contemporary ecclesiology. In other words, while drawing on the inspiration of Vatican II, synodality offers something new in the form of an impetus for innovation and aspiration. The examples are many, but a few would suffice, such as the principle of co-responsibility of all the faithful for the life and mission of Church without creating a division of labor between bishops and clergy, who govern the Church, and lay women and men, who operate in the secular sphere; the imperatives of relationality, listening, and discernment for the Church; and the importance of interiority as the sources of synodal aspirations and conversion.

Unlike the tendency in Vatican II to assign church leadership to the ordained and "secular duties and activities" to the laity—"citizens of two cities," according to *Gaudium et spes*—synodality calls us to acknowledge that the People of God, through their baptismal identity and dignity, are also called and commissioned to exercise responsibility for mission within the Church. *Gaudium et spes* articulates this when it states, "The laity are called to participate actively in the whole life of the Church" (43). The key phrase here is "the whole life of the Church." Achieving such participation counts as an essential objective of synodality.

Thus synodality hardly repackages Vatican II. While there is inspiration in Vatican II, there is aspiration and innovation in synodality. There is tension as well, particularly in relation to the triangulation of papal primacy, episcopal institution, and synodal ecclesiology. How these three elements intersect and interact remains an open question that neither the Final Document nor the bishop of Rome, as "guarantor of synodality," can resolve (131). In a true synodal fashion, the ensuing tension, friction, and dissonance may eventually be resolved only in the course of the journey,[7] for the path is made only by walking it.

Ecclesial Metaphors

The language of synodality proffers a feast of metaphors: path, journey, way, tent, and road. Some of these have served as inspiration for the initiatives of local churches, for example, the

---

[7] Massimo Faggioli, "The End of the Synod … and the Beginning of Synodality," *Commonweal*, November 13, 2024, www.commonwealmagazine.org/end-synod.

Introduction: Of Roots and Trees　　　　　　　　　　　　　　　　　xiii

Synodal Path in Germany and the Plenary Council in Australia. These metaphors are important for several reasons. First, there is a dynamic quality about them: they presuppose a goal and a destination. A synodal path is neither an aimless enterprise nor a meaningless endeavor, much less pointless banter simply for the sake or for the fun of it. "We think that doing synodality is joining hands and going for a walk, partying with the boys … or doing a survey of opinions" (Pope Francis, 29 November 2019). Walking the path of synodality represents a purpose-driven effort to become the community called Church according to the mind of God.

Second, the imagery suggests a diversity of participants and charisms of the Body of Christ engaged in the synodal journey and who "seek to recognize together 'what the Spirit is saying to the churches'" (Revelation 2:7; FD 82). The entire People of God are co-travelers at different points or stages of the journey, but no one is left behind, excluded, or marginalized on account of his or her status; see the story of John racing ahead of Peter to the tomb but waiting for Peter to enter first (John 20:1–9). "A synodal style allows local Churches to move at different paces. Differences in pace can be valued as an expression of legitimate diversity and as an opportunity for sharing gifts and mutual enrichment" (FD 124).

Third, in a synodal Church, answers to matters of consequence are not determined ahead of the dialogue; we make the way by walking. On the synodal path, the People of God place themselves on a journey toward the truth; the truth is no longer the acquired and exclusive preserve of the ordained or the consecrated. One of the primary features or graces of synodality lies in the fact that it relativizes the presumed power by the clerical class to determine the agenda of the ecclesial community. Charting the course, clearing the path, and setting the direction is a shared task of the People of God. The agenda is the fruit of a collective discernment, of the Church on the road. "A mother teaches her children to walk by walking alongside them" (FD 24).

The variety of images illustrates and points to the dynamic nature of a synodal Church. "Synod" is a verb, not a noun. Walking together on the road. It is not merely abstract or theoretical.[8] The original vision of Vatican II was codified into a Synod of Bishops as a periodic convening of bishops around the pope to address topical matters. No matter how fulfilling and consoling these ordinary or special intermittent gatherings in Rome were, they neither approximated the meaning nor fulfilled the promise of synodality as a dynamic process. Used in its proper form as a verb, "to synod" points to the ongoing tasks of practicing listening, discernment, and dialogue in a dynamic, creative, and innovative manner, and to foster participation, deepen communion, and enhance mission.

> Synodality is the walking together of Christians with Christ and towards God's Kingdom, in union with all humanity. Orientated towards mission, synodality involves gathering at all levels of the Church for mutual listening, dialogue, and community discernment. It also involves reaching consensus as an expression of Christ rendering Himself present, He who is alive in the Spirit. (FD 28)

Rather than being a one-off event, "the Synod is a process that engages the whole Church and everyone in the Church, each according to his or her function, charism and ministry."[9]

As a constitutive dimension of the life and mission of the Church, synodality envisions a shared experience to which the entire People of God are called as valued stakeholders. It bears reiterating that we make the path by walking it. This process of "synodification" will require a sustained level of work on the part

---

[8] General Secretariat of the Synod, *Instrumentum Laboris* (IL) for the second session of the Sixteenth Ordinary General Assembly of the Synod of Bishops, September 7, 2024, 18.

[9] Cardinal Mario Grech, "Opening Address to the 1st General Congregation," October 2, 2024, www.synod.va.

of the People of God. This kind of work is capable of renewing the missionary and prophetic dynamism of the Church as light to the nations.

From the journey so far, certain characteristics and signs of a synodal Church have emerged. These are categorized variously as the primacy of baptismal dignity of the People of God, a capacity for listening and learning, encounter and dialogue, inclusion and welcome, and certitude and tension.[10] It is possible to further distill these characteristics and signs into three distinct, defining, and interrelated marks that are constitutive of a synodal Church, namely, listening, discernment, and relationality.

Marks of a Synodal Church

Listening

"A synodal Church is a listening Church."[11] Listening is the action most commonly associated with the understanding, knowledge, and practice of synodality. Considered a mark of a synodal Church, listening is inclusive, multidirectional, and Spirit-inspired: "The faithful people, the college of bishops, the Bishop of Rome: all listening to each other, and all listening to the Holy Spirit."[12] More important, the purpose of this exercise is clear: "Everyone has something to learn." This implication is twofold: First, no ecclesial institution, structure, office, or person exercises a monopoly over the process. The qualifying criterion for participation is the baptismal dignity of all the People of God: "By virtue of Baptism, women and men have equal dignity as members of the People of God" (FD 60). Second, learning and listening are indissociable

---

[10] IL, 19–31.

[11] Pope Francis, address commemorating the fiftieth anniversary of the institution of the Synod of Bishops, October 17, 2015.

[12] Pope Francis, address commemorating the fiftieth anniversary of the institution of the Synod of Bishops, October 17, 2015.

and essential components of synodality. On this point, the path to understand synodality has been marked by frustration. From the experience of the Synod on Synodality, while we acknowledge listening as an art and dialogue as a crucial part of synodality, they can also lead to misunderstandings and tensions.

Synodal learning requires conversion and a change of mind-set. It is conceivable that the community called Church has not fully grasped all the implications of synodality yet; it remains a work in progress that requires a disposition to listen and learn with humility, patience, and respect. "Synodality is not a manifesto, a creed, a platform for reformist initiatives; it is a process of ecclesial engagement, a maturing of a church assembly supported by the pillars of deep listening, reverencing the other and deploying silence as a tool of encounter."[13] Although the synod has concluded, there is still a long way to go in cultivating the requisite dispositions.

Discerning

A synodal Church is a discerning Church. Listening is linked to discernment and discernment with accompaniment as ordinary dimensions of the life of a synodal Church. A missionary synodal Church discerns the will of God through humble listening to the voices of all and accompanies them in their service and mission.

As Anne Arabome points out in her contribution, discernment is one of the most commonly used words in the Final Document (FD) of the synod. The frequency of its use is indicative of its pertinence as a constitutive dimension of a synodal Church. It harkens back to the fundamental conviction that synodality is primarily a spiritual disposition. The belief that God's will is discoverable both for individuals and for communities is the primary underlying assumption of discernment. As such,

---

[13] Michael W. Higgins, "Inverting the Pyramid," *Tablet*, November 9, 2024, 9.

discernment is the privileged means by which the synodal Church discovers and receives what the Spirit "says to the Churches" (Revelation 2:7) "in order to put it into practice" (FD 27). The integration of prayer and discernment into decision-making processes is an important part of the goal to become a more synodal Church that is more discerning in its ways of proceeding—in other words, a prayerful, humble, and listening Church. In essence, synodality is about how the community goes about addressing the issues that matter to it, resolves differences, and diffuses our tensions in a way that is informed by listening (to the Spirit), dialogue (with one another), and discerning (the will of God).

A basic presupposition is that discernment requires the consultation of the People of God in all matters relating to the life of the Church. "In the synodal Church 'the whole community, in the free and rich diversity of its members, is called together to pray, listen, analyse, dialogue, discern and offer advice on taking pastoral decisions' (ITC 68) for mission" (FD 87). Devoid of such consultation, discernment degenerates into a cover for authoritarian imposition of preferred views on the community of the faithful. The synodal process has given greater depth and prominence to the practice of discernment as a constitutive dimension of a synodal Church. Embedding a culture of discernment constitutes an imperative for the synodal Church. It is a path to consensus that is informed by the inspiration of the Holy Spirit. "The art of spiritual discernment is the fruit of a contemplative approach to reality, of contemplative prayer."[14] As Pope Francis states, "What characterizes the synodal path is the role of the Holy Spirit. We listen, we discuss in groups, but above all we pay attention to what the Spirit has to say to us."[15]

---

[14] Tomáš Halík, "Catholicism's Unknown Future," *Tablet*, September 7, 2024, 10.

[15] Pope Francis, *Let Us Dream: The Path to a Better Future* (New York: Simon and Schuster, 2020), 85.

Synodality without spirituality, without a life of interiority, devolves into a hollow exercise of unproductive and unimportant talking, discussion, and communicating that goes on for too long.

Relationality

A synodal Church is a relational Church; it exists as "a web of relationships,"[16] comprising people who walk and make the path together. Before structures and institutions, there was the People of God, who, united by a shared baptismal identity, constitute the subject of a synodal Church. The community called Church is above all "God's home and family," from which no one is excluded (FD 28). To be authentic, a synodal Church refrains from imposing limits or setting boundaries on the experience of God's grace by the People of God on matters of ethics, ministry, and responsibility for the mission of the Church.

> The vision of a Church capable of radical inclusion, shared belonging, and deep hospitality according to the teachings of Jesus is at the heart of the synodal process: "Instead of behaving like gatekeepers trying to exclude others from the table, we need to do more to make sure that people know that everyone can find a place and a home here."[17]

To conceive of the Church as "home" is to concede that "it is not thought of as a closed space, inaccessible, to be defended at all costs; the image of home evokes the possibility of welcome, hospitality, and inclusion." As such, a critical imperative for synodality "is to ensure that the Church is perceived as a welcoming home, a sacrament of encounter and salvation, a school of communion for all the sons and daughters of God" (FD 115).

---

[16] IL, introduction.

[17] "Enlarge the Space of the Tent": Working Document for the Continental Stage, Synod 2021–2024, 31.

Introduction: Of Roots and Trees

The model par excellence of relationality is the triune God.[18] The ecclesial community is a community of brothers and sisters endowed with charisms that are personal, communal, and missionary.[19] "So the challenge for the Church is to become the community of God's friends. This is incompatible with 'clericalism,' the elevation of the ordained above the baptised into a superior caste."[20]

Taken together, these marks of a synodal Church further validate the principle and practice of co-responsibility: All the baptized People of God are capable of listening, discerning, and relating. While formation can help refine particular skills and develop capacities for the concrete manifestations of these marks, they are first and foremost graces conferred on the People of God.

The journey of synodality entails the People of God walking together as the community of the risen Christ listening to the Spirit, to the Word of God, and to one another. The development of a solid spirituality of synodality rests on the ability to initiate and develop formation in and fostering the following aspects in the way of working and living as a synodal Church.

1. Intentional, communal, nonjudgmental, and inclusive listening to what the Spirit is saying in and through all members of the Church without exception—women, men, children, young, old, and all of creation regardless of their status, position, or situation.
2. The practice of discernment in common, which uses the simple method of conversation in the Spirit or spiritual conversation as a means of finding the will of God for the synodal Church in all consequential issues.
3. Welcoming and learning from the varied modes of listening to the Holy Spirit that is developed in the local churches,

---

[18] IL 23.
[19] IL 23.
[20] Timothy Radcliffe, "The Spirit of the Synod," *Tablet*, April 13, 2024, 4.

cultures, and contexts that constitute the synodal Church such as the spirituality of Ubuntu, which prioritizes mutuality and relationality.

A truly synodal Church would exist and find meaning only if its values and practices are deeply rooted in the Holy Spirit.

The Gift of Diversity

Listening, discernment, and relationality connote plurality; these are communal practices in a synodal Church. Judging by the experience of the Synod on Synodality, a synodal Church embraces and thrives in diversity. It does not exist in a vacuum but thrives within the diverse cultures and contexts of the People of God.[21] One basic insight from the synodal process is the realization that the Church is a composite of traditions and cultures existing in a variety of local contexts, historical circumstances, and sociological spaces. There is nothing new in this realization except that the synodal process emphasized and heightened its visibility as inherent in the understanding and function of the community called Church. The idea that plurality is a gift and harmony a horizon of ecclesial pilgrimage has a long tradition in the history of ecclesiology. It applies to the understanding of charisms and ministries. Also, it denotes a richness that is characteristic of the meaning of Catholicity (FD 38).

Yet, as previously mentioned, this understanding of diversity can generate unease and foment tension because it relativizes any pretension to a privileged authoritative center in relation to subordinate margins or peripheries of the community called Church. A synodal Church is a constellation of peripheries rather than a consolidation of a presumed center of importance and dominance. In reality, the challenge of becoming a synodal

---

[21] IL 11–12.

Church entails a commitment to "resist the temptation of being at the centre, and open oneself to the acceptance of other perspectives" (FD 42).

The synod reflected the Church's remarkable diversity; it served as a microcosm of its global identity—from vibrant sartorial displays to sharp differences in opinion, from warm conviviality to intense debates. Synodality has highlighted the plurality of contexts within local churches. As mentioned, a synodal Church thrives in diverse cultural contexts, with culture shaping synodality, which in turn is deeply rooted in these contexts. In this sense, it may be more appropriate to speak of "synodalities" (rather than "synodality") as creative responses to circumstances of local churches. Synodality does not have one embodiment; it is culturally contextualized and will look different in different places. An inculturated synodality may generate tension, yet it can also surface successful innovative practices and models that can be learned and adopted in other contexts. "The synodal development of the Church will show, in the words of Pope Francis, many new ways of being Christian, and new—and unexpected—ways of being the Church in the world."[22] This approach calls for a deep reverence for the spaces and bonds that connect the diverse peoples and cultures in the global Church (FD 110).

If the goal of synodality is a more inclusive, listening, participatory, humble, and prayerful Church, there are various paths for reaching that goal by drawing on the contextual realities and the diversity of gifts available to the Church from various ecclesial communities. In practical terms, this might mean that while some practices are allowed to all, they are not imposed on all. Thus, structurally, a synodal way of being and living as a Church implies that local churches walk at different paces and do not necessarily toe the line on every issue. In reality, "Differences

---

[22] Halík, "Catholicism's Unknown Future," 11.

in pace can be valued as an expression of legitimate diversity and as an opportunity for sharing gifts and mutual enrichment. This common horizon requires discerning, identifying and promoting concrete practices which allow us to be a synodal Church on mission" (FD 124).

Thus, the assumption that there is only one synodal path is not supported by the diversity of gifts and graces rooted in the generosity of the Spirit, as suggested in scripture and tradition. Differences and disagreements and competing visions of synodality—its meaning, practice, and implications—exist and are part of the synodal tradition. The view that synodality is or ought to be a smooth, seamless, and uncontroversial experience is an anodyne perception that barely exists in lived reality. A robust conversation, creative tension, and sharp disagreements are not inconsistent with the spirit and practice of synodality.

As mentioned, there may not be one way of being synodal; hence, it is about synodalities. This plurality is a grace and a gift of the Spirit. As some contributors to the chapters of this book show, in Africa, there are appropriate locally discerned and culturally relevant ways of being a synodal Church because synodality correlates with key African concepts and practices. Yet it is critical to stress that synodality is not a sociological task to be completed but a spirit to be incarnated and lived, a habitual way of life, and an ecclesial culture that God expects of the Church in the third millennium. The process is as important as its outcome. As such, synodality offers a chance for ecclesial renewal and conversion. Beyond the diatribes, controversies, and divisions, the fundamental question remains how to *synod* (verb), how we walk together as one body, the Body of Christ. The baptismal dignity of the People of God must be the foundation, root, and basis of a synodal Church. This principle is the antithesis of a hierarchical stratification of the Body of Christ demarcated along lines of clerical station, status, and situation.

Introduction: Of Roots and Trees

In the final analysis, a synodal Church is precisely that—a Church on the way. The journey begun, it remains open to new discoveries and humbly expresses its vulnerability and humility, which allows it to experience conversion that makes it more and more conformed to God's dream for God's Church undeterred by its sense of a "healthy restlessness of incompleteness."[23]

The chapters of this book have been developed in response to the twin calls of Pope Francis and the Synod on Synodality "to take a courageous step forward and to develop a theology of synodality" and "to continue research aimed at clarifying and deepening the meaning of synodality" (FD 67). The primary purpose is to develop the requisite materials for such a theology to clarify and deepen the understanding, knowledge, and practice of synodality in the local churches.

Anne Arabome's lead chapter draws strong parallels between African religion, spirituality, and culture and the knowledge, understanding, and practice of synodality. Her main thesis is the fundamental relationship between synodality and spirituality. Synodality is rooted in spirituality and needs to be. She offers illustrations by exploring the nexus of discernment, the palaver ethics of communication, where all people together discuss matters that pertain to the Church under the guidance of the Holy Spirit, and the concept of Ubuntu, which recognizes the dignity and mutuality of human beings and the importance of treating one another as humans and listening to all regardless of status.

Her analysis allows us to see the constitutive elements of the spirituality of a synodal Church, specifically, spiritual interiority, inclusive discernment, and conversation in the Spirit. As she demonstrates, discernment entails a capacity to listen with openness and honesty and to speak with courage and charity. The necessity and practice of discernment represent a communal

---

[23] IL 29.

process rather than an isolated, individual act or an event decreed from a hierarchical pedestal. This has implication for the foundational understanding of the Church as the People of God on the way. One of the fundamental principles of synodality is the prioritization of co-responsibility in governance and the inclusion of laypeople in processes leading to consequential decisions. It is a process of, by, and for the People of God. In a synodal Church, lay women and lay men have a right to be listened to, and this right is rooted firmly in our shared baptismal grace as equal members of the Body of Christ, which is a deep font of synodal spirituality.

Marcel Uwineza locates synodality in the foundational journey of creation when God journeyed with humanity and invited humanity to return the process. The defining principle of this single reciprocal synodal movement is God's love, which reveals the life of the triune God. This foundational understanding transforms the meaning of synodality understood as journeying or walking together into an imitation, albeit imperfect, of God's action.

Using several examples, illustrations, and references, he explores the sources and resources of synodality in scripture and Christian tradition. Readers would easily recognize the striking points, especially the exploration of the historical and theological trajectory of synodality as a foundation for other chapters in this book. Also discernible are the innovation and creativity that he underscores in the aspiration toward building a synodal Church. Of salience is Jesus's way of being with people and fulfilling his mission. His life and ministry unfold in a synodal manner because Jesus welcomes and includes everybody without marginalizing anyone.

The community that gathers around Jesus and extends his mission in time and space retains and propagates its synodal identity. Eventually, though, this synodal vision of the community of Jesus's disciples is eclipsed by an ecclesiology rooted in the pursuit of power and domination. The loss of synodality is a feature of the Middle Ages. The long road back to synodality passes through the creative contributions of many theologians that culminated in Vatican II, and with this, new seeds of synodality were sown. We find in the Final Document no dearth of examples of the claim that synodality is the heart of Vatican II. Quite clearly, Pope Francis has emerged as the champion of synodality by his visionary and prophetic summoning of the Church to walk a synodal path and courageously modeling this journey and task. Finally, Uwineza turns to the African Church to discover synodal cognates, including the practice of inclusive consultation and dialogue and a holistic spirituality.

Chijioke Azuawusiefe leans into the African reality of orality and its rich landscape of symbolism, in particular *ngiga*, to delineate an understanding of communication as a practice of sharing that aligns with the principal dimensions of synodality, notably communion, participation, and mission. The triad of communication, communion, and community functions as a representation of synodality. He stresses the importance of communication in a synodal Church and the centrality of listening. Dialogue, communication, and community are mutually reinforcing. His essay contains a critique of cultures of obstruction, including patriarchy and clericalism, that undermine nourishing forms of communication, communion, and community. He makes a strong case for the vital need to promote, with creativity and imagination, a missionary synodal Church that embraces the challenge to sanctify, use, and evangelize digital spaces, environments, and cultures as places of interiority, where genuine and real personal relationships with Jesus Christ can be cultivated, nourished, and deepened for everyone who needs it, young and old alike. Central to the understanding of synodality is a model of spirituality of communication that practices inclusive or participatory communication rooted in the respect for the dignity and equality of the baptized People of God.

Josée Ngalula undertakes a creative reflection on synodality and God. As does Uwineza, she locates synodality at the core of God's relationship with humanity and creation. The Trinity is ultimately the foundation of synodal living and working as the People of God. Walking and journeying together offer a fitting description of what God does as the Trinity. This insight aligns with the idea of relationality as a distinguishing mark of a synodal Church. Creation and redemption are compelling examples of a triune God, who is synodal in their relationship and who work synodally in relation to humanity. It further confirms the pivotal theological insight that a missionary synodal Church exists as "a web of relationships" and that we are saved as a community: "No one is saved alone."[24] From this understanding, she derives the intuition that creation is a mission for women and men to live in communion and participate with equal dignity in the mission of the Church. The imperatives for mission, communion, and participation as essential dimensions of synodality are rooted in scripture. From this and some insights from research and pastoral experiences relating to the understanding of the Trinity in an African context, she also discerns the practical necessity of facilitating access to the Bible and guarding against misinterpretation as part of a formation program for a synodal Church.

José Minaku examines synodality as a transformative approach to ecclesiology rooted in Pope Francis's vision for a participatory Church. His creative approach harks back to one of the classic texts of ecclesiology in the twentieth century, namely, Avery Dulles's *Models of the Church*. He uses this framework to explore the capacity for synodality to renew traditional ecclesiological paradigms and models through the practice of listening, dialogue, discernment, and inclusivity. The critical question is how to delineate the shape or form of Pope Francis's new model of a synodal Church, which appears as a continuation

---

[24] IL, introduction.

if not a fulfillment of the inspiration sown by Vatican II. Through a critical appraisal of Dulles's approach, he demonstrates how synodality fosters theological reflection and praxis, addressing contemporary challenges to reimagine or remodel the Church for the third millennium.

A synodal ecclesiology is dynamic rather than static; it prioritizes the creation of lasting processes over the habit of temporarily occupying spaces, and a lived reality over a theoretical construct. Rather than juxtapose Dulles's models and Pope Francis's model of the Church, he argues that constitutive elements of the latter, such as listening, dialogue, and discernment, provide critical resources for reforming, reactivating, and remodeling the former. Additionally, synodality provides a path for combating clericalism and the abuse of power and authority. His position aligns with Francis's idea of synodality as the quest for a different rather than a new Church.

Anthony Egan explores the ethics of synodality and highlights dialogue, discernment, and trust as its constitutive elements for the emergence of a truly synodal Church. His essay is a strong reminder that synodality in theory and practice is a contested narrative. Expressions or the lack thereof of synodality are mapped along the ideological fissures of the opposing narratives. It falls to the Church that aspires to be synodal to generate and prioritize effective means such as the Eucharist, a source and expression of lived synodality, for transforming the polarizations. As developed in several parts of this volume, specific African values including palaver and Ubuntu provide a path, albeit imperfect, toward overcoming these polarizations and establishing trust at the core of the synodal Church. The search for truth and the practice of prayer are important expressions of dialogue and prayerful discernment in a synodal Church. He makes a strong case for cultivating trust among the people invested in synodality. In the absence of this linchpin, synodality is impracticable if not impossible. The outcome of the Synod on Synodality as expressed in the Final Document that Pope Francis made available immediately as a guide for synodal action offers hope for the emergence of a genuine synodal ethics.

Léocadie Lushombo outlines the giftedness and wisdom of women in many activities and ministries. She also underlines the theological impulses and biblical examples that illustrate and motivate their pastoral and ministerial engagement and their status as leaders and protagonists of a truly synodal Church. Important female personalities in the Hebrew Bible, Jesus's practice in the New Testament, and several women leaders in the early Christian communities and churches provide compelling warrants for adopting a synodal and inclusive vision of Church that welcomes everyone into the ecclesial community. These examples are vital for creating a listening Church that values women's gifts and reflects Jesus's care for the marginalized. These examples summon women and men to practice a form of humility, without which empathetic listening can be hindered. Additionally, these examples offer lessons for a listening Church to enable it to recognize the diverse gifts of religious women, empower them for ministry, and promote their full participation and equal dignity. The synodal process provides an auspicious opportunity to renounce alienating, discriminatory, and skewed narratives in order to retrieve and reenact women's role in the Church as exemplified in the scriptures and modeled by lay and religious women. As teachers of synodality, African women draw on their culturally informed theological perspectives to engender creative and constructive approaches to the understanding of the relationship between religion and culture. Also, they exercise important synodal practices such as solidarity, mutual support, culture of care, and listening to people at the grassroots. This is amply attested by the example of the Circle of Concerned African Women Theologians, which offers a platform for women to walk together as a community. She concludes with the insight that the reimagination of motherhood offers a key to agency and social transformation that allows women to advance synodal initiatives with significant social impact.

Ludovic Lado begins his analysis of the understanding and exercise of authority in a synodal Church by revisiting the conception of authority according to Vatican II, the key features of which are collegiality and primacy and the patriarchal and clerical monopoly over authority to the near exclusion of "those faithful called the laity" (*Lumen gentium* 30). The vision of synodality as an inclusive and participatory exercise of authority serves as an antidote to this warped view of authority. This vision affirms and embraces God's plan for humanity that is both female and male, women and men. Accordingly, he advocates renaming the Synod of Bishops as the Synod of the Church. This tension over the nomenclature, legitimacy, and authority of a Synod of Bishops that includes people other than bishops featured prominently during the Synod on Synodality. Additionally, he presents models of authority in African cultures that align closely with the synodal approach in the Church, albeit tending to be dominated by men. This evolving model of synodality challenges patriarchal structures and promotes a discernment-based approach to governance, which is slowly reshaping African societies toward a more inclusive practice of governance.

Synodality is founded on an exercise of authority that prioritizes and practices ecclesial discernment, co-responsibility, transparency, and accountability in the exercise of authority. The gift of authority rests in the community on whose behalf and in whose interest holders exercise it. In a synodal Church, the axis of authority runs through accountability, relationality, participation, transparency, and evaluation. The call for a conversion to a more synodal manner of exercising authority is more acute in the context of the Church in Africa, which is steeped in cultures of patriarchy and hierarchy. In a synodal Church, a radical shift is necessary to facilitate genuine co-responsibility and a recognition of the charisms and gifts of the People of God in decision-making for an exercise that is healing and life-affirming for the community.

Veronica Rop looks at the important contribution of consecrated women religious to synodality, using the experience of the Association of Consecrated Women in Eastern and Central Africa serving within the Association of Member Episcopal Conferences in Eastern Africa. She offers some examples of the multiple ways that these women enrich the life and contribute to the mission of the Church by their prophetic lives and heroic ministries, often inhibited and undermined by the excesses of patriarchy, hierarchy, and sexism. The values they profess and live are concrete embodiments of the life of the synodal Church. To deny women their rightful place in the Church is a disservice to the goal of developing a synodal Church.

To make progress, she identifies practical steps, including the integration of women in formation and training of those seeking ordained ministries, participation in discernment and consultation, decision-taking and decision-making, and improving existing mechanisms, structures, systems, and procedures that ensure accountability, transparency, and evaluation. These conditions and requirements relate to the exercise of authority in local churches and in religious institutes. They also relate to the participation of young people in the Church.

Ultimately, the goal is to create a culture or cultures that embody and promote the values and principles of synodality in the Church and in all the communities, institutions, and structures of the Church, especially those aspects that inflict harm on women and hinder their desire to be members of the Church with equal dignity. The needs, challenges, and gifts of young people in the Church are no different from those of young, consecrated women

Introduction: Of Roots and Trees xxxi

religious. They have gifts, including knowledge of digital media, that can be utilized for evangelization, education, and formation, and more important, to promote a culture of synodality.

David Kaulemu argues for love as agape as the foundation of co-responsibility in a synodal Church. Baptism empowers co-responsibility albeit not as an end in itself but for service of the life and mission of the community. The charisms bestowed on us by the Holy Spirit are a response to the needs of the Church and the exigencies of mission rather than private possessions. The ensuing "baptismal ministries" that are open to any baptized woman or man need to be recognized, promoted, and valued through an ecclesial act that is rooted in listening.

As an aspect of ecclesial identity, the practice of co-responsibility imposes ethical and spiritual obligations of being our sister's and brother's keeper. Co-responsibility extends to mission beyond the confines of the Church as a call to proclaim the good news of the Gospel of Jesus Christ in socioeconomic and political contexts and conditions and on pertinent issues such as climate change. It values the gifts and charisms of all and allows us to participate fully in the life and mission of the Church. Ultimately, the connectedness modeled on the example of trinitarian life provides a strong rationale and call for embedding co-responsibility in ecclesial life. Local church communities provide the needed space to practice co-responsibility and fulfill the important responsibilities it confers on the People of God. He furnishes concrete illustrations of these insights by briefly mentioning several ecclesial leaders who have tried to live the life of synodality before the synod as models of co-responsibility.

As her starting point, **Sheila Pires** underlines the key teachings of the encyclical *Christus vivit* ("Christ Is Alive") to emphasize the critical importance of walking with young people as the vibrant now of a synodal Church. This awareness has implications for the formation of young people. Using examples from the Southern African Catholic Bishops Conference, she argues for the formation of young people as a priority for the synodal Church. One of those important spaces for formation and the exercise of the gifts of young people in the Church are the Small Christian Communities. Yet they face difficulties, struggle with generational gaps, and are challenged by socioeconomic difficulties that impact their well-being, mental health, and capacity to thrive. The opportunity of the moment is a call to the Church to create spaces for the giftedness of young people to emerge and flourish, for their voices to be heard, and for their leadership to be exercised. One area where this is crucial is the use of digital media and technologies. Embracing the opportunities without overlooking the potential for harm will enable young people to become digital missionaries, as illustrated by the life of teenage Saint Carlo Acutis.

What characterizes these essays is a deep reverence for the Church that manifests in a shared desire for reforming the Church and the imperative of formation as an impetus for a paradigm shift and for reimagining new ways of being Church. At times, the essays take on the quality of a commentary on important documents on synodality. In all instances, they are intended as resources for formation in synodality. Essentially, this is not an attempt to explain but to live synodality.

Depending on people's expectations of the synod, consolation or desolation greeted the Final Document in equal measure. While the former disposition will foster a true synodal spirit and practice, the latter will likely limit the efficacy of the synod in part due to the entrenched and endemic clericalism in the Church. It is important to take the full measure of the importance of this moment. The outcome of the Synod on Synodality was hard-won, and the synod is not a dream deferred but an act of trust in the slow work of God. The journey is being guided by the Holy Spirit. The synodal process generates hope for the emergence of a different Church, and this book makes a contribution from Africa; it is an act of hope for the Church. The goal is to contribute to the creation of a synodal Church by engaging in a synodal theology focusing on some important issues. The journey continues.

This volume is neither comprehensive nor exhaustive. Many issues dealt with at the synod have not been addressed in this volume. The problem of clericalism both of the clergy and of the laity persists as one of the big challenges in Africa. Nor have we sufficiently and substantially explored the promises and prospects of the co-responsibility of all the People of God. In a modest way, this volume aims to make the understanding, knowledge, and practice of synodality more accessible to members of the Church. The contributors take an interdisciplinary approach that connects many issues such as spirituality, communication, leadership, ethics, authority, religious life, African spirituality, and young people.

In the final analysis, these chapters show that there are some uniquely African ways of being community and doing things that we can offer to the Church to enhance synodality and so become more creative in engendering a constitutively synodal Church. The synodal theology of this volume models the art of theology reimagined as not the work of an inspired individual but a palaver that is outgoing and ongoing. The African voice is important; it is not the only one, but it is an important voice of influence. Its absence would mean the loss of something precious to the Church.

1

A Spirituality of Synodality

Drawing from the Wells of African Spirituality

Anne Arabome

Pope Francis has declared that there is no synodality without the Holy Spirit: "If the Spirit is not present, there will be no Synod."[1] The pope's conviction aligns with the insight of the Final Document of the Synod on Synodality that

> synodality is primarily a spiritual disposition. It permeates the daily life of the baptised as well as every aspect of the Church's mission. A synodal spirituality flows from the action of the Holy Spirit and requires listening to the Word of God, contemplation, silence and conversion of heart. (Final Document [FD] 43)

Accordingly, spirituality offers a necessary starting point and a fertile ground for synodality to take root, grow, and thrive.

Vatican II also teaches that at the heart of synodality is the action of the Holy Spirit under whose guidance, direction, and inspiration

---

[1] Pope Francis's address for the opening of the synod, October 9, 2021, www.vatican.va/content/francesco/en/speeches/2021/october/documents/20211009-apertura-camminosinodale.html.

the Church journeys together as "a people made one with the unity of the Father, the Son and the Holy Spirit" (*Lumen gentium* 4). Participation, communion, and mission are preeminently spiritual dispositions. Considered as graces, these dispositions are gifts of the Holy Spirit. "The renewal of the Christian community is possible only by recognizing the primacy of grace. If spiritual depth at both personal and communitarian levels is lacking, synodality is reduced to organizational expediency" (FD 44).

This essay explores particular resources that the synodal Church can draw from African culture, religion, and spirituality. It begins by considering key aspects of African religion and identifies the major components of African spirituality. The combination of religion and spirituality in an African context provides substance and support for the spiritual values, practices, and resources that undergird the emergence of a truly synodal Church, especially listening, discernment, dialogue, prayer, and spiritual conversation or conversation in the Spirit. To understand, know, and live synodality, these practices are indispensable and offer the possibility of transforming the Church in its journey of synodality.

The central idea of my essay is the awareness that synodality is connatural with African spirituality. Contrary to some perceptions, synodality is not an invention or imposition by Pope Francis. Nor it is something exterior and a personal ecclesiology of Francis. As mentioned, synodality is essentially a spiritual experience on personal and communal levels. Considered as such, it is not exterior to human spiritual experience as expressed in different cultures. In every culture, we can find this link of human experience of spirituality aspiring to communal experience.

As foremost African theologian Mercy Amba Oduyoye once stated, quoting a Yoruba proverb, "If you do not know where you are going, at least you know where you are coming from."[2] The

---

[2] Mercy Amba Oduyoye, "Acting as Women," in *African Theology Today*, ed. Emmanuel Katongole (Scranton, PA: University of Scranton Press, 2002), 179.

Church is on a journey of synodality. The People of God have embarked on a journey, to walk together as the community of Jesus Christ, listening to the Spirit and listening to one another. A truly synodal Church would exist and find meaning only in its spiritual values and practices deeply rooted in the actions of and inspired by the gifts of the Holy Spirit. African religion and African spirituality offer some foundational elements that foreground the meaning and practice of synodality. These elements are worth exploring in order to situate synodality in the space of African ecclesial life as its animating principle.

African Religion, Spirituality, and Culture

Religion has been part of life in Africa over many generations. It is worth recalling the key aspects of African religion.

> In general, traditional religion in Africa is characterized by belief in a supreme being who created and ordered the world but is often experienced as distant or unavailable to humans. Lesser divinities or spirits who are more accessible are sometimes believed to act as intermediaries. A number of traditional myths explain the creation and ordering of the world and provide explanations for contemporary social relationships and norms. Lapsed social responsibilities or violations of taboos are widely believed to result in hardship, suffering and illness for individuals or communities and must be countered with ritual acts to re-establish order, harmony and well-being.[3]

---

[3] See "Tolerance and Tension: Islam and Christianity in Africa" (Pew Research Religion and Public Life Project, April 15, 2010), http://www.pewforum.org/2010/04/15/executive-summary-islam-and-christianity-in-sub-saharan-africa/; and Agbonkhianmeghe E. Orobator, *Theology Brewed in an African Pot* (Maryknoll, NY: Orbis Books, 2008).

In addition to the foregoing features, one of the defining characteristics of African religion is the absence of formal creeds, proclaimed dogmas, or sacred texts comparable to the Bible in Christianity or the Koran in Islam. Oral traditions, myths, rituals, festivals, shrines, art, and symbols are preeminent forms of expression of African religious beliefs and spirituality. Historically, Western missionaries disparaged these forms and expressions as animism, paganism, magic, or simply superstition.[4] Several scholars acknowledge the existence of sophisticated African religion that prioritizes the well-being of humanity in the present as opposed to offering salvation in a future, yet-unrealized world.

Because beliefs and practices vary across ethnic groups and regions, some experts perceive a multitude of different religions in Africa. My preference for the term "African religion" is premised on the observation that there are unifying themes and common elements across a wide diversity, hence the possibility of considering African religion as a single expression of belief albeit with contextual and geographical varieties, particularities, manifestations, and differences.

In terms of its main elements, as noted in the Pew research on religion in Africa, belief in a supreme being who created and ordered the world is paramount.[5] Depending on the context or situation of adherents, such a being can be perceived as distant, remote, inaccessible, or unavailable to humans. In the traditional African worldview, God is an experience rather than a fixed and definite image cast in a rigid, unbreakable mold. This experience

---

[4] Agbonkhianmeghe E. Orobator, *Religion and Faith in Africa: Confessions of an Animist* (Maryknoll, NY: Orbis Books, 2018) explores this phenomenon comprehensively.

[5] The section draws largely on chapter 3 of the Pew Research report "Traditional African Religious Beliefs and Practices," www.pewresearch.org/religion/2010/04/15/traditional-african-religious-beliefs-and-practices-islam-and-christianity-in-sub-saharan-africa/.

can be found in many expressions.[6] Lesser divinities or spirits that are more accessible are sometimes believed to act as intermediaries. A number of traditional myths explain the creation and ordering of the world and provide explanations for contemporary social relationships and moral norms. Infringements of social norms and violations that affect personal and communal relationships are widely believed to occasion misfortune and calamity for individuals or communities and must be countered or neutralized with ritual acts to reestablish order, harmony, and well-being among human beings and between them and their physical and metaphysical environments.

Ancestors, considered to be in the spirit world, are believed to be part of the human community. Adherents hold that ancestors sometimes act as emissaries between living beings and the Supreme Being, helping to maintain social order and withdrawing their support if the living behave wrongly. Religious specialists such as diviners, herbalists, and healers are called upon to discern what infractions or violations are at the root of misfortune and to prescribe the appropriate rituals or traditional medicines to set things right.

African religion tends to personify evil. Believers often blame witches or sorcerers for attacking their life-force, causing illness or other harm. They seek to protect and fortify themselves with ritual acts, sacred objects, and traditional medicines.

Taking the foregoing into account, when we turn to African spirituality, the main contours are also quite easily discernible. In the first place is the belief that we are meant to be one community and family. This communal dimension is the only way to be fully human. Although colonialism and the coming of the

---

[6] See Orobator, *Theology Brewed*, 24–25. This is one of the central affirmations of Laurenti Magesa in his book *What Is Not Sacred? African Spirituality* (Maryknoll, NY: Orbis Books, 2013).

missionaries tried to teach Africans how to relate in a personal way to God, Africans practiced and believed in a communal way of being. According to an African proverb, "It is by the strength of their number that the ants in the field are able to carry their prey to the nest." For Africans, community is paramount. This understanding is a radical feature of life in the spirit in Africa, rendering spirituality fundamentally communal.

Similarly, African spirituality is a lived reality. Like African spirituality in the American and Caribbean diaspora, it is "embodied in music and song, dance, prayer, instrumentation, works of social justice, and relationships."[7] Laurenti Magesa adds architecture to this list.[8] There is so much vitality and life in African spirituality that informs the way that African Christians worship and celebrate their faith. Seen in this embodied sense, and despite rapid changes occasioned by new and emerging technologies, African spirituality continues to influence and shape patterns of belief, worship, and life in the religious space. With the intensification of urbanization, these patterns are shifting from rural areas to urban centers. In cities such as Nairobi and Dar es Salaam, it is not uncommon to encounter publicly advertised services of *Nganga wa kienyeji* ("traditional healers"), whose ritual practices, especially beliefs in the protective powers of objects and sacrifices to ancestors, derive from African religion.

Besides embodiment, there is also the participative, interactive, and integrative dimensions of African spirituality. Everybody sings, everybody prays, and everybody worships. There is no place for spectators. This is another key element of African spirituality, and it consists of being present in mind, body, and spirit to the actions and presence of the Divine.

---

[7] Therese Taylor-Stinson, "Black Spirituality and the Art of Spiritual Direction," *Presence: An International Journal of Spiritual Direction* 15, no. 4 (December 2009): 48–49.

[8] Magesa, *What Is Not Sacred?* 69–80.

From experience, I have vivid memories of the participative, interactive, and communal dimensions of faith and worship. I can still recall my paternal grandmother's storytelling. She would tell us stories, and there was always a call and response built into every story. In a sense, we became the story as well. We grew into the story. The same applied when it came to worship; it involved everyone. In reality, there is hardly a private worship in African spirituality.

Pneumatology in African Religion

To reinforce some of the points made above, it is important to underscore, albeit briefly, the role of spirits in relation to the central role accorded the Holy Spirit in the understanding of synodality.

Many African communities strongly believe that there are connections between all that makes up the universe, including their ancestors. Because of these attitudes, many natural resources have been preserved because they are considered sacred. Some forests are considered sacred, and certain trees are not to be harmed. Certain mountains, streams, rivers, and hills are seen as intrinsically connected to the community's survival. These sacred places are the dwellings of the deities, ancestors, gods, goddesses, and their messengers. Some animals are also seen as sacred and connected to the community's survival. "The African universe is charged with a palpable spiritual energy; this energy comes from faith in the existence of many spiritual realities: gods, goddesses, deities, ancestral spirits, and so on."[9]

One fascinating observation is the strong similarity between the African worldview of spirits and the biblical view of the Holy Spirit. Stephen Bevans illustrates this similarity in his anthropological model in which he describes Robert Hood's understanding of it. He affirms,

---

[9] Orobator, *Theology Brewed*, 141.

> The biblical worldview regarding the Spirit of God . . . is very similar to the African worldview regarding the spirits. It is the Spirit that "will not speak on his own authority, but whatever he hears he will speak" (Jn 16:13), and this is similar to the African belief that the spirits are given authority by God to act in certain ways in the world.[10]

Just as the prophets were driven by the Spirit to speak God's Word, so in African religion, the spirits give power and inspiration. Like the spirits that stand before God's throne ready to do God's bidding, so the spirits in African religion serve as messengers to human beings.[11] This correlation between the Holy Spirit and spirits calls for more analysis.

In their conclusion to *Towards an African Narrative Theology*, Joseph Healey and Donald Sybertz affirm that "the Holy Spirit is at work in the African local churches and in local communities everywhere. The 'Unsurpassed Great Spirit' is active in Africa, helping people to write new narrative theologies of inculturation and liberation."[12] This view of the Holy Spirit as active in the lives of Africans honors the realities from which African lives emerge. However, it is also a reality that spirits have a place in African religion and culture.

Viewed in the foregoing manner, a picture emerges of the holistic nature of African spirituality. It encompasses everything and everybody. It permeates every space. The Divine is always present even when we are not aware. This God is with us in the streets, in fields, in the gathering, and in our homes. This God is everywhere, present in the smallest events of our everyday lives and at work

---

[10] Stephen Bevans, *Models of Contextual Theology* (Maryknoll, NY: Orbis Books, 2002), 63.

[11] Bevans, *Models of Contextual Theology*, 63.

[12] Joseph Healey and Donald Sybertz, *Towards an African Narrative Theology* (Maryknoll, NY: Orbis Books, 1996), 377.

in them. The fundamental vision of a holistic spirituality in the African context reveals the harmony of the sacred and the secular. There is nothing else but God and us and our cosmic space. This understanding is at the heart of African spirituality.

To further this holistic understanding, one unique aspect of African spirituality is the belief that there is neither separation nor a compartmentalization of the various dimensions and aspects that constitute and give meaning to people as individuals and as communities. Simply put, we bring our whole selves into every aspect of life. This holistic approach establishes a rich confluence and deep connections between the individual and the communal, the sacred and the profane, contemplation and action, and human ecology and environmental ecology in such a way that eliminates the polarization, antagonism, and alienation of binary juxtapositions. The resonances of this kind of holistic spirituality with the practice of synodality are strong. In a synodal Church, "No one can progress along the path of authentic spirituality alone; we need accompaniment and support, including formation and spiritual direction, both as individuals and as a community" (FD 43).

The African religious worldview perceives the natural order as infused with palpable energy and vitality. This order, whether human, animal, or vegetal, emerges as sacred, a junction that connects transcendence with immanence. It thrives on relationality. As Magesa describes this worldview, "It is based on interactive relationships among human beings and between humans and the entire order of existence. It understands this relationship to be the essence of religion, the sacred."[13] Life rooted in relationality is central to the self-understanding of Africans and their praxis of mutuality and encounter. This understanding exemplifies

---

[13] Magesa, *What Is Not Sacred?* 24; see Elochukwu Eugene Uzukwu, *God, Spirit, and Human Wholeness: Appropriating Faith and Culture in West African Style* (Eugene, OR: Pickwick Publications, 2012), 151–79.

the core of African spirituality, because "this perception of life is at the very heart of African spirituality; it is an approach that is absolutely relational and completely unitary."[14] Here as previously, there is a correlation between African spirituality and the practice of synodality. A synodal Church is constitutively relational—"a Church that is God's home and family" (FD 28, 136).

The principles and values of African religion engender practices that further define the experience of spirituality. The main elements of the latter are evident in the foregoing. Equally important is the understanding of culture. Without going into an in-depth analysis of the meaning of culture in Africa, suffice it to state that culture refers to unique, multifaceted, complex, and dynamic ways of expressing deeply held beliefs and regulating relationships within personal and communal spaces and contexts. Understood in this sense, the understanding, knowledge, and practice of culture will vary from one place to another. Yet in each instance, religious factors and spiritual practices blend to provide the framework for how cultures are expressed and evaluated. "The appreciation of contexts, cultures and diversities, and of the relationships between them, is key to growing as a missionary synodal Church and to journeying, prompted by the Holy Spirit, towards the visible unity of Christians" (FD 40).

In light of the foregoing, what form or shape does the spirituality of synodality take? What are the defining characteristics and constitutive elements of the spirituality of synodality? In the following section, I provide and highlight two practices or models that foreground synodality in African spirituality, namely, communal discernment and palaver. My aim is to show how African spirituality provides a fertile ground for the practice of synodality, or to put it differently, how synodality finds a home in African spirituality.

---

[14] Magesa, *What Is Not Sacred?* 24.

Spirituality of Synodality as Communal Discernment

Synodality entails intentionally listening to all members of the Church without exception—women, men, children, young, old, and all creation—as a means of finding the will of God, who dwells in all things.

> A synodal Church is a Church which listens, which realizes that listening "is more than simply hearing." It is a mutual listening in which everyone has something to learn. The faithful people, the college of bishops, the Bishop of Rome: all listening to each other, and all listening to the Holy Spirit, the "Spirit of truth" (Jn 14:17), in order to know what he "says to the Churches (Revelation 2:7)."[15]

This art or practice of finding God's will for the community, in this case, the ecclesial community, is what is commonly referred to and understood as discernment. Discernment is a constitutive dimension of synodality.

> Orientated towards mission, synodality involves gathering at all levels of the Church for mutual listening, dialogue, and community discernment. It also involves reaching consensus as an expression of Christ rendering Himself present, He who is alive in the Spirit. (FD 28)

Discernment is a synodal act, and synodality is an act of discernment.

The multiple references to ecclesial discernment or discernment in common in the Final Document underscore the importance of discernment as a constitutive dimension of synodality. The document is suffused with discernment, which is mentioned at least sixty-seven times. Ecclesial discernment is one of the most widely discussed

---

[15] Pope Francis's address for the ceremony commemorating the fiftieth anniversary of the institution of the Synod of Bishops, October 17, 2015.

subjects in the Final Document, making it a foundational element in the understanding and practice of synodality:

> Ecclesial discernment is not an organizational technique but rather a spiritual practice grounded in a living faith. It calls for interior freedom, humility, prayer, mutual trust, an openness to the new and a surrender to the will of God. It is never just a setting out of one's own personal or group point of view or a summing up of differing individual opinions.... As this discernment entails the contribution of everyone, ecclesial discernment is both the condition and a privileged expression of synodality, in which communion, mission and participation are lived. The more everyone is heard, the greater the discernment. (FD 82)[16]

For participation, communion, and mission to be concretely manifested, they must be grounded in ecclesial discernment. Proper formation of the People of God on "how to practice ecclesial discernment" represents one of the essential tasks of a synodal Church (FD 148).

As has become evident, the practiced method of ecclesial discernment is the use of conversation in the Spirit or spiritual conversation. "Conversation in the Spirit is a tool that, even with its limitations, enables listening in order to discern 'what the Spirit is saying to the Churches' (Rev 2:7)" (FD 45). During this experience, participants take turns to respectfully express and listen to the fruit of their prayer. This instance is reinforced by sharing how this expression of each person's experience of prayer shapes, determines, shifts, or changes the position or opinions of the other members of the group or community. In the final instance, the participants seek a consensus, common ground, to discover what the Holy Spirit is revealing to the community as

---

[16] The Final Document identifies "the steps of ecclesial discernment" (84).

the will of God. Thus, finding the will of God is at the heart of discernment, which in turn is at the core of synodality.

The disposition to "listen to the other person" respectfully without contradicting the movement of the Holy Spirit in that person's own reflection aligns with the embodied, communal, and holistic nature of African spirituality. In listening to the other, we can engage in dialogue rather than monologue. We become deeply rooted in a circle of relationality and mutuality. The practice is inclusive of all the voices of members of the community listening to the Holy Spirit as the latter speaks through its members.

As mentioned above, in keeping with the practice of African religion and African spirituality, in an ecclesial context, discernment is always a communal action rather than an ecclesiastical fiat resulting from isolated, individual thought processes no matter how sophisticated. During conversation in the Spirit, even when personal prayer is prescribed as the starting point, there is the strong awareness that the entire community is at prayer. The community as a whole is attuned to the stirrings of the Holy Spirit because discernment in common is a spirit-led experience that involves personal and communal prayer. It is a way of being Church that is inclusive of all its members endowed with the *imago Dei*. This is particularly important for the synodal Church as it seeks to become inclusive, especially of women and the marginalized, knowing that whatever is shared or planned affects every member of the Body of Christ called Church.

Spirituality of Synodality as Palaver

One of the key outcomes of the Synod on Synodality is the insight that

> the word "conversation" expresses more than mere dialogue: it interweaves thought and feeling, creating a shared vital space. That is why we can say that conversion is at play

in conversation. This is an anthropological reality found in different peoples and cultures, who gather together in solidarity to deal with and decide matters vital to the community. Grace brings this human experience to fruition. Conversing "in the Spirit" means living the experience of sharing in the light of faith and seeking God's will in an evangelical atmosphere within which the Holy Spirit's unmistakable voice can be heard. (FD 45)

A widely attested experience of this "anthropological reality" known as conversation in the context of African cultural practices is the communicative practice of *palaver*. In general, this practice is perceived as an ethics of communication. At its core lie key elements of African spirituality that provide the basis for the spirituality of synodality. The practice of palaver can be a resource for generating a deep and powerful practice of spirituality for the synodal journey.

African spirituality is marked by relationality, embodiment, rootedness, and communal participation. There is a strong belief in Africa that human beings are not closed entities—a person is a person through and because of other people. This is what is commonly referred to as the principle or ethics of Ubuntu.[17] This understanding of relationality is the foundation of palaver as a form and practice of the spirituality of synodality.

What is palaver? The term comes from the Portuguese *palavra*, "word," even though dictionary definitions tend to trivialize it as "talking unproductively and at length" or "talk or discussion that goes on for too long and is not important."

---

[17] Josée Ngalula explores the relationship between Ubuntu and synodality in her essay "Ubuntu and Synodality," in *Toward a Synodal Church in Africa: Echoes from an African Christian Palaver*, ed. Ikenna Okafor, Josée Ngalula, Nicholas Segeja, and Stan Chu Ilo (Maryknoll, NY: Orbis Books, 2024), 85–121.

Like any process of discernment, the practice of palaver involves talking, discussion, and communicating, but it is hardly unproductive or unimportant.[18]

I understand palaver as a communicative practice that includes the voices of all members of the community in the discussion, discernment, and resolution of matters of consequence affecting the entire community. This practice is preceded by and rooted in a shared universe of mutual belonging and relationship with the source of life both for the individual and for the community. The community that gathers in conversation and dialogue is first and foremost a community of faith and belief. In this sense, palaver is a spiritual practice, moment, and experience in the life of the community. Like the practice in African spirituality, no member of the community is considered to be a bystander or a spectator. This practice of communal discernment has some key dimensions. Let me emphasize the salient ones.

First, in keeping with the spiritual nature mentioned above, the practice of palaver is a form of discernment in common, because to be engaged in palaver is to be engaged in a process of discerning how the community grows as an organic reality in particular contexts and in awareness of the relationship that holds the community together and with its ancestral forebears. To use a biblical analogy, as a process of discernment, palaver allows the Holy Spirit to blow wherever the Holy Spirit wills through the members of the community. The primary attitude that this process calls forth is listening not only to the leaders but also to

---

[18] See Stan Chu Ilo, "Exploring the Possible Contributions of the African Palaver Towards a Participatory Synodal Church," in *Toward a Synodal Church in Africa*, 123–36. Like some African writers, this author presents palaver as simply an adaptation or instantiation of a sociological phenomenon of conversation and dialogue. There is a tendency to miss its deeply spiritual foundation and characteristic.

the category of people whom Jesus would have described as the least of his sisters and brothers (Matthew 25). As such, palaver is inclusive just as synodality is inclusive.

Second, a community that engages in the communicative ethics and spiritual practice of palaver is enriched by the process precisely because speaking and listening as a community of discernment is always healing, renewing, and liberating. The word that is spoken and shared during discernment is neither oppressive nor violent; it is ever new and always renewing. In this sense, palaver appears as an experience of synodality, which is a dynamic process of speaking and listening under the guidance and animation of the Spirit. As Pope Francis states in his book *Let Us Dream*, "What characterizes the synodal path is the role of the Holy Spirit. We listen, we discuss in groups, but above all we pay attention to what the Spirit has to say to us."[19] The key lesson here is that a community that practices this process of collectively paying attention to the revelations of the Holy Spirit is dynamic and vibrant because the word never rests and the Holy Spirit is never dormant.

Third, because of its inclusive nature, the practice of palaver entails a widening circle of conversation, relationality, and engagement. Nobody is left out or left behind. The spirituality of synodality is a grassroots process in local churches, families, neighborhoods, Small Christian Communities, parishes, and dioceses. It is not a monopoly of the ordained clergy or of bishops. Rather, it is a space of discernment of, by, and for the People of God. In this sense, synodality is more authentically a dynamic movement "from the 'I' to the 'we.'"[20]

However, this third point needs to be nuanced. As we know, society is not perfect; palaver may not always function

---

[19] Pope Francis, *Let Us Dream: The Path to a Better Future* (New York: Simon and Schuster, 2020), 85.

[20] Synod of Bishops, First Session, October 4–29, 2023, Synthesis Report: "A Synodal Church in Mission," 2a.

as ideally as it should. For example, women are often excluded from participating in decision-making processes. This is one of the shortcomings of African religion and cultures. With this in mind, the practice of palaver is an ideal that calls the Church to conversion—to strive consistently for an inclusive practice of conversation and discernment as the People of God and the Family of God. In regard to women's participation, "There is no reason or impediment that should prevent women from carrying out leadership roles in the Church: what comes from the Holy Spirit cannot be stopped" (FD 60).

Fourth, the palaver circle is open-ended; it creates an unbounded space—ever widening and always including more participants in its primary goal to achieve consensus and overcome division with reconciliation. Here, I would add that although palaver refers to a word that is spoken and shared, this is not the only medium of communication. Like the embodiment of African spirituality described above, palaver can take various forms, including dance, storytelling, mime, mythology, and even silence. In line with what Ludovic Lado calls the "pedagogy of listening and silence" in his essay, silence is particularly important because listening in silence is quite often the most creative disposition in the context of palaver as a practice of discernment that allows us to hear the small, still voice of the Holy Spirit (1 Kings 19:12). "A synodal spirituality flows from the action of the Holy Spirit and requires listening to the Word of God, contemplation, silence and conversion of heart" (FD 43). This recalls the insightful remarks of Pope Francis that synodality "is an exercise of mutual listening, conducted at all levels of the Church and involving the entire People of God.… It is not about garnering opinions, not a survey, but a matter of listening to the Holy Spirit."[21]

---

[21] Pope Francis's address to the faithful of the Diocese of Rome, September 18, 2021.

As a practice of communal discernment in Africa, palaver entails the key elements of the spirituality of synodality, namely, encounter, dialogue, and listening. Far from being a mere exchange of words, there is a transcendent dimension in the practice of palaver. The spoken word originates in an experience of encounter with the Word of God, that is, Jesus Christ, not as text but as a personal encounter. Hence, "listening to the Word of God is the starting point and criterion for all ecclesial discernment" (FD 83). In the beginning was the Word of God (John 1). Sharing the Word of God in the process of ecclesial discernment constitutes a path of deeper encounter with God because "when we listen to our sisters and brothers, we are participants in the way that God in Jesus Christ comes to meet each of us" (FD 51).

In its authentic sense, palaver expresses the synodal path as defined by Pope Francis: it "makes room" for every member of the Body of Christ, that is, all women, men, and children, so that the community called Church can hear more clearly the voice of the Holy Spirit. It is important to reiterate the point that the inclusion of everybody in the synodal journey of participation, mission, and communion represents an ideal or aspiration rather than a lived reality. As the synodal process has revealed, the exclusion of many people on account of their lived situation, including gender, sexual orientation, and identity, poses a real challenge to the aspirations of synodality.

> The Church, both at the local level and by virtue of its Catholic unity, aspires to be a network of relationships which prophetically propagates and promotes a culture of encounter, social justice, inclusion of the marginalized, communion among peoples and care for the earth, our common home. (FD 121)

Creating room for the voices of all to be heard in a synodal Church ensures "that the Church is perceived as a welcoming home, a sacrament of encounter and salvation, a school of communion for all the sons and daughters of God" (FD 115). A patently patriarchal and hierarchical mode of exercising authority to the exclusion of women and young people is antithetical to the meaning of synodality.

As tools for ecclesial discernment, conversation in the Spirit and palaver offer the Church in Africa an effective means of practicing synodality. Formation in the understanding and application of these synodal tools is a prerequisite for the emergence of a truly synodal Church in Africa.

> It is essential to offer formation opportunities that spread and nourish a culture of ecclesial discernment focused on mission in local Churches, as well as in small ecclesial communities and parishes. This is particularly necessary amongst those who hold leadership roles. It is equally important to encourage the formation of facilitators, whose contribution is often crucial to the process of discernment. (FD 86)

The practice of ecclesial discernment opens the Church to receive the abundant gifts of the Spirit present in the community of believers: "This discernment draws on all the gifts of wisdom that the Lord bestows upon the Church and on the *sensus fidei* bestowed upon all the baptized by the Spirit" (FD 81).

Furthermore, this approach of palaver in the context of Africa confirms the meaning of synodality:

> In its broadest sense, synodality can be understood as Christians walking in communion with Christ toward the Kingdom along with the whole of humanity. Its orientation is towards mission, and its practice involves gathering in assembly at each level of ecclesial life. It involves reciprocal listening, dialogue, community

discernment, and creation of consensus as an expression that renders Christ present in the Holy Spirit, each taking decisions in accordance with their responsibilities.[22]

As Pope Francis states, "What characterizes the synodal path is the role of the Holy Spirit. We listen, we discuss in groups, but above all we pay attention to what the Spirit has to say to us."[23] Thus, spirituality is the soul of synodality, without which the latter becomes a hollow exercise of unproductive and unimportant talking, discussion, and communicating that goes on for too long.

Spirituality of Synodality: A Synthesis

Seen through the lens of African religion, African spirituality is contextual; it delineates the locus of encounter between the human and the Divine, the space where God encounters human beings and vice versa. In a similar vein, synodality is the praxis of encounter of both human beings and the Divine animated by the shared goal and desire to discover the will of God for the Church. This spirituality of encounter prioritizes mutual respect, listening, and dialogue. For synodality to become rooted in the Church, these elements ought to be prioritized. This spiritual approach to synodality renders it a more dynamic and transformative ecclesial exercise:

> We are called not only to translate the fruits of a personal spiritual experience into community processes. We are also called to experience how practicing the new commandment of reciprocal love is the place and form of encounter with God. In this sense, while drawing on the rich spiritual heritage of the Tradition, the synodal perspective contributes to renewing its forms: a prayer

---

[22] Synthesis Report, 1h.
[23] Pope Francis, *Let Us Dream*, 85.

open to participation, a discernment lived together, and a missionary energy that arises from sharing and that radiates as service. (FD 44)

The foregoing provides the basis for concluding that African spirituality has significant contributions to make to the universal Church in this journey of synodality. The Church would be richer if it draws from the deep wells of African spirituality to nourish the understanding, knowledge, and practice of synodality:

It is proposed that the Churches should experiment with and adapt conversation in the Spirit, and other forms of discernment in ways they may consider appropriate, drawing from diverse spiritual traditions relevant to the needs and cultures of their contexts. Appropriate forms of accompaniment can facilitate this practice, helping to grasp its logic and overcome possible resistance.[24]

It is unhelpful to disregard the gifts of African spirituality on account of prejudiced notions or views of Africa. To recall the words of Robert Schreiter, dwelling

on the problems that plague contemporary Africa is to see only some of the faces that it presents to the world today.... One cannot escape the feeling that a fulsome energy underlies what is going on in Africa today, both in the problems it confronts and the prospects it displays.[25]

In the practice of synodality, the Church can discover new roots in and draw insights from African spirituality to strengthen mission, communion, and participation as essential dimensions of synodality. Complemented by the respectful recognition of

---

[24] Synthesis Report, 2j.
[25] Robert J. Schreiter, *Faces of Jesus in Africa* (Maryknoll, NY: Orbis Books, 1991), viii.

the baptismal dignity of each member of the Body of Christ, synodality will fulfill its promise and transform the community called Church into a community rooted and anchored in the love of God and the love of one another, "so that it can walk with every man and woman, radiating the light of Christ" (FD 28).

2

Theological Foundations of Synodality

Marcel Uwineza

The concept of synodality has received exceptional and increasing attention in contemporary theology. It reflects the essence of what it means to be human and the nature of the Church in particular. Life with God is a synod par excellence. As far as one can trace the creation of human beings, one discovers a God who journeys and encounters humanity and vice versa. The God who creates is the God who journeys with, restores, heals, challenges, leads God's creatures, and gives them life. Human beings discover their true identity when they realize that they are oriented toward God, who remains mystery.

While the human person can still say something about the ineffable God, God remains greater and mysterious. This discovery is a journey that persons cannot make alone. They journey with others, learn from others, and ultimately realize that they are the addressees of God's love. Karl Rahner expressed this idea eloquently: "When we have said everything which can be expressed about ourselves, . . . we have not yet said anything about ourselves unless . . . we have also included that we are beings who are oriented toward the God who is incomprehensible."[1]

---

[1] Karl Rahner, "Theology and Anthropology," in *Theological Investigations*,

Foundationally, synodality is thus rooted in the sense that humanity journeys together toward God as it discovers that God has first journeyed toward creation.

Some people may co-opt God for their own interests. The question is then how to ensure that humanity is open to the "right" God. The criterion is a particular kind of love.

> What the Christian tradition maintains is the least inadequate expression for God finds its clearest, sharpest, simplest statement in . . . the first letter of John. There we read that "God is love" (1 John 4:8, 16). This love is *agapē*, that is "other-directed, love which seeks no return, love which does not want anything back." Ultimately, it is love which is pure self-gift. This love reveals God as incomprehensible mystery, revealing that God's love has no bounds and so urges humanity not to put bounds on love.[2]

As David Kaulemu also points out, the vision of synodality is primarily rooted in this love of God.

> At the heart of synodality is the Triune God. We find communion of the Father, the Son, and the Holy Spirit. This communion is foundational and a model of ecclesial relation and participation. Communion with the Triune God does not erase diversity. The three persons of the Trinity are distinct with different missions. Yet, they are united. The "Church is seen to be 'a people brought into unity from the unity of the Father, the Son, and the Holy Spirit.'"[3]

---

vol. 9, trans. G. Harrison (New York: Seabury, 1972), 216; see also Karl Rahner, "On the Theology of the Incarnation," in *Theological Investigations*, vol. 4, trans. K. Smith (New York: Crossroad, 1982), 108.

[2] Michael Himes, *Doing the Truth in Love: Conversations about God, Relationships, and Sacrifice* (New York: Paulist Press, 1995), 9–12. Some words of this quotation have also been used in my forthcoming book, *Healing a Wounded World* (2025).

[3] St. Augustine, *Sermon* 71, 20, 33.

Similarly, the Church is a community called by God, who has revealed Godself in Jesus Christ and the Spirit. It is a communion of communities, sustained by the memory of Jesus Christ inherited from the apostolic tradition. It embodies the stories and Christian *theopraxis* of pilgrims in need of redemption. The Church is rooted in the theological conviction and belief that "this body of people, this nation of pilgrims, in and for the world, is a fundamental part of God's plan in history, guided by the Holy Spirit."[4] It is not, therefore, a community of mere well-wishers or a syndicate of the like-minded. God calls us to journey together as the vulnerable people we are and inseparable from our fellowship and encounter with God. Therefore, to live in Christian community is to share in the life and love of the three persons in one God. *Lumen gentium* places the origin and sustenance of the Church in the ongoing work of the Father, Son, and Spirit. The Church must also be considered "as forming one complex reality comprising a human and divine element" (*Lumen gentium* 5).

While emphasizing the foundational mystery of God, who journeys with humanity, this essay also examines multiple sources in the tradition and historical practices of the Church, including Vatican II and Pope Francis's speech on the fiftieth anniversary of the establishment of the Synod of Bishops, that support and illuminate the vision of synodality in the third millennium. It also discusses the unique feature and ecclesiology of a synodal Church in our contemporary world that distinguishes it from previous conceptions and practices. Further, it explores the promises and prospects of synodality, its challenges and limitations, by showing what is African about synodality.

Ultimately, this essay brings forth resources from our Christian tradition, and it offers hope. Hope empowers humans "to have trust enough to undertake anew an exodus out of the

---

[4] Richard Gaillardetz, *Ecclesiology for a Global Church: A People Called and Sent* (Maryknoll, NY: Orbis Books, 2008), 91.

present into the future."⁵ At the heart of synodality is the desire to sow seeds of hope in an increasingly divided world, to notice those who are missing at the table, to go out in search of them, and proclaim with audacity the promises of God's reign of justice, peace, love, and reconciliation.

Foundations of Synodality in Scripture

The term *synod* stems from two Greek words: *syn*, which means together, and *hodos*, which means way, in other words, to come together, to walk together. In the Old Testament, the Hebrew word עֵדָה/קָהָל (*qahal*), often translated into Greek as ἐκκλησία, means assembly. This assembly manifests elements of synodality:

> This assembly . . . ratified in the Sinai covenant (cf. Exodus 24:6–8; 34, 20ff.), makes the People freed from slavery important and worthy to speak to God; in the exodus journey they gather around their God to celebrate His cult and live by His law, recognising that they belong to Him alone. (See Deuteronomy 5:1–22; Joshua 8; Nehemiah 8:1–18)⁶

In the assembly, the Lord remains at the center. In that assembly, men, women, children, and foreigners are welcome, and they journey together. That is why the International Theological Commission adds this.

> עֵדָה/קָהָל (qahal/'edah) is the first form in which the People of God's synodal vocation is disclosed. In the desert, God orders the census of the tribes of Israel,

---

⁵ Karl Rahner, "On the Theology of Hope," in *Theological Investigations*, vol. 10, trans. David Bourke (New York: Seabury Press, 1977), 250, 257.

⁶ International Theological Commission, *Synodality in the Life and Mission of the Church* 6, 2018, www.vatican.va/roman_curia/congregations/cfaith/cti_documents/rc_cti_20180302_sinodalita_en.html, 13.

giving each its place (cf. Numbers 1–2). At the centre of the assembly, as its only guide and shepherd, is the Lord, who becomes present through the ministry of Moses (cf. Numbers 12:15–16; Joshua 8:30–35), with whom others are associated in a subordinate and "collegial" way: the Judges (cf. Exodus 18:25–26), the Elders (cf. Numbers 11:16–17, 24–30), and Levites (cf. Numbers 1:50–51). The assembly of the People of God consists not only of men (cf. Exodus 24:7–8) but also women and children and even foreigners (cf. Joshua 8:33–35).[7]

The prophets used the language of their time to call for synodality. They invited the People of God to live in love and "justice in their relationships with their neighbours, often the poorest, the oppressed, foreigners, as a tangible witness to God's mercy."[8]

In the New Testament, the first synodal act of Christian mission is to be with and to know Jesus, or at least to have the desire and to act on it. Jesus journeyed with and gathered "a community of the unexpected."[9] His company did not exclude women. There are several examples. The former tax collector Matthew listens to the Word, laughs with him, "breaks bread with him, and in this finds his true identity. Adam was the friend of Yahweh before becoming, through his own fear and pride, Yahweh's enemy. Now Jesus, Yahweh made flesh, seeks to reestablish this lost friendship with Adam's descendants."[10] It is reasonable to think that other sinners were inspired by this encounter between Jesus and Matthew and yearned to enjoy table fellowship with Jesus.

---

[7] International Theological Commission, *Synodality in the Life and Mission of the Church*, no. 13.

[8] International Theological Commission, *Synodality in the Life and Mission of the Church*, no. 14.

[9] Bernard P. Prusak, *The Unfinished Church: Ecclesiology through the Centuries* (Mahwah, NJ: Paulist Press, 2004), 10.

[10] Robert Barron, *Eucharist* (Maryknoll, NY: Orbis Books, 2012), 41.

Or consider the story of Zacchaeus, who also experiences table fellowship with Jesus (Luke 19:1–10). Jesus invited those who had been excluded from society. One may recall how he listened to the cry of Bartimaeus, a blind man and a beggar (Mark 10:46–52). Unlike the crowd that attempted to silence him, Jesus did not silence him. He asked Bartimaeus to come closer.

If we place these encounters alongside the multiplication of bread and fish (Matthew 13:14–21), in which a great crowd is fed, we understand that in Jesus God journeys with "the hungry human race, starving from the time of Adam and Eve for what will satisfy."[11] We rediscover the synodal way of Jesus. In his meeting with sinners, lepers, or the woman at the well in Samaria (John 4:1–42), Jesus affirms that the "way" he teaches accords no significance to a person's race, ethnicity, culture, or country. The way Jesus teaches announces God's exclusive power and desire to create and name *us all* as God's sons and daughters.

Table fellowship reveals Jesus's synodal motive to renew God's friendship with humanity. "God sanctifies the world in Christ and men [and women] worship the Father as they adore him through Christ the Son of God" (*Sacrosanctum concilium* 10). Jesus makes God's friendship clearer in his words to his friends and disciples during the Johannine Gospel's farewell discourse: "No longer do I call you slaves, for the slave does not know what his master is doing; but I have called you friends, for all things that I have heard from My Father I have made known to you" (John 15:15). Consequently, Jesus's ministry was done in a synodal way.

From New Testament witnesses, one finds that the Church is a community of God's people who walk together in faith, hope, and love. The public ministry of Jesus was communal. It involved others as exemplified by the calling of his disciples, and Jesus's teaching called for mutual service, which is synodal. The final judgment in Matthew 25 is based on how well one has journeyed with others, especially those on the margins.

---

[11] Barron, *Eucharist*, 43.

Synodality and the Theological Trajectory in the Church

Journeying with the Lord is not done in isolation. It leads to the formation of a community, the Church, which is the visible symbol and continuation of the ministry of Jesus. The early Christian community solved its problems by coming together. One recalls how the initial problem of admission of Gentiles came through a common discernment (Acts 15). The Church and synodality are mutually inclusive. Saint John Chrysostom (CE 347–407) noted that "the Church and Synod are synonymous."[12] A few centuries earlier, Saint Ignatius of Antioch had stressed the synodal nature of the Church.

> Ignatius of Antioch describes the synodal understanding of the various local Churches, which saw themselves as jointly embodying the one Church. In his letter to the community in Ephesus, he says all its members are σύνοδοι, "companions on the journey," by virtue of the dignity of baptism and their friendship with Christ. Furthermore, he stresses the divine order that makes the Church a single body.[13]

The Church is a community of Christ's disciples who understand that their historical journey with God extends to all creation; a community transformed by the presence of the Holy Spirit (Romans 8:23; 2 Corinthians 2:4; Titus 3:5, 7). The Fathers emphasized the importance of unity and collective discernment prior to making decisions. The universal communion of such churches was mediated via the communion of their bishops, who assembled for general or ecumenical councils, convoked by the Christian emperors, to respond to serious threats to the unity of

---

[12] Preparatory Document for the Synod (2021), 14, www.synod.va/content/dam/synod/common/preparatory-document/pdf-21x21/en_prepa_book.pdf.

[13] Preparatory Document for the Synod (2021), no. 25.

the faith and of the newly Christian empire.[14] Regional synods were summoned to address doctrinal and pastoral issues. This practice continued through the Middle Ages and ecumenical councils; despite their limitations in participation, the councils served as concrete and visible symbols of ecclesial commitment to journeying together.

In the development of the Church during the Middle Ages up to Vatican II, with a few exceptions, the synodal nature of the Church lost its way. Church leaders struggled for power and imitated the structures of the Roman Empire. Bishops "ruled over their subjects who were expected to give them the kind of respect given to secular rulers."[15] A pyramidal ecclesiology ruled the day. It emphasized authority and hierarchy over synodality. The Church was conceived as a "perfect society"[16] without need of reform, and the "teaching church" took ascendance over the rest of the faithful. A distinction of ranks among the People of God became strong. The clergy were in charge, and the laity were to follow their orders. However, some theologians such as Johann Adam Möhler (1796–1838) and John Henry Newman (1801–1890) realized that the Church was and still is deeply impoverished if it does not celebrate the diversity of the gifts of all the People of God and if it does not consult the faithful.

On the one hand, Möhler remarks that all believers are bound in unity, but individuality is not suspended. He invites us to think of the Church as an organic body, a living organism with different parts or functions, or as a harmonious choir with different voices and a choirmaster who ensures the harmony of voices and rhythm. Möhler brought back the "lost" notion of the

---

[14] Prusak, *The Unfinished Church*, 130.
[15] Prusak, *The Unfinished Church*, 181.
[16] Prusak, *The Unfinished Church*, 249.

universal priesthood of all the faithful.[17] Möhler's ecclesiology distanced itself from the medieval Catholic ecclesiology, which was primarily juridical. He emphasized a spiritual communion among human beings with God. Möhler's theology affirms the synodal nature of the Church; not least is its recovery of the central role of the Holy Spirit.

On the other hand, John Henry Newman called Church leaders to rediscover the lost notion of consultation of the faithful manifest in the early Church. When asked why the faithful should be consulted, Newman responded, "The answer is plain, because the body of the faithful is one of the witnesses to the fact of the tradition of revealed doctrine, and because their consensus through Christendom is the voice of the Infallible Church."[18]

It is this consultation that the contemporary synodal way seeks to foster. For Newman, *consult* is "a word expressive of trust and deference, but not of submission."[19] Newman's call to journeying together with all the faithful is stronger in the following words: "Let us pay attention to the judgement of all the faithful, because the spirit of God breathes into every faithful."[20] What is clear is that the faithful have an important role in the Church—"the Church would look foolish without them"—and the concept of *consensus fidelium* was important to him. Newman challenged the pyramidal ecclesiology of the Middle Ages that ruled the Church for many centuries. In his writings, one finds the call for going back to the synodal sources of the early Church. Newman was ahead of his time; Vatican II, the institution of the Synod of Bishops by Paul VI, and the Synod on Synodality advance the ideas of Newman.

---

[17] John Henry Newman, *On Consulting the Faithful in Matters of Doctrine* (New York: Rowman and Littlefield, 1961), 74.

[18] John Henry Newman, "On Consulting the Faithful in Matters of Doctrine," 6, http://www.jstor.org/stable/90012581.

[19] Newman, *On Consulting the Faithful*, 70.

[20] Newman, *On Consulting the Faithful*, 68.

Vatican II and Synodality

Vatican II (1962–1965) was an event that brought a new style, a new approach, a new understanding, a spiritual and optimistic view of the Church. It challenged those who saw nothing but calamity in the world and in the Church, those whom Pope John XIII called "prophets of doom."[21] Beyond the conception of the Church as a "perfect society" that had prevailed, Vatican II reconceived the Church as a pilgrim People of God in need of constant reform. It is a church better understood primarily from its trinitarian roots than its external structures. Vatican II emphasizes that the hierarchy of the Church is at the service of communion. At the heart of Vatican II is the paradigm shift that explains its synodal and theological style. Jesuit historian John O'Malley summarizes it as follows.

> I will summarize in a simple litany some of the elements in the change in style of the Church indicated by the council's vocabulary: from commands to invitations, from laws to ideals, from threats to persuasion, from coercion to conscience, from monologue to conversation, from ruling to serving, from withdrawn to integrated, from vertical and top-down to horizontal, from exclusion to inclusion, from hostility to friendship, from static to changing, from passive acceptance to active engagement, from prescriptive to principled, from defined to open-ended, from behavior-modification to conversion of heart, from the dictates of law to the dictates of conscience, from external conformity to the joyful pursuit of holiness.[22]

---

[21] John XXIII, "Opening Address to the Council," October 11, 1962, www.catholicculture.org/culture/library/view.cfm.

[22] John W. O'Malley, "The Style of Vatican II," *America* 188, no. 6, February 24, 2003, 12–15.

The synodal nature of Vatican II is thus evident in its shift in style to invitation and to ensure that all Catholics find a home in the Church. There is a clear shift of "focus from *what* the council said to *how* it said it."[23] The documents of Vatican II heighten appreciation for a person, an event, an institution, and they excite emulation of an ideal. I shall briefly give some theological examples that reveal how synodality is at the heart of Vatican II.

An in-depth reading of *Lumen gentium* shows the reversal of pyramidal structures to communion ecclesiology in which all the baptized are equal because of their baptism. The Church is a mystery, not primarily an institution or organization. It is the whole People of God, not just the hierarchy. All the People of God participate in the mission of the Church, not just in the mission of the hierarchy. The Church is a communion of all the baptized, who are all equal before God. The Church is not primarily defined as a hierarchical institution. Vatican II thus gave a new orientation that offered the basis for an inclusive and decision-making process.

Lumen gentium affirms that the Church is also "related to those who have not yet received the Gospel" (16) and calls for continuous journey together and search for understanding of other religions. Similarly, *Nostra aetate* reverences what is true and holy in other religions:

> The Church, therefore, exhorts her sons [and daughters] that through dialogue and collaboration with the followers of other religions, carried out with prudence and love and in witness to the Christian faith and life, they recognize, preserve and promote the good things, spiritual and moral, as well as the socio-cultural values found among these men [and women]. (2)

---

[23] John W. O'Malley, *What Happened at Vatican II* (Cambridge, MA: Harvard University Press, 2008), 46–52.

Vatican II emphasized the use of vernacular languages in liturgy. This is explicit in *Sacrosanctum concilium*, which calls for greater participation and accessibility of public worship for all the faithful. This understanding of the Church is possible only when the People of God journey together and feel that they belong. The Church is the People of God made into one body in Christ, and it "takes citizens from all races" (*Lumen gentium* 1).

At the heart of Vatican II is an appeal for collegiality that calls bishops, clergy, and laity to shared responsibility in the governance of the Church. In line with Ludovic Lado's essay in this volume, collegiality is a synodal expression through which the bishops walk and work together for the good of the Church with the bishop of Rome. Pope Paul VI established the Synod of Bishops in 1965 to directly accentuate Vatican II's emphasis on communal concern for the life of the Church.

Furthermore, Vatican II reemphasized the role of the laity in the mission of evangelization, and the hierarchy must ensure that lay ministry is acknowledged and promoted (*Apostolicam actuositatem* 2, 3). This recognition is foundational for synodality. *Gaudium et spes* reiterated the synodal need of embracing "the joys and hopes, the griefs and anxieties" of the present age, especially the poor and the marginalized, to be "the joys and hopes, the griefs and anxieties of the followers of Christ" (*Gaudium et spes* 1). This radical solidarity is practically impossible without synodality. At the heart of *Gaudium et spes* is the desire to build a synodal Church that is not indifferent to the problems of the world but journeys with all humanity as salt and light for the world. Although this discussion on Vatican II is not exhaustive, it is fair to conclude that a redefinition of ecclesiology rooted in Vatican II lays down the foundations for synodality that has found its strongest reception in the theology of Pope Francis.

Pope Francis and Synodality

Among the theological threads that mark the pontificate of Francis, synodality stands out. Since the inception of his papacy, the following synods have taken place.

1. The Synod on the Family (2014–2015) with Francis's apostolic exhortation *Amoris laetitia* (2016), addressing the Church's role in accompanying families with mercy and compassion.
2. The Synod on Youth (2018) with Francis's postsynodal apostolic exhortation *Christus vivit* (2019), encouraging young people and the Church to embrace their energy and potential.
3. The Synod on the Amazon (2019) with Francis's apostolic exhortation *Querida Amazonia* (2020), emphasizing care for the environment, social justice, and cultural respect.
4. The Synod on Synodality (2021–2024), which represents a transformative effort to renew the Church's structures and practices.

These gatherings have demonstrated his desire for listening, open dialogue even about contentious issues such as divorced and remarried Catholics, clerical celibacy, and the role of women in the Church. The preparatory and consultative phases preceding these synods involved unprecedented levels of lay participation, with surveys and consultations conducted worldwide.

Francis's emphasis is rooted in his vision of the Church as the People of God as expressed in *Lumen gentium* at Vatican II. Listening and dialoguing internally and with the broader world are hallmarks of Francis's leadership. He has reached out to those on the fringes of society such as migrants and sexual minorities. He has promoted a culture of encounter with people of other religions. Francis offers a clear historical and theological rationale, and he underscores the fundamentals of synodality. For him, synodality is an indispensable dimension of the Church's way of being, born from the Church's ability to discern the will of God by listening to the Spirit of God, which speaks through the faithful.[24]

Synodality fosters collaboration among bishops. It seeks to promote the unity and vitality of the Church. Thus, a synod is not simply an administrative entity that regulates the relationship among the pope, bishops, and laity, but a process of discernment, listening, participation, and dialogue in view of seeking better ways of fulfilling the mission to announce the Gospel.

In his vision of synodality, Pope Francis makes it clear that the pope does not stand above the Church but is within it, as one whose mission is to preside in love and unity.[25] The structure of the synod works hand in hand with the authority of the pope in a collegial spirit with bishops, which echoes the teachings of Vatican II. However, Francis also recognizes that living out synodality comes with its challenges. He warned against two temptations: "rigid centralization, which stifles dialogue, and unchecked decentralization, which risks fragmentation." The pope stressed the need for a synodal Church to be "open to constructive debate, respectful of diverse perspectives, and attentive to the needs of the world."[26]

Pope Francis highlights the central dimension of lay participation, particularly that of young people and women, in the life of the Church and in decision-making processes. For him, "listening to the laity is not a concession but a reflection of the Church's mission to engage the entirety of God's people."[27]

---

[24] Pope Francis, address on the fiftieth anniversary of the institution of the Synod of Bishops, Vatican, October 17, 2015.

[25] Pope Francis, address on the fiftieth anniversary of the institution of the Synod of Bishops.

[26] Pope Francis, address on the fiftieth anniversary of the institution of the Synod of Bishops.

[27] Pope Francis, address on the fiftieth anniversary of the institution of the Synod of Bishops.

Listening to all People of God is essential, and its nurtures the Church's outward-looking gaze. It calls for humility as one listening to challenging voices, and it responds to the signs of our times. Ultimately, Francis's vision of synodality holds that it must be the Church's way of being and acting as we walk together to foster unity and diversity in service to the world. We may also ask if there is anything African about synodality. The following section turns to this theme.

What Is African about Synodality?

Although synodality is universal, its expression in Africa is intensely cultivated by the continent's rich cultural, social, and spiritual heritage. As Anne Arabome demonstrates in her essay, in the African context, one can find a unique perspective or lens "through which the essence of synodality can be explored and enriched." The African communal worldview, rooted in the philosophy of Ubuntu and often encapsulated in the phrase "I am because we are," is an important synodal lens that underscores interconnectedness, mutual care, and the centrality of community in individual and collective life. Synodality, which calls for the Church to walk together in unity and solidarity, finds a natural home in this communal ethos.

In Rwanda and Burundi, decisions are made after collective consultation and dialogue involving families, community leaders, or those who are considered to be *inyangamugayo* in Rwanda (or *abashingantahe* in Burundi), that is, people of incontestable integrity. This decision-making method is also obtainable in many African cultures. There are thus parallels to the synodal method of listening and discerning together in order to be actively attentive to every voice and to seek consensus. In many African societies, the tradition of storytelling and oral dialogue carries within it the requirement of listening and communal understanding—a point that Chijioke Azuawusiefe explores in his essay.

Since there are always competing voices, and God does not speak with one univocal voice, how do leaders discern and recognize God's voice and do what is right? One has to assess the role of traditional leadership in Africa. Following the lead of the Nigerian theologian Elochukwu Uzukwu,

> The metaphor of listening . . . is drawn from the experience of the *Manja* of Central African Republic. The totem of the *Manja* chief is the rabbit because it has "large ears." The idea of listening . . . should inform and transform ministry in the church community.[28]

The point from this Central African worldview is that a leader must listen and speak only after he or she has "recorded the discussions going on in the community, so that his speech releases the healing Word of which he [or she] is the principal custodian, a word which makes the community stand erect."[29] The point is that chiefs and elders, honored for their wisdom and authority, must be servants of harmony and reconciliation and be decision-makers for the benefit of all. Implicit in this model is servant-leadership, which involves service as opposed to domination. Those who participate in synodal processes can learn from African traditional practices in order to encourage full participation and inclusive leadership in the Church. This is what has been at the heart of Francis's call for a synodal Church.

Synodality is also rooted in the vitality of African spirituality, as Arabome explains in her essay. Many Africans have great respect for the sacred, the ancestors, and communal rituals. The vibrancy of African liturgies involves the whole person and community. The African inclusion of both young and old, men and women in ritual celebrations is an inspiration for an ongoing synodal process.

---

[28] Elochukwu E. Uzukwu, *A Listening Church: Autonomy and Communion in African Churches* (Maryknoll, NY: Orbis Books, 2006), 11.

[29] Uzukwu, *A Listening Church*, 129–30.

Africa faces many historical and ongoing challenges including poverty, exclusion, corruption, injustice, conflict, genocide, tribalism, nepotism, and dysfunctional leadership. These challenges offer the African Church some opportunities to take seriously its traditional values and to prioritize the voices of those who feel excluded. In many African countries, the Church's care for the elderly and refugees, its advocacy for justice, and its education institutions are but examples of the call to journey with those on the margins.

The Church can further draw from the African approach to reconciliation and healing. Methods of healing and reconciliation, such as the truth and reconciliation commissions of South Africa and Rwanda, restorative justice such as *gacaca*,[30] and avenues for truth-telling are close to the synodal invitation to dialogue and listening. The Church in Africa can draw on these traditions to foster unity and renewal in the global Church.

Promises and Prospects: The Unique Feature and Ecclesiology of a Synodal Church

The Synod on Synodality has caused a paradigm shift in the understanding of what it means to be Church. Its emphasis on communion, participation, and mission as foundations of ecclesiology cannot be exaggerated (FD 3, 6, 16). Synodality has rearticulated the vision of *Lumen gentium*, which illustrates the sacramental nature of the Church in its communion with the triune God. Further, *Lumen gentium* also reemphasized the shared

---

[30] The word *gacaca* means tall grass. In the past, a village sat on the grass to settle community disputes. Village elders heard the disputes and resolved them according to local customs. Modern gacaca is a contemporary Rwandan traditional and legal structure that tried many genocide cases. For further exploration, see Paul Christoph Bornkamm, *Rwanda's Gacaca Courts: Between Retribution and Reparation* (New York: Oxford University Press, 2012).

Christian responsibility of all the baptized in the mission of the Church (FD 9). The chapter on the People of God comes before that of hierarchy to underscore the co-responsibility (FD 30a) and vocation of all the baptized: "The whole People of God is an agent of the proclamation of the Gospel. Every baptised person is called to be a protagonist of mission since we are all missionary disciples" (FD 4).

As José Minaku points out in his essay, communion, participation, and mission reflect a renewed ecclesial model capable of reforming and transforming the overly rigid hierarchical model. The unique feature of synodality is thus the "participation of the whole People of God in its life and mission, on all levels and distinguishing between various ministries and roles" (FD 30a). Synodality offers "the most appropriate interpretative framework for understanding the hierarchical ministry itself."[31] The call for and practice of dialogue, discernment nurtured in spiritual conversation, and inclusion align the synodal Church with the challenges and realities of our contemporary world.

Another feature of the contemporary synodal Church is rooted in the priority given the collective journey of God's people. This shared journey challenges clericalism and encourages the shared responsibilities of laity, clergy, and bishops. This journey deepens the *sensus fidei*, the innate sense of faith of God's people, as Ludovic Lado points out in his essay, who must not be overlooked in ecclesial decision-making. The theology born from a synodal Church must prioritize inclusion as an integral part of what it means to be Church. This includes particular attention to the marginalized, youth, women, migrants, single mothers, different categories of the poor, and those in search of meaning for their lives.

Another distinctive feature of the synodal Church is its openness and authentic interchange within and beyond ecclesial

---

[31] Francis, address in commemoration of the fiftieth anniversary of the institution of the Synod of Bishops.

borders. The ecumenical exchanges that enriched conversations during the 2021–2024 Synod on Synodality are unparalleled. Pope Francis invited leaders of other faith traditions to join in an interfaith prayer at the beginning of both sessions of the synod in 2023 and 2024. This openness to dialogue will enrich other areas of common interests such as social and ecological justice and human rights. Synodal leaders have a lot to learn from experts in fields other than the ecclesiastical disciplines to respond to the challenges of our contemporary world in an interdisciplinary and effective manner.

At the heart of the synodal Church is a mission-oriented ecclesiology. This is a fulfillment of Vatican II's *Ad gentes*: "Divinely sent to the nations of the world to be unto them 'a universal sacrament of salvation' (*Lumen gentium* 1), the Church, driven by the inner necessity of her own catholicity, and obeying the mandate of her Founder (cf. Mark 16:16), strives ever to proclaim the Gospel to all [people]" (1). This mission begins with an inward examination of what the Church is. It is then followed by an outward movement toward others in solidarity and service to all men and women. Thus, synodality invites the Church to shift from a self-referential ecclesial institution to a mission-driven community that brings hope and renewal. "Synodality is not an end in itself. Rather, it serves the mission that Christ entrusted to the Church in the Spirit" (FD 32). To evangelize is "the essential mission of the Church.… It is the grace and vocation proper to the Church, her deepest identity" (*Evangelii nuntiandi* 14). The unique feature of a contemporary synodal Church is expressed in Pope Francis's invitation to labor for a Church that is a "field hospital,"[32] healing the wounds and confronting the struggles of humanity (FD 56). "Synodality and mission are intimately linked: mission illuminates synodality and synodality spurs to mission" (FD 32).

---

[32] Antonio Spadaro, "A Big Heart Open to God: The Exclusive Interview with Pope Francis," *La Civiltà Cattolica,* September 30, 2013.

Finally, the distinguishing features of a synodal Church include the call to shift from hierarchy to collaboration and co-responsibility, from uniformity to diversity, and from ecclesial maintenance and self-referentiality to mission-driven Church and renewal of ecclesial life. These features challenge old, institution-centered paradigms to become more inclusive, discerning, participatory, transparent, dynamic, listening, mutually respectful, trustworthy, humble, prophetic, and mission-centered to proclaim the Gospel to the world. These new models offer hope, renewal, promises, and prospects beyond the boundaries of the Church in order to respond to the needs of our increasingly divided world.

Challenges and Limitations of Synodality

The reading of the Final Document of the synod reveals that there has been and still is resistance to change: "We cannot deny that we have faced fatigue, resistance to change and the temptation to let our own ideas prevail over listening to the Gospel and the practice of discernment" (FD 6). The fathers and mothers of the 2024 synod acknowledged the need to change and the resistance that comes from change, and the needed repentance:

> Acknowledging this, we began the Second Session of the Assembly with a penitential vigil, through which, feeling our shame, we asked forgiveness for our sins, and we lifted up our prayers for the victims of the evils of the world. We identified our sins: against peace, against Creation, against indigenous peoples, migrants, children, women, and those who are poor, in our failure to listen and to seek communion. We were brought to a renewed understanding, namely, that synodality requires repentance and conversion. (FD 6)

Alongside resistance to change are the inequality of voices and risk of division. It remains to be seen how different voices made a difference at the synod. The consultation of those on the margins is important, but it is also important to ensure that these voices do not simply remain simple gestures of inclusion without meaningful impact. Also, cultural minorities find it difficult to have their voices genuinely heard and respected. In the same manner, dialogue needs clear guidance because without careful coordination, differences can become reasons for further division rather than unity (FD 53–54).

Finally, there are challenges of clericalism, power dynamics, complexity of decision-making, and global disparities. These and other challenges need to be seriously discerned, discussed, and confronted if synodality is to bear more fruit for the future. The means of conducting this discernment emerge from within the practice of synodality.

Conclusion

This chapter discussed the theological foundations of synodality. Drawing on scripture and tradition, it has located synodality within the whole journey of humanity with the triune God. Synodality evokes the human story with God. With reference to several magisterial documents and theologians, the chapter has offered the resources of synodality. It underscored the inclusive mission of Jesus's way of being and journeying with people, including the unexpected: sinners and prostitutes. The synodal Jesus still asks, Who is missing at your table when you gather as Church? How much effort have you put into bringing them back or making them feel at home and inviting them to conversion?

The chapter further explored how the synodal vision of the community that gathered around Jesus lost its originality because of power and domination during the Middle Ages.

Post-Reformation theologians challenged the Church of the Middle Ages and sought to bring back the lost synodal spirit, which was recovered at Vatican II. What has emerged from Pope Francis is that synodality remains the embodiment of what it means to be Church. It is a path to conversion, a healing of wounds, mercy, and pastoral care.

Finally, the chapter turned to African wisdom to discover synodal cognates, including the practice of inclusive consultation and dialogue and a holistic spirituality. Ultimately, synodality is now a sacrament of hope for the Church. Despite the challenges and limitations of synodality, it still offers hope that will not deceive or disappoint (Romans 5:5).

3

COMMUNICATION AND THE SYNODAL CHURCH

Ngiga as an African Symbol of Synodality

CHIJIOKE AZUAWUSIEFE

This essay examines the interconnections of communication and synodality and assesses the role and challenges of communication in a synodal Church from an African perspective. It begins with an illustration of *ngiga* as a central symbol of its analysis and explores synodality at the intersection of communication, communion, and community. It also analyzes Pope Francis's emphasis on dialogue and listening as an appropriate and recommended communication style of the synod as well as how the particular nonverbal communication procedure of the synod's roundtable approach promotes and enriches synodality.

This essay further evaluates the reality and challenges of synodality for the Church in Africa and concludes by looking ahead to some of the key values essential for that synodality to become a way of living and working of the Church. For the Church in Africa to continue to respond meaningfully to the needs of the faithful in the twenty-first century, it needs to embrace the synodal process of open, honest, and inclusive dialogue and conversations; free itself from the restrictions of clericalism as well as unhealthy hierarchy and patriarchy; and not only respect the dignity and equality of the baptized but also listen to and incorporate the voices of those often consigned to the periphery by race, gender, age, migration, climate change, inequality, and injustice.

Communication informs a synodal process. It animates the ongoing conversations on the approaches to living out the reality of the Church as *ecclesia*, the People of God, in light of the ecclesiology of Vatican II and as articulated by the magisterium of Pope Francis, under the inspiration and guidance of the Holy Spirit.

In October 2021, Pope Francis called for a Synod on Synodality and a synodal Church. His call inaugurated a process of communication and reflections that continue to invite the Church, as the People of God, to journey together in communion with one another, acknowledging and respecting the dignity and equality of the faithful.[1] The two-part Synod on Synodality (October 2023 and October 2024) was marked by terms that express the synod's theme of "communion, participation, and mission." They include words and phrases such as dialogue, listening, assembly, and roundtable as well as discernment, conversation in the Spirit, and sharing of life experiences.

These terms indicate the vision of the Church that Pope Francis wants his papacy to embody. He understands and talks about synodality as a dynamic process, a journey, an evolving and ongoing engagement that is anchored on the word *synod*, "walking together." This vision of synodality dates back to the start of his pontificate. In 2013, he described synodality as a dynamic engagement that "should be lived at various levels" and must involve the walking together of the people, the bishop, and the pope.[2] Addressing the

---

[1] See General Secretariat for the Synod, "Synod and Communication: A Pathway to Develop" (2022); Congregation for the Doctrine of Faith, "Synodality in the Life and Mission of the Church" (2018).

[2] Francis, "A Big Heart Open to God: An Interview with Pope Francis," by Antonio Spadaro, SJ, *America* (September 30, 2013).

faithful of the Diocese of Rome in 2021, Pope Francis reiterated this vision, describing synodality as "a dynamism of mutual listening, conducted at all levels of the Church, involving the whole People of God."[3]

Both synodality and its articulation by Pope Francis underscore a fundamental element of the Church: communication. The Church is communication that reflects the communication and communion of the community of the Trinity.[4] Communication is not only vital and foundational to the Church; it is also particularly indispensable to the synodal process. On the one hand, it calls for an active presence and participation of the faithful as members of the ecclesial community. On the other hand, it informs the Church's self-understanding and its mission as it continues to seek better ways to dialogue and communicate as a community of the faithful in communion with one another (see Acts 6:1–7).

Ngiga: An African Symbol of Synodality

When [the disciples] climbed out on shore, they saw a charcoal fire with fish on it and bread.... Jesus said to them, "Come, have breakfast." ... Jesus came over and took the bread and gave it to them, and in like manner the fish. (John 21:9–13 RNAB)

An African proverb from the Igbo people of southeast Nigeria says, *E zuo ka aha eri aja, a totuo ngiga*, "Once the gathering of those who share a common sacrificial meal convenes, they lower the *ngiga*." An ngiga is a spherical basket with a lid used to store and preserve meat, fish, and other cooking items. It is usually

---

[3] Francesca Merlo, "Pope to Rome's Faithful: Synodality Expresses the Nature of the Church," *Vatican News* (September 18, 2021).

[4] See Federation of Asian Bishops' Conferences Office of Social Communication (FABC-OSC), "27th Annual Bishops' Meet 2022 Communication and the Synodal Church" (November 6–10, 2022).

hung over a hearth to keep its contents perennially dry with the heat from the cooking below. The sacrificial dish here refers to the meat of animals sacrificed to particular divinities.

The ngiga analogy expresses the reality of a community gathered together around a common meal—in a manner similar to the way those baptized in Christ, the faithful, are gathered around the Eucharist, the perfect sacrifice, the source and summit of the Christian life. More important, it symbolizes the post-resurrection gathering of the disciples around a meal of fish and bread prepared for them by Jesus Christ on a charcoal fire on the lakeshore and how that nourishment represents a part of the initial invitation and gathering of his disciples around a common meal by the risen Christ. In reference to the Prophet Isaiah, the Final Document of the Synod on Synodality calls this meal a "banquet," "a feast for all peoples," "a superabundant and sumptuous banquet prepared by the Lord on the mountaintop, a symbol of conviviality and communion intended for all peoples" (Isaiah 25:6–8 [RNAB]; FD 153). It signifies the beginning of an eschatological banquet that finds its fullness in heaven.

Keeping the above elaboration in mind, and without any attempts to extract exact equivalences out of the analogy, one could say that the hearth symbolizes the altar and the ngiga symbolizes the tabernacle. In that sense, the coming together of the members becomes a eucharistic gathering around the altar. However, in the sense that the content of ngiga is an assortment of items, the content differs tremendously from the body and blood of Jesus Christ, the Eucharist. Nevertheless, to the extent that the lowering of ngiga for such a symbolic and ceremonial communion gathers members together for a common meal, a meal that nourishes the community and fosters communion, one might draw parallels.

Hence, the proverb speaks to the community and communion into which the risen Christ continues to invite the Church (FD 152). It indicates that once those who dine together, those who break bread together gather, they open their common dish. To dine together is to share communion; to share communion is to communicate with one another on a deeper level. As presented by Anne Arabome in her essay about the spirituality of synodality, community and communion are central to the ways that Africans conceive of and engage with their worldviews. The ngiga ritual becomes symbolic of the African palaver, with dialogue at its heart, and dialogue fosters collaboration, communion, and community. Prioritizing these values in a synodal Church enables the Church to communicate as well as ensure and promote communication at different levels within its diverse communities (and with the Church's external publics—men and women of good will). This experience of communication enriches and advances community and communion not only at the center but also between the center and the peripheries.

Communication, Communion, Community: Toward a Dynamic Synodality

In the beginning was the Word, and the Word was with God and the Word was God. He was in the beginning with God. All things came to be through him, and without him nothing came to be. (John 1:1–3 RNAB)

For cultures in Africa that are traditionally steeped in orality, the spoken word remains central. It constitutes an essential ingredient of the African palaver, which deriving from the Portuguese *palavra*, equally means "word." In his classic novel *Things Fall Apart*, Chinua Achebe popularizes an African proverb that underscores the significance and preeminence of the spoken word: "Among the Igbo the art of conversation is regarded very highly, and proverbs are the palm-oil with which words are eaten."[5]

---

[5] Chinua Achebe, *The African Trilogy: Things Fall Apart, No Longer at Ease, Arrow of God* (New York: Everyman's Library, 2010 [1958]).

In other words, for a conversation, a palaver, a dialogue to have an enduring and meaningful outcome, the words have to be metaphorically consumed with the aid of proverbs, adages, and sayings to guarantee a smooth passage and easy digestion of their inherent message.

In the Bible also "word" primarily refers to the spoken word, and words represent the predominant means of communication. Hence, the meal and palaver of the ngiga metaphor privilege the spoken word in a way that establishes and connects its cultural import to the overarching context of the eternal Word in the opening passage of John's Gospel. In the ritualized ngiga experience of the Church—the Eucharist—both the Word and the spoken word remain central, as Jesus Christ, the incarnate Word, communicates the essence and love of God to the members of his body sharing in the meal of his body and blood. Hence, word is essential to communication; the phrase "Word of God" represents the most eloquent and preponderant expression of divine communication in the Bible.[6]

Understood as a symbolic process that produces, maintains, repairs, and transforms reality, communication has two nineteenth-century Western culture–influenced conceptions that derive from both secular and religious origins, namely, the transmission and the ritual views of communication.[7] The former and more common is often conveyed through terms like "imparting," "transmitting," "sending," or "giving information to others." It is informed by a metaphor of transportation, in a similar sense of the movement of information being likened to

---

[6] See Jose Punamadam, "Biblical Understanding of Communication," n.d., https://marthoma.in/biblical-understanding-of-communication-rev-jose-punamadam/.

[7] The essay's analysis of these conceptions and categorizations of communication is informed and enriched by the treatment of the subject by James Carey in *Communication as Culture: Essays on Media and Society* (Boston: Unwin Hyman, 1989).

the movement of people and goods. The idea of associating communication with transportation and transmission dates back to the ancient human desire to move messages faster across time and space as well as to increase their impact in the process. However, although the ritual understanding of communication represents a minor thread, it predates the former. Informed in part by Emile Durkheim's work,[8] the ritual view of communication connects to terms like "sharing," "participation," "association," "fellowship," and "the possession of a common faith." It shares roots with words such as "commonness," "communion," and "community." To a great extent, this conception of communication contributes to building society. As James Carey puts it,

> A ritual view of communication is directed not towards the extension of messages in space but toward the maintenance of society in time; not an act of imparting information but the representation of shared beliefs.... The archetypal case [of communication] under a ritual view is the sacred ceremony that draws persons together in fellowship and commonality.[9]

The ritual view of communication and the terms that articulate its reality underscore not only the relationship of communication with communion and community; they also highlight the connectedness of that understanding of communication to the theme of the Synod on Synodality: communion, participation, and mission. They evoke the dynamic nature of synodality as a journey, a process of dialogue, assembly, listening, and roundtable. Likewise, the roundtable-esque feature of the ngiga symbol fosters a similar reality and process. It focuses on the connectedness of communication with communion and community. The three

---

[8] Emile Durkheim, *The Elementary Forms of Religious Life* (New York: Free Press, 1995 [1912]).

[9] Carey, *Communication as Culture*, 18.

intersect at the rituals of communal experience centered around the ngiga and its content, evoking not only memories but also invitations to and actions of association, participation, and fellowship in dialogue and conversations equally rooted in mutual, dynamic, and respectful listening.

For the Church, communication, communion, and community reflect and derive from God's self-manifestation, especially in the scriptures. Although the word "communication" is not used in the Bible, communication remains central in the Bible, and the entire Bible is an account of God's communication, acts, and actions in relationship with God's people. Even though in everyday human conversations, one hardly hears of God spoken of as a communicator, as a God of communication, the Bible represents an unambiguous documentation and communication of God's love, judgment, and mercy to God's people. Since communication remains an integral part of the Bible, the Bible becomes the divine communication articulated in human language. From the Old Testament, God reveals God's self through words, deeds, and God's presence, manifesting the everlasting presence of divine communication.[10]

From the first pages of the Bible, we encounter God as God of communication, God who communicates. Genesis, for instance, begins by telling us that God created the heavens and the earth through communication; God communicated the world into existence. The opening verses of the first creation account tell us that in the beginning, when God created the heavens and the earth, the earth was without form or shape, and darkness covered the face of the earth. That introduction primes us for our first and resounding encounter with God's communication: "Then God said: Let there be light, and there was light" (Genesis 1:3, RNAB). The first communication of the creator God not

---

[10] See Margaret M. Mullan, *Seeking Communion as Healing Dialogue: Gabriel Marcel's Philosophy for Today* (Lanham, MD: Lexington, 2021).

only commands form and order unto the universe; it also dispels darkness, bringing life into existence.

Throughout the scriptures, God continues to communicate awe, order, love, compassion, and even jealousy and fury. God continues to communicate with God's people, communicating and manifesting God's self to us through words, revelation, actions, interactions, and ultimately—in the New Testament—through Jesus Christ, the eternal Word of God made flesh (John 1:14). Given that the essence of the incarnation is to communicate God's love to humanity, God primarily and particularly communicates the divine love in a special way through Jesus Christ, who is both the medium and the message of God's communication. Jesus Christ, the Word that was with God in the beginning and through whom God created the world (John 1:1–3), becomes the communicative self-expression of the Trinity, communicating God as well as God's love and compassion not only through his own life but also, among other things, through parables and stories, and subsequently—following his passion, death, and resurrection—through the Church.[11]

As an incarnational reality, the Church exists to communicate. It "exists in order to bring men [and women] into communion with God and thereby to open them up to communication with each other."[12] It mirrors the rich variety of modes of communication employed by Jesus Christ in the words and message of the Gospel of God's love to the cultures it serves and ministers to. Beyond formal doctrinal teachings, the Church also teaches through its being, presence, and actions. The baptized—

---

[11] John Navone, "Communion, Community, and Communication," *Homiletic and Pastoral Review* (2014); Agbonkhianmeghe E. Orobator, *Theology Brewed in an African Pot* (Maryknoll, NY: Orbis Books, 2008); Marshall McLuhan, *The Medium Is the Message: An Inventory Effect* (New York: Bantam Books, 1967).

[12] Avery Dulles, "The Church and the Media," *Catholic Mind* 69, no. 1256 (1971): 6–16.

clergy, religious, or lay—advance this communication mission of the Church, the community, in communion with one another.

As several contributors to this volume, particularly Josée Ngalula and Marcel Uwineza, demonstrate, the communion of the Church among its members and with God draws from the trinitarian community as its source, model, and goal. The Trinity, through their self-communication, create and sustain the community of the Body of Christ, thereby offering to humanity an image of their triune life and love. The Trinity share their triune love through the mission of the Son and the Holy Spirit to unite all humankind in communion, community, and communication. The awareness of this communion and community rooted in the Trinity fosters interdependence among the members of the Church as the People of God and avoids individualistic notions of personhood as well as the promotion of unfettered autonomy and infinite freedom—all of which undermine the sense of dialogue and conversation at the root of the African palaver that animates the ngiga meal.

The ngiga symbol presupposes a community, in this case, a community of the Church, the People of God, where the Trinity remains present and central, inviting the baptized to sacrament, communion, community, and friendship. Jesus continuously draws and inaugurates us into this new community, his body, the Church—the abiding sacrament of God's love for the incorporation of humanity into the life and love of the Trinity. This community informs the Church's desire for a true and authentic communion with the baptized, those at the margins, as well as with men and women of good will, while communicating the redemptive message of the Gospel.

Given the understanding of communication as a process of achieving and fostering communion and community, one can say that the Church is communication. In that sense, the Church becomes an extensive and expansive communication network designed to bring the community of the People of God into communion with God. If, then, the Church is communication and exists to communicate, part of the responsibility of leaders in the Church should be to ensure adequate and proper communication. Communication in the Church is essential for building community and fostering communion. The apostles and the early Christians built a community of believers and fostered communion among themselves partly because of their ability to communicate to one another and to others the manifestations of the message of the Gospel in the life, passion, death, and resurrection of Jesus Christ. They in turn modeled this community-building, communion-fostering communication after the approach of Jesus Christ, their master and teacher, who oriented them into the communion, community, and communication of the Trinity by calling and gathering them into a community and by teaching them the good news of the Kingdom.

Listening with the Heart: Roundtable of Dialogue and Conversations in the Spirit

In a synodal Church the whole community is called together to pray, listen, analyse, dialogue, discern and offer advice on making pastoral decisions which correspond as closely as possible to God's will.[13]

Another African proverb from southeast Nigeria is *Nti bu ogaranya*, "The ear is a rich or wealthy individual." But that is not all that the proverb says. *Nti bu ogaranya* means that one is enriched through listening, that through active listening, one gains substantially. For an oral culture, like most preliterate African cultures, one would understand why active listening was important to such a society. In the period when nothing was written down, one had to pay attention and listen attentively to register and retain whatever was being communicated so as

---

[13] General Secretariat of the Synod, "What Is Synodality," synod.va.

to remember and later recall it. The ability to retain, remember, and relay oral messages was counted and lauded as social and cultural capital for the individual who possessed it and deployed it efficiently.

Even when our contemporary society and communities have become literate, attentive and active listening still remains important in our world. The Bible teaches that such listening establishes an important connection in the relationship of dialogue between God and humanity. The *Shema* of Deuteronomy 6:4 (Hear, O peoples!) illustrates the point that the knowledge and love of God start with hearing the Word of God with one's heart. Spotlighting the importance of listening to communication in his 2022 Message for the 56th World Day of Social Communications, Pope Francis invites the faithful to "[listen] with the ear of the heart."[14]

The pontiff calls listening "the first indispensable ingredient of dialogue and good communication" and insists that "the true seat of [such] listening is the heart."[15] To listen with the heart, then, is to listen with empathy, to listen with a mind-set that helps us understand others' words and their meanings as well as to genuinely respect their humanity, dignity, and freedom. Both the synod's *Instrumentum Laboris* (Organizing Document) and Final Document underscore the importance of listening when they emphasize dynamic listening and use the word "listen" sixty-five times and fifty-two times, respectively.[16] The Final Document (3) further centers listening when it notes, in reference to the richness and fruitfulness of the entire synodality journey, "We began by

---

[14] Message of Pope Francis for the fifty-sixth World Day of Social Communications, "Listening with the Ear of the Heart," January 24, 2022.

[15] Francis, "Listening with the Ear of the Heart." See also Matthew MacDonald, "Synod on Synodality's Communication Style: Don't Debate—Listen, Says Pope Francis," *National Catholic Register*, October 12, 2023.

[16] *Instrumentum Laboris* for the First Session, October 2023, Final Document.

listening, taking care to grasp in the many voices 'what the Spirit is saying to the Churches' (Rev. 2:7)." The fruit of such a dynamic and intentional listening helps both the Church and humanity build a better world, because the human need for listening is to communicate better. By listening to hear and to understand, we put ourselves in a better position to have a meaningful and respectful dialogue. As Pope Francis notes, "It is only by paying attention to *whom* we listen, to *what* we listen, and to *how* we listen that we can grow in the art of communicating, the heart of which is not a theory or a technique, but the 'openness of heart that makes closeness possible.'"[17]

This openness of heart that informs intentional listening and genuine communication speaks to the Church's commitment to nurturing dialogue. As *Communio et progressio* notes, "The Church looks for ways of multiplying and strengthening the bonds of union between her members. For this reason, communication and dialogue among Catholics are indispensable."[18] Furthermore, "The Church does not speak and listen to her own members alone; her dialogue is with the whole world" (*Communio et progressio* 122).

Although the Church's commitment to dialogue predates Vatican II, the documents of Vatican II illustrate further its mission to communication and dialogue. Besides *Gaudium et spes*, whose commitment to dialogue manifests through its address to "the whole of humanity," Vatican II equally issued *Dignitatis humanae*, the Declaration on Religious Liberty, to further underscore the significance of dialogue in communicating the truth without disregard for human dignity. Also, the postconciliar document "On Dialogue with Unbelievers" articulates dialogue

---

[17] "Listening with the Ear of the Heart."
[18] "*Communio et progressio*: Pastoral Instruction for the Application of the Decree of the Second Vatican Council on the Means of Social Communication" (1971).

as "any form of getting together and communication between persons, groups or communities, in a spirit of sincerity, reverence for persons, and a certain trust, in order to achieve a greater grasp of truth or more human relationships."[19] Through *Inter mirifica*, the Decree on Means of Social Communications, the Church continues to assert not only its duty and right to proclaim the Gospel, instruct the People of God, and labor for the salvation of souls with the help of those media of social communications, but also its responsibility to facilitate dialogue using the same media.[20]

The advancement of dialogue and human relationships remains essential to communication. However, the dynamics of the art of communication and the cultivation of the trust necessary for realizing it are not always verbalized. Owing to the prominence given to verbal communication in our world today, the tendency to either ignore or relegate nonverbal communication to the background remains strong. Research shows that average adults spend about 70 percent of their time engaged in one form of communication or the other; 45 percent of this 70 percent goes to listening, even though we remember only about 20 to 50 percent of everything we hear. What this means is that in every twenty-four hours, we spend about seventeen hours engaged in one form of communication or the other. Out of these seventeen hours, we use approximately eight hours for just listening. However, we retain only between one and a half hours to four hours of what we hear. If we spend eight hours of our day listening to a lot of things but retain as little as just one and a half hours or at most four hours of those, it goes to show the importance of learning how to listen more attentively, more purposefully, and more dynamically while paying attention

---

[19] "On Dialogue with Unbelievers" (1968). See also "Pastoral Constitution on the Church in the Modern World, *Gaudium et spes*" (1965); "Declaration on Religious Liberty, *Dignitatis humanae*" (1965).

[20] "Decree on the Means of Social Communication, *Inter mirifica*" (1963).

to the nonverbal cues of human interactions so that we can retain more and communicate better.[21]

By centering the Synod on Synodality on collaborative communication and conversation in the Spirit as well as by inviting the synod participants to listen (with the heart) more than to discuss and debate, Pope Francis highlights the significance of nonverbal communication in the life of the Church today. Within the context of the synod, much more than the words uttered by the participants, the nonverbal communication component of the eleven-person roundtable seating arrangement of the participants enhances dynamic listening, fosters community, and enriches dialogue. This communal dialogue harkens to the Genesis account of creation, which highlights elements of dialogue in divine communication: "Let us make human beings in our image" (Genesis 1:26, RNAB).

Reality and Challenges of Synodality of the Church in Africa

We are a Church learning to journey together.[22] As stated above, "synod" in its simplest understanding refers to "walking together." Pope Francis emphasizes that such a journey benefits the Church in the twenty-first century more if it includes not only the hierarchy and the clergy but also religious brothers and sisters as well as lay men and women who journey together as they dialogue and listen to one another, discerning the life and the mission of

---

[21] See Gema Bellido, ed., *A Church in Dialogue: The Art and Science of Church Communication* (Rome: Edizioni Santa Croce); Roffey Park Institute, "The Art of Listening" (2021); Roland B. Adler, Lawrence B. Rosenfeld, and Russell F. Proctor, *Interplay: The Process of Interpersonal Communication* (Fort Worth, TX: Harcourt, 2001).

[22] Agbonkhianmeghe Orobator, in Andrew Kaufa, "As Africa Celebrates Its Synodal Moment: Where Does It Go from Here?" *Vatican News*, March 4, 2023.

the Church. The tradition of ngiga fosters dialogue, but at the same time, it opens up conversations with regard to the level and degree of access to and participation in that dialogue among the participants. It raises the question of whether the Church in Africa really has an open, free, and honest culture of communication. It equally brings to the fore the concerns of how committed the Church is to listening to and incorporating the voices of those at the periphery (periphery engendered by race, class, gender, age, migration, climate change, inequality, and injustice) into the decision-making and activities at the center.

In resonance with the image of Church as the People of God, the ritual of ngiga becomes a vital symbol of the synodal Church in Africa engaged in open and honest conversation with members concerning issues that affect the life of the ecclesial community. Through multiple initiatives, the synodal process has been evident at different levels of the Church in Africa. Bishops, clergy, religious sisters and brothers, laity, and theologians have all been engaged in the process. While the process reflects the many voices (male and female, old and young, liberal and conservative, traditional and contemporary) that continue to vocalize the desires and concerns of the faithful, it also acknowledges some challenges in the Church in Africa.[23]

Within this Family of God, for instance, one has to acknowledge patriarchal and hierarchical authority as well as gender and age biases that are deep-seated in African sociocultural structures and the challenges they introduce into the dynamics of familial relationships and interactions. The Church in Africa comprises people who live the realities of these structures and exhibit similar mind-sets, often internalized and expressed unconsciously and nonverbally. It is evident that some people in the Church "including clergy, hesitate to embrace change for fear of the

---

[23] See African Synodality Initiative, "A Vision of Synodality Rooted in an African Ecclesial Context" (2022).

unknown and how that will affect the position of the church and its leaders."[24] Pope Francis acknowledges, "Even on the concept of 'the people of God,' there can be rigid and antagonistic hermeneutics, remaining trapped in the idea of an exclusivity, of a privilege."[25] How does the Church in Africa respond to what the pope calls "much resistance to overcome the image of a Church rigidly divided between leaders and subordinates"?[26]

As Christians, members of the People of God on the continent are then called to challenge these structures in the Church and in African cultures that prevent people, especially women, from fully participating in decision-making processes that develop and advance the Church and the cultures. True synodality would continue to be undermined by the absence of full participation of women in the Family of God as equal partners.

Similarly, in line with the argument put forward by Sheila Pires and David Kaulemu, in a world steeped in digitalization, a world in which the Church continues to address the realities of digital culture, the Church in Africa has a duty to pay attention to the voices and contributions of its young members, channeling their distinctive perspectives and energy to the benefit of the Church's life and mission.[27] One effective way to engage the youth is through the media and communication technologies. In the new era of communication where the internet and social media have altered the way people connect and communicate with one another, and where the digital world constitutes "a significant part of young people's identity and way of life,"[28] it becomes imperative for the

---

[24] African Synodality Initiative, "A Vision of Synodality," 2.

[25] Address of Pope Francis for the opening of the synod, 2021.

[26] Address of Pope Francis for the opening of the synod, 2021.

[27] See Dicastery of Communication, "Towards Full Presence: A Pastoral Reflection on Engagement with Social Media," May 28, 2023; CCEE-SECAM, "Synodality: Africa and Europe Walking Together" (2024).

[28] Synod of Bishops, Final Document from the Pre-Synodal Meeting in

Church in Africa to be mindful of and understand these changes in order to better communicate with its members, especially the youth who are at the forefront of the new media.

Equally, the roundtable dimension of the Synod on Synodality has been present in how the Church understands and articulates the use and role of the media of social communications. As *Communio et progressio* (19) puts it, "The modern media of social communication offer men [and women] of today a great round table." But beyond the connections and the interactions that these media offer at the digital roundtable, Pope Benedict XVI notes that they also promote a "culture of respect, dialogue and friendship."[29] Hence, it is imperative that modern media and new media technologies help the Church initiate and sustain an expanded dialogue and conversation space made possible by the democratization of these technologies.[30] Nevertheless, given the growing influence of artificial intelligence on communication, it becomes necessary that the Church continue to rediscover the human encounter that primarily underlies communication.[31]

The synodal roundtable and the ngiga rituals foreground this human encounter. New media technologies ensure that these two are no longer limited to and by physical space, thereby challenging and at the same time enabling the Church to invite and include the people previously at the margins of the table. The promise and goal of synodality is to ensure that everyone is engaged at all levels

---

Preparation for the XV Ordinary General Assembly, "Young People, Faith, and Vocational Discernment" (March 19–24, 2018), para. 1.

[29] Message of Pope Benedict for the forty-third World Communications Day, "New Technologies, New Relationships: Promoting a Culture of Respect, Dialogue and Friendship," May 24, 2009.

[30] See also Justin Wise, *The Social Church: A Theology of Digital Communication* (Chicago: Moody, 2014); Daniella Zsupan-Jerome, *Connected Toward Communion: The Church and Social Communication in the Digital Age* (Collegeville, MN: Liturgical Press, 2014).

[31] See Dicastery of Communication, "Towards Full Presence," 1.

at the same time with the lowering of the ngiga. While everybody would not be engaged with presiding over the ceremony of the ngiga ritual at the same time, in the intimate, warm, and welcoming setting of that human encounter, everyone present participates in the dialogue, conversation, and listening that are essential to building community and fostering communion. As Pope Francis maintains, in this journey of synodality, "everyone is a protagonist. No one can be considered a mere extra."[32]

Looking Ahead

We, though many, are one body, for we all partake of the one loaf. (1 Corinthians 10:17, RNAB)

Synodality exists in actions that transcend the Church's present engagements to call for and enable the walking together of the people, in dialogue and conversation, in listening, and in discernment. The ngiga ritual signals and promotes horizontality in the relationship and interaction that fosters dialogue among the faithful. It symbolizes the vision of synodality that bears a particular meaning for the Church in Africa: "In particular, our contribution to the Synod on Synodality must include our African cultural values (expressed in terms like Ubuntu, Ujamaa, Baraza, Palaver, etc.), reverential dialogue that is inspired by the family spirit and related to nature, our ancestors, and the desired future for Africa."[33]

In the spirit of synodality, it is important that the Church in Africa bears the following values and responsibilities in mind. First, the communion dimension of the 3Cs of this essay (communication, communion, and community) hinges on the trinitarian communion. In order for the Church in Africa to reflect this trinitarian communion and to "communicate

---

[32] Francis, address on the opening of the synod.
[33] African Synodality Initiative, "A Vision of Synodality," 3.

in the most profound sense" (*Communio et progressio* 11), its communication, by necessity, has to encourage and promote an inclusive and participatory community. Second, given the central place of communication in the community of the faithful, the Church in Africa should encourage a "spirituality of communication"[34] among the faithful, educating them on the understanding of communication that transcends its mechanical and transmission dimension to emphasize its connectedness to community and communion. Third, a genuinely participatory Church has to recognize, respect, and promote the dignity and equality of all the baptized in communion with one another in the community.

In the light of the foregoing, living the call for the Church to "[listen] to one another with the 'ear of the heart'"[35] becomes manifest in the synodal Church that communicates in a way that fosters participatory community among the communion of the faithful.

---

[34] See FABC-OSC, Communication and the Synodal Church.
[35] Francis, "Listening with the Ear of the Heart."

4

SCRIPTURAL FOUNDATIONS OF A SYNODAL CHURCH

JOSÉE NGALULA

Synodality in the Church is journeying together in faith as the pilgrim and listening People of God. The ecclesiology of the People of God and some biblical narratives such as the Council of Jerusalem (Acts 15) help the Church organize processes and institutions of walking together, reciprocal listening, community discernment, participation, and co-responsibility as the "modus *vivendi et operandi* of the church."[1]

Looking for biblical foundations of synodality does not mean simply searching for words, expressions, or narratives that would justify or encourage the Church to adopt a process of reform to be more faithful to its founder, Jesus Christ. Such a task must be a more profound approach because the Bible contains the Word of God, that is, revelation where "the invisible God out of the abundance of His love speaks to people as friends and lives among them, so that He may invite and take them into fellowship with Himself" (*Dei verbum* 2). Consequently, deepening scriptural foundations of synodality is a process of opening oneself to this fellowship, this great source of the divine gift of love and joy.

---

[1] International Theological Commission, *Synodality in the Life and Mission of the Church* (2018), 6, 43, 70.

> Indeed, sharing in the life of God, a Trinity of love, is complete joy (cf. 1 Jn 1:4). And it is the Church's gift and inescapable duty to communicate that joy, born of an encounter with the person of Christ, the Word of God in our midst.... There is no greater priority than this: to enable the people of our time once more to encounter God, the God who speaks to us and shares his love so that we might have life in abundance. (cf. John 10:10; *Verbum domini* 2)

Synodality that is intimately linked to mission[2] "translates the trinitarian dynamism with which God comes to meet humanity into spiritual attitudes and ecclesial processes."[3] Indeed,

> the ultimate meaning of synodality is the witness that the church is called to give to God, Father, Son and Holy Spirit, the harmony of love that pours Himself out, to give Himself to the world. We can live the communion that saves by walking in a synodal way, in the intertwining of our vocations, charisms and ministries. By going forth to meet everyone in order to bring the joy of the Gospel we can live the communion that saves: with God, with the entire humanity and all of creation. It is then that we will begin to experience, through sharing, the banquet of life that God offers to all peoples. (Final Document 154)

This essay will focus on the fact that this fellowship and joy offered by the triune God appear in the Bible to be synodal because humanity was created and redeemed by a synodal God

---

[2] International Theological Commission, *Synodality in the Life and Mission of the Church*, 31.

[3] Synthesis Report of the Sixteenth Ordinary General Assembly of the Synod of Bishops (2023).

in order to empower human beings to walk on this earth in a synodal way. I will successively develop these three dimensions and stress some insight from Africa.

Created by a God Who "Journeys" Together

In Genesis 1:26, God said, "Let us make human beings in our image, after our likeness" (NABRE).[4] What is the nature of this God in whose image human beings have been created? Many biblical texts show that we were created in the image of a God who is synodal in essence and who systematically acts and works synodally. While speaking about the glory and the love he had with God before the creation of the world (cf. John 17:5, 24), Jesus presented it as a walking together of the Father and the Son. Everything the Son has comes from the Father, that is, the name, the glory, the Word, the mission of salvation, and the disciples (see John 17:7–8:11, 12:22–25). All that the Son has is the Father's, and all that the Father has is the Son's (John 17:10). The disciples the Father gave to the Son were "of the Father," but he entrusted them to the Son (see John 17:6–9) because the Father "is in" the Son and the Son "is in" the Father (John 17:21).

In this dynamic and intimate relationship, the creation of the world was made synodally, because some biblical texts affirm that when the Father created the universe, God walked together with the Son: "In him were created all things in heaven and on earth: everything visible and everything invisible, thrones, ruling forces, sovereignties, powers—all things were created through him and for him" (Colossians 1:16; see also John 1:3; John 1:10; 1 Corinthians 8:6; Hebrews 1:2). The Father also walked together with the Holy Spirit: "In the beginning God created heaven and

---

[4] All scriptural quotations are taken from the New Jerusalem Bible, unless otherwise noted.

earth. Now the earth was a formless void, there was darkness over the deep, with a divine wind sweeping over the waters" (Genesis 1:1–2; see also Job 33:4; Psalm 104:30). The Holy Spirit is in the very "depths of God" (1 Corinthians 2:10–11). In light of this, the synodal assembly of 2024 draws the following conclusion.

> As a spiritual being, the human creature is defined through interpersonal relations. The more authentically he or she lives these relations, the more his or her own personal identity matures. It is not by isolation that humans establish their worth, but by placing themselves in relation with others and with God. Hence, these relations take on fundamental importance. We recognize a synodal Church by flourishing interpersonal relationships flowing from the mutual love that constitutes the "new commandment" left by Jesus to His disciples (cf. Jn 13:34–35). The Church as "a people made one by the unity of the Father and the Son and the Holy Spirit" (LG 4) can witness to the power of relationships founded in the Trinity especially where individualism pervades cultures and societies. Differences that are found in every Christian community with respect to age, vocation, sex, profession and social belonging provide an opportunity for an encounter with otherness that is indispensable to personal growth and maturity. (FD 34)

Redeemed Synodally in Jesus Christ

Like creation, the redemption of the world, the divine action was also a walking together of the Father (who sent the Son, John 5:36–37, 6:44, etc.), the Holy Spirit (who deployed a divine power for the incarnation, Luke 1:35), and the Son (who obeyed the Father, Luke 22:42; John 14:31; Philippians 2:8, also accepted to be led by the Holy Spirit, Matthew 4:1).

During his ministry of saving this world through his incarnation, death, and resurrection, Jesus Christ never worked alone: the beginning of his ministry with the baptism by John the Baptist was marked by the presence of the Father and the Holy Spirit (Luke 3:22). After that, the Father was always with him, and he stood with the Father (John 8:16, 29, 32). All he did was in concert with his Father because of the love between the Father and the Son (John 15:19–22). Jesus also walked together with the Holy Spirit: for his incarnation, the whole of his ministry (Luke 4:14, 18–19), and for the consolidation and continuation of his work of salvation (Luke 24:49; John 4:14, 14:16; Acts 1:4–5, 2:1–11; Galatians 4:6). That is why the Christian baptism is a synodal act of the Father, the Son, and the Holy Spirit (Matthew 28:19). For this reason, Vatican II stresses, "It has pleased God, however, to sanctify and save men and women not individually and without regard for what binds them together, but to set them up as a people who would acknowledge Him in truth and serve Him in holiness" (*Lumen gentium* 9).

Created and Redeemed to Walk Synodally

As mentioned, Genesis narrates that "God created humanity in the image of himself, in the image of God he created him, male and female he created them. God blessed them" (1:27–28). The fifth chapter is more explicit: "In the day that God created Adam he made him in the likeness of God. Male and female he created them. He blessed them and gave them the name Man, when they were created" (Genesis 5:1–2). In creation, male and female human beings are created conjointly and equally in God's image. Nobody is the image of God alone, not the man (male) alone, nor the woman (female) alone, but they are together the image of God, and they are human companions walking together on this earth, fulfilling their human vocations.

In the opinion of some, Genesis 2:22 (that says that God fashioned the rib he had taken from the man into a woman and brought her to the man) represents some inequality between men and women. Where there is inequality, it is not possible to walk together in communion, because there will be only hierarchical relationships between masters and servants, superiors and inferiors. Fortunately, Adam himself corrects this way of thinking by asserting joyfully the equality of flesh and bones, that is, the equality of humanity: "And the man said: This one at last is bone of my bones and flesh of my flesh! She is to be called Woman, because she was taken from Man" (Genesis 2:23). That means that neither man nor woman is perfect or complete without the other; they complement each other in equal respect, mutual love, and mutual help, as intended in the act of creation. In 1999, Pope John Paul II explained it this way.

> This statement is the basis of Christian anthropology, because it identifies the foundation of man's dignity as a person in his creation "in the likeness" of God. At the same time, the passage clearly says that neither man nor woman separately are the image of the Creator, but man and woman in their reciprocity. Both are equally God's masterpiece. In the second account of creation, through the symbolism of the creation of woman from man's rib, Scripture stresses that humanity is not in fact complete until woman is created (cf. Gn 2:18–24). She is given a name whose verbal assonance in Hebrew indicates a relationship to man (*is/issah*). "God created man and woman together and willed each for the other" (*Catechism of the Catholic Church*, n. 371). That woman is presented as a "helper fit for him" (Gn 2:18) should not be interpreted as meaning that woman is man's servant—"helper" is not the equivalent of "servant"; the psalmist says to

God: "You are my help" (Ps 70:5; cf. Ps 115:9, 10, 11; Ps 118:7; Ps 146:5); rather the whole statement means that woman is able to collaborate with man because she complements him perfectly. Woman is another kind of "ego" in their common humanity, which consists of male and female in perfectly equal dignity.[5]

This paradigm of the creation of man and woman as equals in dignity stresses also the call of their creator to communion. "It is not right that the Man should be alone" (Genesis 2:18):

From the beginning, God, who is love, created us for communion and endowed us with an innate capacity to enter into relationships with others. Our lives, reflecting in the image of the Trinity, are meant to attain fulfillment through a network of relationships, friendships, and love, both given and received. We were created to be together, not alone. Precisely because this project of communion is so deeply rooted in the human heart, we see the experience of abandonment and solitude as something frightening, painful and even inhuman. This is all the more the case at times of vulnerability, uncertainty and insecurity, often caused by the onset of a serious illness.[6]

Several verses of the Bible emphasize the importance of walking and working together as human beings: "Two are better than one, because they have a good return for their labor: if either of them falls down, one can help the other up. But pity anyone who falls and has no one to help them up" (Ecclesiastes 4:9–10; see also Psalm 133:1; Romans 12:4–5; Ephesians 4:3–6). When

---

[5] Pope John Paul II, general audience, November 17, 1999, 1.
[6] Pope Francis, message for the XXXII World Day of the Sick, "It Is Not Good That Man Should Be Alone." Healing the Sick by Healing Relationships (February 2024), 1.

Jesus began his ministry as the Son of God who took on our humanity, he did not walk alone. Not only did Jesus choose many disciples and apostles; he also sent them "two by two" (Mark 6:7).

What about other creatures? Through the act of creation, humanity is called to walk together with all the creatures, because human beings are not alone in creation. There exists an interconnection of all things that implies that "everything is related, and we human beings are united as brothers and sisters on a wonderful pilgrimage, woven together by the love God has for each of his creatures and which also unites us in fond affection with brother sun, sister moon, brother river and mother earth" (*Laudato si'* 92). According to *Laudato si'*, in this journey with all the creatures, "We must forcefully reject the notion that our being created in God's image and given dominion over the earth justifies absolute domination over other creatures" (67). Consequently, a total technical dominion over creation is incompatible with the meaning of creation (*Laudato si'* 115–16).

Because of this idea of journeying together with other creatures, some scholars have proposed the possibility of expanding the concept of the *imago Dei* to include animals. Having examined biblical texts and the theological tradition, Eva van Urk-Coster concludes,

> We must admit that nonhuman animals may have their own relationships to God, hidden from our observations, but most probably do not reflect on their own identity and place in the world like we do. As humans we search for meaning, we need to make sense of our own lives—and a notion like imago Dei is particularly helpful in this case. Already in the biblical stories, we see that God addresses humankind, and seeks a relationship with humans. In turn, humans respond to God's call, and even dare to question God occasionally. In this sense, it

can be said that humans are in structural, relational and functional ways God's counterpart in creation, although the imago Dei does not ultimately reside in some kind of quality but is grounded in God's call.... Accordingly, the imago Dei is best understood as the cornerstone of a developing story of humans as particular creatures of God, who above all are called to live responsible lives in harmony with their fellow creatures, and who—like no "other animals"—have to navigate ethical tensions in how to act appropriately in this creaturely world.... I conclude that only humans are created in the image and likeness of God. As we have seen, such a moderate position does not need to be diminishing to other animals.[7]

The New Testament goes further, announcing the good news that human beings are redeemed in Jesus Christ to journey together. Christian baptism transforms believers as "journeyers" on the way (Acts 9:2), that is, in the paths of Jesus Christ, the "Way, Truth and Life" (John 14:16). This Christian journey is made in the light of Jesus Christ himself (John 8:12; 1 John 1:7) and toward the final participation in the glory of the Son of God (John 17:24; Romans 8:29–30; Ephesians 2:5–6), the day God will be "all in all" (1 Corinthians 15:28; Hebrews 10:24–25). This Christian journey is made by the baptized as together "one body" in Jesus Christ (1 Corinthians 6:15, 10:16, 12:12–13:27; Romans 12:4–8; Ephesians 1:22–23, 4:4, 12–16, 5:23; Colossians 1:18, 24). They journey together as brothers and sisters in the Family of God, united in Christ, drinking of the one Spirit, who unites them across all lines of human, social, and ministerial diversity (Romans 10:12; Galatians 3:27–28; Colossians 3:11). They journey together moved by God's gift

---

[7] Eva van Urk-Coster, "Created in the Image of God: Both Human and Non-Human Animals?" *Theology and Science* 19, no. 4 (2021): 356–57.

of fellowship rooted in God's love (John 15:10; Acts 2:42–44, 4:32; Philippians 2:2; 1 John 1:3). They journey together as joyful witnesses and missionaries of God's marvelous love and salvation for all creation (Mark 16:15; John 15:14–17, 17:21; 1 Peter 2:9). Being synodal is therefore a natural characteristic of the Christian life and institutions: Those baptized in Jesus Christ and walking on earth in his footsteps can think, live, and organize themselves only synodally.

Jesus Christ has given a full guarantee of his presence: "Where two or three meet in my name" (Matthew 18:20). That means that common faith and unity in Christ are the basis of the "walking together" (John 17:21; Ephesians 1:10; Colossians 1:19–20). In this context, discerning situations in the presence of the Holy Spirit in an attitude of listening to God and to one another without exclusion (Matthew 24:3–31) will become possible. This will also guarantee a self-comprehension and organization of Christian communities as united in the respect of diversities and servant leadership (1 Corinthians 12:4–7) according to the example of Jesus Christ. In this dynamic, the 2024 synod stressed,

> To be a synodal church, we are required to open ourselves to a genuine relational conversion that redirects each person's priorities and we must once again learn from the Gospel that attending to relationships is not merely a strategy or a tool for greater organizational effectiveness. Relationships and bonds are the means by which God the Father has revealed Himself in Jesus and the Spirit. When our relationships, even in their fragility, allow the grace of Christ, the love of the Father, the communion of the Spirit to shine through, we confess with our lives, our faith in God the Trinity. (FD 50)

Some Insights from African Theology and Pastoral Experience

As the Sixteenth Ordinary General Assembly of the Synod of Bishops recalled, "The whole of Christian existence has its source and horizon in the mystery of the Trinity, which brings forth in us the dynamism of faith, hope and love" (FD 15). In this dynamic, Christopher Mwoleka has argued that in Christianity the Trinity is not a puzzle to be solved but rather an example to be followed; consequently, it can be proposed as a model both for the Church and society in Africa.[8] Motivated by this vision, some African theologians have focused their exploration on the attempt to unravel the implications of trinitarian theology for Christian life in the Church and society. A first group draws from the African traditional understanding of community that can help Africans better interiorize the relationality in the Trinity and its implications for the daily life in Church and in society.

For Mwoleka, the African philosophy of Ujamaa is helpful for understanding that the Trinity is about the sharing of life together in such a way that the persons in God are not three gods but one. Accordingly, Jesus prayed that his followers may be one just as the three are one.[9]

Okechukwu Ogbonnaya is inspired by the trinitarian thought of Tertullian, who interpreted the Trinity as a theory of divine community. For African contexts, Ogbonnaya proposes to focus on the notion of divine communalism in the triune God because there is a community of equality in which the Father, Son, and Holy Spirit are related to one another and ontologically equal while at the same time distinct from one

---

[8] See Christopher Mwoleka, "Trinity and Community," *African Ecclesiastical Review* 17, no. 4 (1975): 203–06.

[9] Mwoleka, "Trinity and Community," 203–06.

another by their personhood and functions.[10] That is why Small Christian Communities in Africa are grounded in the trinitarian understanding of the Church as "the People of God, the Body of the Lord and the Temple of the Holy Spirit" (*Lumen gentium* 17). In the archdiocese of Kinshasa, for example, the diocesan Day of the Small Christian Communities is the liturgical solemnity of the Holy Trinity because the life of the triune God is both the source and the inspiration: "To be Church means to live the intimate love and sharing which characterizes the Trinity and this can be experienced more in a tangible way in small communities than in large anonymous communities."[11]

A second group challenges some aspects of the patriarchal system in African traditions that harm African church and societies. Starting from Christian baptism into the name of the Trinity, Mercy Amba Oduyoye argues that the Trinity offers an egalitarian model of female-male relations. Therefore, those baptized in the name of the trinitarian God should promote a participatory model of the Church and stand against monarchical and hierarchical understandings of the relationships in the Church.[12]

Ibrahim S. Bitrus is a forceful critic of the evils of patriarchal domination that distort African communalism, including ethnic and religious exclusivism. He proposes the egalitarian and inclusive life of the triune God as an inspiring model that can build African society in a way that embodies individuality without libertarian individualism, communality without patriarchy, and mutual multiethnic and religious relations without nepotism and domination.[13]

---

[10] See A. Okechukwu Ogbonnaya, *On Communitarian Divinity: An African Interpretation of the Trinity* (New York: Paragon House, 1994), 23–89.

[11] James O'Halloran, *Small Christian Communities, Vision and Practicalities* (Dublin: Columba Press, 2010), 17.

[12] See Mercy Amba Oduyoye, "Jesus Christ," in *The Cambridge Companion to Feminist Theology*, ed. S. Parsons (Cambridge: Cambridge University Press, 2002), 143–45.

[13] See Ibrahim S. Bitrus, *Community and Trinity in Africa* (New York: Routledge, 2018), 56–159, 189.

Indeed, many African scholars have denounced the fact that "the deeply entrenched patriarchal and hierarchical nature of most African societies" has a negative impact not only on biblical interpretation but also on the reception of the fraternity and communion in God proposed by the Gospel.[14]

A third group tries to find African imagery or concepts that challenge the patriarchal system. Agbonkhianmeghe Orobator proposes an appropriation of the Yoruba maternal imagery *Obirin meta* (that expresses the idea of a multifunctional woman of unmatched depth and unbounded substance) as suitable to illuminate our comprehension of the Trinity as the abundant and radical open-endedness of God in God's self and metaphor for God's involvement in the experience of humanity.[15] J. Kombo draws on the African metaphysics of *Ntu* and proposes to speak of the triune God as the "Great Muntu who has the oneness of *Ntu*, of Vital Force and of activity."[16]

A fourth group explores these intuitions in a deeper way by making a link between Ubuntu and Trinity.

> The participatory humanism that is the foundation of ubuntu aligns well with a view of the human person as made in the image of the Trinity. Gabriel Setiloane contends that "the essence of being is participation in which humans are always interlocked with one another.... The human being is not only vital force, but more vital force in participation." ... Given that the human person is created imago Trinitatis, it is legitimate to claim that ubuntu and Christian theological views of the human

---

[14] See Frederick Mawusi Amevenku and Isaac Boaheng, *Biblical Exegesis in African Context* (Wilmington, DE: Vernon Press, 2021), 99.

[15] Agbonkhianmeghe E. Orobator, *Theology Brewed in an African Pot* (New York: Orbis Books, 2008), 31–32.

[16] See J. Kombo, *The Doctrine of God in African Christian Thought: The Holy Trinity, Theological Hermeneutics, and the African Intellectual Culture* (Leiden: Brill, 2007), 46, 232–47.

correlate. According to this view, we were created for participation; it is a virtue that we need to live out in every domain of our existence.... Furthermore, participation is a virtue that we humans are also called to enact. If the doctrine of the Trinity has anything to teach us about authentic existence, it is that communion rather than individualism is the goal of human life. Participation, then, is a Trinitarian virtue that marks our human existence.[17]

Linking the foregoing theme of Trinity, Ubuntu, communion, and participation to the process of synodality, I have argued,

> It is the whole Church of Christ, in its universal and local aspects, which is a family in which Ubuntu must reign, that is: the mutual respect and promotion of the human dignity of the other. In relations between local Churches, some must not believe that they are superior to others in dignity, because they have more material means or other assets. For Ubuntu philosophy and spirituality, considering that the other is no less human than me, and building interpersonal relationships on this basis, is a matter of ethical honesty. Living in the dynamics of true synodality, that is, imbued with Ubuntu, is ultimately a matter of honesty before God, who has revealed his Trinitarian dimension so that we may discover how to live truly as humans and embark on the path of spirituality of communion. And this, at the individual and institutional levels.[18]

---

[17] Neil Pembroke, "An Ubuntu-Inspired Approach to Organisational Spirituality," in *Practicing Ubuntu: Practical Theological Perspectives on Injustice, Personhood and Human Dignity*, ed. Jaco Dreyer, Yolanda Dreyer, Edward Foley, and Malan Nel (Zurich: Lit Verlag GmbH, 2017), 230.

[18] Josée Ngalula, "Ubuntu and Synodality," in *Journeying Together for a Synodal Church in Africa: Echoes from an African Christian Palaver*, ed. Ikenna U. Okafor, Josée Ngalula, Nicholaus Segeja, and Stan Chu Ilo (Nairobi: Paulines Publication Africa, 2023), 36.

Finally, these African perspectives on the Trinity aim "to draw implications of the doctrine for Christian life and society. The attempt to place the symbol of the triune God in the public sphere (often on the basis of African communality and relationality) illustrates the importance of the social context in African theological method."[19]

Conclusion

To listen deeply to the scriptures in order to better understand the roots and meaning of synodality is vitally important. As *Verbum domini* puts it, "Each of us is enabled by God to hear and respond to his word. We were created in the word and we live in the word; we cannot understand ourselves unless we are open to this dialogue. The word of God discloses the filial and relational nature of human existence" (22).

A synodal Church is composed of and animated by human beings, but are they aware of the synodal nature of their human identity and their Christian identity? The imperative to be a synodal Church has solid roots in the Bible, in the identity of God as well as in both creation and salvation. We human beings have been created and redeemed not only by a synodal God but also in a synodal manner. So it is important to emphasize the awareness of this aspect of Christian identity.

When Christians meditate on scripture to nourish and transform their daily lives, they have the opportunity to discover the synodal identity of God and of their own identity; they are also at the "school of the synodal process"[20] and way of

---

[19] Teddy Chalwe Sakupapa, "The Trinity in African Christian Theology: An Overview of Contemporary Approaches," *HTS Theological Studies* 75, no. 1 (2019), 6; a5460; https://doi.org/10.4102/hts.v75i1.5460.

[20] Margit Eckholt, ed., *Synodality in Europe—Theological Reflections on the Church on Synodal Paths in Europe* (Autriche: LIT, 2023), 279.

living synodally. As stated by Chijioke Azuawusiefe in his essay, underscoring the primacy of orality in Africa, even when our contemporary society and communities have become literate and attentive, active listening still remains important. The Bible teaches that such listening establishes an important connection in the relationship of dialogue between God and humanity. The Shema of Deuteronomy 6:4, which was mentioned above, illustrates the point that the knowledge and love of God starts with hearing the Word of God with one's ears.

Consequently, the following challenges emerge for all local churches around the world. First, scripture is a basic nourishment to help interiorize the synodal dimension of God's and Christian identities. Unfortunately, the Bible has not yet been translated into all languages. In addition, despite the fact that many dioceses already have organized biblical apostolates, many Christians remain without any contact with the Bible, sometimes because of illiteracy, the high price of Bibles, legal interdiction, or the difficulty involved in understanding at once the many books of the Bible. This situation becomes critical in light of the fact that

> God wants to dialogue with human beings. When we read the scriptures, we show our readiness to welcome God's teaching.... It is therefore necessary to learn, if not relearn, how to read and celebrate the word of God individually and in community to allow it to give shape to our lives.... The purpose of God's Word is to enlighten and build communion. Forming ourselves in synodality is inspired by God's Word.[21]

---

[21] Philippe Abraham Birane Tine, "Forming Ourselves in Synodality," in *A Pocket Companion to Synodality: Voices from Africa*, ed. Josée Ngalula, Wilhelmina Uhai Tunu, et al. (Nairobi: African Synodality Initiative, 2022), 61.

Second, misinterpretation of the Word of God can occur either by removing all connection with everyday life, thus preventing its power of conversion and union with the true identity of God, or by making contextual readings that make scripture say the opposite of its intention, or by ideological interpretations. That is why Vatican II has appealed for scripture to be read in the Church (*Sacrosanctum concilium* 7), that is, with the true hermeneutic inherited from the apostles. The Word of God read solemnly, understood communally, and updated in the present context is at the heart of the eucharistic celebration. Thus, caring for the liturgy of the Word is indispensable for the emergence of a truly synodal Church. Not only can it happen that the liturgy of the Word is poorly cared for; there are also many places where Christian communities do not have the opportunity to celebrate the Eucharist for several reasons. That is why

> each member of Christ's faithful should grow accustomed to reading the Bible daily! An attentive reading of the recent Apostolic Exhortation *Verbum Domini* can provide some useful pastoral indications. Care should be taken to initiate the faithful into the ancient and fruitful tradition of *lectio divina*. The word of God can lead to the knowledge of Jesus Christ and bring about conversions which produce reconciliation, since it is able to sift "the thoughts and intentions of the heart" (Hebrews 4:12). The Synod Fathers encouraged Christian parish communities, Small Christian Communities, families and associations and ecclesial movements to set aside times for sharing the word of God. In this way, they will increasingly become places where God's word, which builds up the community of Christ's disciples, is read, meditated on and celebrated. This word constantly enlivens fraternal communion (cf. 1 Peter 1:22–25). (*Africae munus* 150–51)

The emergence of a true synodal Church formed by a synodal God and schooled in God's synodal methods in creation and redemption requires us to take seriously the Christian doctrine that teaches that the People of God are the receivers of the Word of God, as Vatican II explains it: "Sacred tradition and sacred Scripture form one sacred deposit of the word of God, entrusted to the Church. Holding fast to this deposit, the entire holy people, united with its pastors, remains steadfastly faithful to the teaching of the apostles" (*Dei verbum* 10). Individual Christians, through the help of the Holy Spirit, can have their hearts "burning" (Luke 24:32) when they pray the scripture in the context of their personal lives. That is why it is so important to make the Word of God accessible to all the faithful by enabling access to the Bible and good commentaries on it during the eucharistic liturgy and outside of it. The task of the pastors and ministers is crucial: They are called to assist the faithful (*Evangelii nuntiandi* 57–58) in their effort to understand and discern how the Word of God is enhancing and empowering them to achieve their synodal identity as the image of God as well as the synodal impulse of the People of God for the salvation of the world.

5

Synodality or the "Remodeling" of the Church

José Minaku Lukoli

"The path of synodality is the path that God expects of the Church of the third millennium."[1] This seemingly terse declaration of Pope Francis on commemorating the fiftieth anniversary of the institution of the Synod of Bishops was decisive because it heralded the movement of synodality as he perceived it and has tenaciously pursued it. Synodality appears as an ecclesial process of listening, dialogue, and consultation as opposed to a rigid system whose features mirror both a hierarchical conception of authority and a clericalist exercise of leadership. Both issues represent significant concerns for Pope Francis in his approach to synodality.[2]

---

[1] Pope Francis, address commemorating the fiftieth anniversary of the institution of the Synod of Bishops, October 17, 2015.

[2] On several occasions, Pope Francis bluntly condemned clericalism. Here are some examples: Chrism Mass (March 28, 2013): In his homily, he emphasized the role of the clergy as servants of the people and stressed the importance of being close to their congregations, echoing his ongoing critique of clericalism. Interview with *La Civiltà Cattolica* (September 2013): He pointed out the discrepancy between clericalism and the true purpose of the priesthood, reinforcing his stance that the clergy should serve the people, not dominate them. General Audience (October 15, 2014): He stressed the need for the Church to be a welcoming, inclusive community free of elitist

Francis's determination to overcome the persistence of a hierarchical and clericalist conception of the Church is anchored in introducing, promoting, and establishing a different model of the Church. From an ecclesiological perspective, this raises the question of whether such an approach is not destined to create another model of the Church that will ultimately prove itself as a system of equal rigidity and self-referentiality as the one that the pope seeks to supersede. As synodality advances, in part through the two-phased Synod on Synodality, it is essential to analyze the different facets of this new model and to enrich it by drawing on diverse ecclesial experiences, especially in local contexts, and to root it more deeply in a theological foundation.

To identify the unique and constitutive elements of synodality as a "new model of the Church," I will use Avery Dulles's *Models of the Church*.[3] This book has a timeless relevance as a classic of ecclesiological literature.[4] Using a descriptive approach, Dulles presents the Church as being at the same time an institution,

---

mentalities. Speech at the Celebration of the Feast of the Presentation of the Lord (February 2, 2015); Homily at Casa Santa Marta (December 13, 2016): He underscored how clericalism leads to a harmful separation within the Church, advocating for openness and genuine pastoral care instead. Letter to the People of God (August 20, 2018): Following the abuse scandals, Francis addressed the deeper issues within the Church's structure, focusing on clericalism as a cause of many of these problems, urging for greater accountability and humility among the clergy.

[3] Avery Dulles, *Models of the Church* (New York: Doubleday, 1987 [1974]).

[4] The field of ecclesiology boasts a rich body of literature spanning centuries. Among classics, I can mention *De Ecclesia Militante* by Nicholas of Cusa (1433), *Summa Theologica (in Segunda Pars and Tertia Pars)* by Thomas Aquinas (1265–1274), *De Ecclesia* (Kirchliche Dogmatik) by Karl Barth (English translations between 1956 and 1975), particularly in volume IV. Vatican II documents (1962–1965), particularly *Lumen gentium* (Dogmatic Constitution on the Church); *The Church*, by Hans Küng (1967); *The Church as the Body of Christ*, by F. J. Leenhardt (first published in 1955); *Corpus Mysticum*, by Henri de Lubac (French edition 1944; English translation 1956). *Models of the Church* by Avery Dulles (1974) finds a place of choice in this prestigious section of ecclesiological literature.

a mystical communion, a sacrament, a herald, a servant, and a community of beloved disciples. His explanation of each model includes a critical analysis, identifying its merits and shortcomings. While seemingly lacking depth and overly simplistic on account of its descriptive approach, this classic of ecclesiology has contributed to succinctly presenting an accessible categorization of ecclesiological discourse and imagery.

In this work, Dulles's models can provide a ground for understanding the synodal model of the Church. Conversely, I demonstrate that the synodal model of the Church offers substantial elements for transforming the various images of the Church and infusing them with new, dynamic, and vibrant elements such as listening, dialogue, and discernment.

A critical reappraisal of Dulles's ecclesiology can enhance, advance, and deepen the process of synodality in an increasingly complex Church. Rafael Luciani accurately expresses it in these terms.

> In this sense, the practice and implementation of synodal Church will have the task of imagining a Church for the third millennium that is, in the words of the Italian theologian Serena Noceti, "open to facilitating complex processes of community discernment involving parishes, priests, the faithful, and theologians."[5]

To achieve this objective, I will critically analyze Dulles's models and then demonstrate how the synodal process constitutes a new and dynamic model of the Church. I will subsequently explore and propose a path by which the synodal process can overcome the weaknesses of preceding models of the Church. In a word, synodality entails a constructive process that "remodels" the Church.[6]

---

[5] Rafael Luciani, *Synodality: A New Way of Proceeding in the Church* (Paulist Press, Kindle edition, 143–72).

[6] After the second session of the Synod on Synodality, Agbonkhianmeghe E. Orobator presented synodality as a "remodeling of the church," http://www.jesuits.global/2024/10/21/reshaping-the-church-for-today-s-world/.

Avery Dulles's Models of the Church: A Cursory and Critical Glimpse

In the aftermath of Vatican II, Dulles wrote his classic when the ecclesiological debate was in full swing. He devised and adopted a clear and straightforward pedagogical means to present the various facets of a complex reality, the Church, systematically and in a structured way. Dulles structured his analysis around six key models, emphasizing different underlying ecclesial theologies and practices. These models are institution, mystical communion, sacrament, herald, servant, and community of beloved disciples. Each model offers a unique perspective on the Church's nature and mission, giving it a strong and specific identity.

Dulles's model has its strengths and weaknesses, revealing the incompleteness of any one model and the necessity of reforming the Church as a living reality. I will briefly review the models.

The model of an institutional Church focuses on the sociological dimension of the Church and its most visible manifestations. Its boundaries are clearly defined, and the criteria for belonging and exclusion are sharply distinguished. This model runs the permanent risk of institutionalizing clericalism. The image of the Church as communion is supported by the idea of a mystical communion that featured prominently in Vatican II. Although this model has a solid biblical foundation, it also runs the risk of easy idealization. For its part, the model of the Church as a sacrament, while rooted in the sacramental nature of the Church, can fall into abstraction. The model of the Church as herald validly expresses the mission of proclaiming the Word of God, but it risks becoming too reductive. Dulles believes that the model of the Church as servant has biblical foundations and warrants, but its identity can be diluted and reduced to the equivalent of a nongovernmental organization. As for the Church as a community of beloved disciples, while it has strong emotional appeal, it can become selective and enclosed.

This presentation of Dulles's models is all too brief, but to his credit, he successfully created a typology that presents a balanced and nuanced view of the Church, thus avoiding oversimplifications. His approach allows for an examination of the Church's mission and identity from various perspectives, each offering valuable insights into what it means to be a Church in different contexts. Concretely, it shows how different contexts and Christian traditions have accentuated or prioritized one aspect over another, depending on a host of circumstances.

It is important to note that Dulles's approach has drawn sharp and significant criticism. The typological approach to analyzing the Church's complex reality has been questioned. Scholars such as George Lindbeck, Hans Küng, Leonardo Boff, Joseph Ratzinger, and Catherine LaCugna have voiced concerns about potential limitations, such as the risk of fostering static or fragmented understandings of the Church. Some further insinuate the risk of promoting relativism that might lead to doctrinal ambiguity, allowing for multiple "truths" about the Church, precisely because of the temptation to see each model as a complete and valid entity in itself depending on the doctrinal leaning of whoever leads the narrative or discourse. These models may not fully encompass the diverse ways the Church understands itself across different times and cultures.

Despite these criticisms, Dulles's work has significantly influenced ecclesiology. He provides valuable tools to articulate and examine the Church's multifaceted nature. The discussion generated by these criticisms continues to enrich theological discourse and reflection on the nature of the Church. One example that comes to mind is the image of the Church as the Family of God, which the first African synod adopted as the best metaphor for the Church in Africa.[7]

---

[7] Agbonkhianmeghe E. Orobator, *The Church as Family: African Ecclesiology in Its Social Context* (Nairobi, Kenya: Paulines Publications Africa, 2000).

Synodality between a Model and a Process

Vatican II made a decisive turning point in many areas, especially in the theology of the Church, as Ludovic Lado and Marcel Uwineza demonstrate in their essays. By conceiving of the Church as the pilgrim People of God, Vatican II dismantled the pyramidal concept of the Church to promote greater participation of the faithful—not limited to only bishops and ordained clergy. More important, the council championed the full involvement of the laity.

Several decades later, the process seems to have assumed a new vitality in the understanding and practice of synodality. In this sense, it can be said that Vatican II opened a path through which the Church has continued to seek new and appropriate ways of expressing its identity and mission in a manner adapted to particular contexts and times.

Without claiming that synodality is particularly new, it can be said that this approach to understanding the Church has given new energy to a seed carefully planted by Vatican II. From its etymological meaning, synodality echoes several elements of *Lumen gentium*, in particular, a people summoned and convoked from a diversity of backgrounds by the Creator and walking the path of life with the Redeemer under the inspiration of the Holy Spirit (LG 2). As other contributors to this volume are keen to emphasize, Pope Francis himself concedes that synodality is ancient in its inspiration; his genius is to have initiated creatively a new phase of reception and implementation of the intuitions of Vatican II. While affirming that the synodal approach is not new, it is a turning point in the history of the Church. One way of holding the tradition of synodality in tandem with the innovation of Pope Francis is to see the latter as inviting the Church to the path of creative fidelity:

> In conformity with the teaching of *Lumen Gentium,* Pope Francis remarks in particular that synodality "offers us the most appropriate framework for understanding

the hierarchical ministry itself" and that, based on the doctrine of the *sensus fidei fidelium*, all members of the Church are agents of evangelization. Consequently making a synodal Church a reality is an indispensable precondition for a new missionary energy that will involve the entire People of God.[8]

We can therefore affirm from a certain point of view that synodality constitutes a "model of the Church." However, the freshness of synodality appears precisely in this way of being, which includes listening, dialogue, and discernment. A synodal Church is a Church that listens. As Luciani states,

> In the synodal Church, we are asked not only to walk together—a simplistic way to understand synodality—but instead, above all, it highlights the relations and the communicative dynamics happening while walking together. It involves praying, meeting, working together, discerning, and making decisions. It is a new ecclesial culture of taking advice and building consensus. By doing so, we can overcome the pyramidal and clericalist model of a Church that teaches and another that learns and follows.[9]

Luciani's insight is echoed in another ecclesiological study undertaken by Alphonse Borras. For Borras,

> the transition toward a new model (of Church) for the third millennium needs to recognize, first, that we are facing a systemic and structural problem that reveals the weakness of the dominant theological-cultural model, which has become outdated and needs not only renewal but also reform.[10]

---

[8] International Theological Commission, "Synodality in the Life and Mission of the Church," March 2, 2018, n. 9.

[9] Luciani, *Synodality*, introduction, 16.

[10] Alphonse Borras, "Votum tantum consultivum. Les limites ecclésiologiques d'une formule canonique," *Didaskalia* 45, no. 1 (2015): 161.

Speaking of synodality, the International Theological Commission mentions the new threshold Pope Francis invites us to cross. These expressions reinforce the idea of a new model of the Church in progress.

If synodality aims to avoid the rigidity of a pyramidal Church, can it also prevent the danger of simply replacing one rigid system with another? This concern echoes criticisms of earlier frameworks such as Dulles's use of models to conceptualize and define the Church, which sometimes led to excessive systematization. Therefore, it is necessary to immediately emphasize that the originality of synodality lies in its dynamic nature, functioning as an internal methodology rather than a static structure. As Francis aptly puts it, in the spirit of synodality, it is more important to initiate processes than to dominate spaces.[11]

The Synod on Synodality proved to be effective in many ways. The simple details of how the space for listening, dialogue, and conversation was configured to facilitate the practice of conversation in the Spirit were more important than any specific outcomes. However, the importance of the latter is to be considered. The approach, therefore, envisions a process that keeps the discourse—whether theological or otherwise—from becoming a mere theoretical exercise. Instead, it ensures that the discourse remains a meaningful expression of the concrete experience of being the Church. More precisely, it reflects the lived reality of the People of God. Thus, ecclesiology is not limited to deploying a systematic discourse but must flow into concrete reality, into praxis. To quote Luciani, "The newness of the current ecclesial epoch is that the Church is in transition, one in which reform is understood as a permanent process, so that

---

[11] Cf. *Evangelii gaudium* (The Joy of the Gospel) 222. In this section, Pope Francis writes, "Time is greater than space." He explains that it is more important to initiate processes that lead to lasting change and transformation than to focus on controlling or occupying positions of power.

ecclesiology becomes ecclesiogenesis, and where the theological and the pastoral cannot be separated."[12]

Therefore, instead of speaking of synodality as a new model, it would rather be better to talk of an activation or revitalization of an underlying reality inherent in the very nature of the Church. Bernard Franks is right when he asserts, "The essence of synodality is a spirit rather than a principle."[13] The International Theological Commission expresses it more poignantly and clearly: "Although synodality is not explicitly found as a term or a concept in the teaching of Vatican II, it is fair to say that synodality is at the heart of the work of renewal the Council was encouraging."[14] Synodality is a dynamic process because it facilitates discernment and dialogue, which allows the most significant participation in the decision-making process and fosters co-responsibility in the Church. Seen in this light, the process of synodality can serve as an interior force and energy that can transform and revitalize existing and familiar models of the Church such as those analyzed by Dulles.

Synodality: The Revitalization of Models of the Church

By all accounts, synodality constitutes an innovative approach to understanding the Church. Therefore, it transcends traditional models' static limitations by introducing a dynamic, process-oriented approach rooted in communal discernment and participation. Unlike models that risk rigidity or idealization, synodality fosters adaptability, ensuring that ecclesiology remains a lived praxis rather than a fixed theoretical construct. As mentioned, this innovation is rooted in a tradition that

---

[12] Luciano, *Synodality*, introduction, 3.
[13] Bernard Franck, "Les expériences synodales après Vatican II," *Communio* 3, no. 3 (1978): 77.
[14] "Synodality in the Life and Mission of the Church," 6.

goes back to Vatican II but as far back as scripture, as Marcel Uwineza, Josée Ngalula, David Kaulemu, and other contributors demonstrate convincingly in this volume. Thus, there is a delicate balance between continuity and discontinuity. Synodality is rooted in the Christian tradition but constitutes something new and appealing.

It is therefore a question of showing how synodality can renew and enrich the models of Dulles and how these models can ensure consistency with the principles of synodality. Each model provides a distinct lens through which to understand today's synodal Church. Without going into depth, as every model can prompt a serious and interdisciplinary study, I will endeavor to open avenues of reflection for each model of the Church about the understanding, knowledge, and practice of synodality.

The institutional model views the Church primarily as a structured, hierarchical organization with clear roles, rules, and authoritative (or patriarchal) leadership. Within this context, the challenges and opportunities for synodality become apparent mainly because it tended to engender clericalism. As we know, Pope Francis is a tireless advocate for the end of clericalism and its incompatibility with a synodal Church: "Enough, it is truly a scandal. Clericalism is a whip, a scourge, a form of worldliness which dirties and spoils the face of the bride of the Lord, which enslaves the holy and faithful people of God."[15] Indeed, on the one hand, the hierarchical structure might initially seem to hinder synodality, as decision-making is traditionally concentrated at the top echelons of the hierarchy. On the other hand, synodality can foster a more collegial and communal expression of authority. This requires reimagining the hierarchy not as a chain of command but as a facilitator of inclusive ecclesial listening to

---

[15] Pope Francis, "Discourse of 25 October 2023," http://www.vaticannews.va/fr/pape/news/2023-10/francois-synode-synodalite-lettre-au-peuple-de-dieu.html.

the Spirit to unify and illuminate the entire People of God. The Final Document (FD) attempts to maintain the delicate balance between the two poles:

> In a synodal Church, the authority of the Bishop, of the Episcopal College and of the Bishop of Rome in regard to decision-taking is inviolable as it is grounded in the hierarchical structure of the Church established by Christ; it both serves unity and legitimate diversity (cf. 13). Such an exercise of authority, however, is not without limits: it may not ignore a direction which emerges through proper discernment within a consultative process, especially if this is done by participatory bodies. (FD 92)

Synodality, as the capacity for listening and consulting, fosters discernment. It relativizes the insularity of power and authority in an institutional Church.

In the model of Church as a mystical communion, the Church is seen primarily as a fellowship of believers united in faith, love, and the Holy Spirit. This model seamlessly aligns with synodal principles that highlight mutual listening, shared discernment, and collective responsibility. Synodality can deepen the Church's lived experience of communion by involving a broader spectrum of the faithful in discerning and responding to the Holy Spirit's movement within the Church:

> As this discernment entails the contribution of everyone, ecclesial discernment is both the condition and a privileged expression of synodality, in which communion, mission and participation are lived. The more everyone is heard, the greater the discernment. Therefore, it is essential that we promote the broadest participation possible in the discernment process, particularly involving those who are at the margins of the Christian community and society. (FD 82)

The multiple and almost unanimous testimonies of the participants in the global process of synodal consultation have confirmed the importance of deep communion as vital to the conception and practice of synodality. The focus of synodal processes through spiritual conversation or conversation in the Spirit to enhance relational bonds and spiritual intimacy among the People of God reflects the profound interconnectedness that characterizes the mystical Body of Christ. Pope Francis put it firmly by asserting, "A synodal Church is a Church which listens, which realizes that listening is more than simply hearing. It is a mutual listening in which everyone has something to learn."[16]

The sacramental model presents the Church as a visible sign of Christ's grace operative in the world. In synodality, sacramental theology can emphasize the communal aspects of the Church's sacramental life—as seen in communal celebrations of the Eucharist and other sacraments, which are inherently participatory. In this regard, the Final Document makes a strong statement about the interrelationship of synodality and sacrament:

> There is a close link between *synaxis* and *synodos*, between the Eucharistic assembly and the synodal assembly. In both cases, albeit in different forms, Jesus' promise to be present where two or three are gathered in His name is fulfilled (cf. Mt 18:20). Synodal assemblies are events that celebrate the union of Christ with His Church through the action of the Spirit. It is the Spirit who ensures the unity of the ecclesial body of Christ in the Eucharistic assembly as well as in the synodal assembly. (27)

Synodal practices can accentuate how sacramental actions are communal and highlight the call for every Christian to contribute to the Church's sanctifying mission actively. Empowering laity

---

[16] Pope Francis, address commemorating the fiftieth anniversary of the institution of the Synod of Bishops, October 17, 2015.

and clergy to discern pastoral responses collaboratively can also enhance the Church's sacramental witness. One of the outstanding achievements of synodality is the very significant involvement of the laity, who have contributed generously and energetically to the progress of the Synod on Synodality, especially during the preparatory phases.

The herald model considers the Church primarily as proclaiming God's Word. Pope Francis said in his address at the fiftieth anniversary of establishing the Synod of Bishops, "We find an intrinsic connection between synodality and evangelization."[17] This link is constitutive of the understanding and practice of synodality:

> Synodality is not an end in itself. Rather, it serves the mission that Christ entrusted to the Church in the Spirit. To evangelize is "the essential mission of the Church.... It is the grace and vocation proper to the Church, her deepest identity" (EN 14).... By appreciating all charisms and ministries, synodality enables the People of God to proclaim to women and men and witness to the Gospel of every place and time, making itself a "visible sacrament" (LG 9) of the fellowship and unity in Christ willed by God. Synodality and mission are intimately linked: mission illuminates synodality and synodality spurs to mission. (FD 32)

For synodality, this translates into viewing the Church's evangelizing mission as communal and involving all its members' contributions. Synodal processes ensure that diverse voices within the Church are heard and integrated into the mission of proclaiming the Gospel. The Good News becomes more productive and contextual when different perspectives and experiences

---

[17] Pope Francis, address commemorating the fiftieth anniversary of the institution of the Synod of Bishops, October 17, 2015.

inform the Church's evangelizing activities. Even the minority and peripheral voices can now be considered in the building of the Church. Furthermore, these processes can foster a sense of shared purpose and collective accountability in proclaiming the Gospel of Jesus Christ mainly through a reimagined understanding and approach to ministry within the Church.

The servant model envisions the Church as a servant to the world, aligning with Jesus's example of self-giving love. Pope Francis has consistently emphasized the Church's mission to serve the poor and marginalized. Many references could be cited, but this one from his apostolic exhortation *Evangelii gaudium* readily comes to mind:

> Each Christian and every community is called to be an instrument of God for the liberation and promotion of the poor, and for enabling them to be fully a part of society. This demands that we be docile and attentive to the cry of the poor and to come to their aid.[18]

In his Apostolic Exhortation *Evangelii gaudium*, Pope Francis emphasizes the Church's mission to engage actively with the world, even at the cost of facing challenges and imperfections. He articulates this vision, stating: "I prefer a Church which is bruised, hurting and dirty because it has been out on the streets, rather than a Church which is unhealthy from being confined and from clinging to its own security."[19]

Synodality in this context amplifies the idea of collaboration in service as well as the diversity and complementarity of Church ministries. By involving various members of the Church in discernment and action, it can more effectively respond to social injustice, poverty, and other societal issues. This collaborative approach encourages identifying needs and pooling resources to

---

[18] Pope Francis, *Evangelii gaudium* (2013), 187.

[19] Pope Francis, *Evangelii gaudium*, 49.

serve humanity. Synodality fosters communal diaconal actions that can be more dynamic and adaptive in addressing the world's needs (FD 73). The preferential option for the poor or the marginalized, even within the Church, highlighted by the Synod on Synodality, is eloquent proof of the movement from the center to the periphery.

Finally, the model of the community of beloved disciples underscores the Church's role as a community that follows Christ together. Pope Francis underlines our commitment as disciples:

> The commitment to build a synodal Church—a mission to which we are all called, each one of us as an essential element—has significant ecumenical implications. For this reason, the term synod calls us to reflect in the broadest sense on the character of the Church as a community of believers, called to the service of humanity, ready to walk together toward the full realization of the kingdom of God.[20]

Synodality resonates deeply with this model as it emphasizes learning, growing, and making decisions together as faithful followers of Jesus Christ. Synodal processes encourage a listening Church, where disciples collectively discern the will of God and are empowered for mission, and where "everyone is an active subject and has something to give to others" (FD 144). Emphasizing discipleship within synodality helps nurture a Church that is humble, teachable, and continually reforming itself and its ministries in alignment with Christ's teachings.

Under the model of the Church as a community of beloved disciples, particular attention can be given to minorities and resistant voices whose perspectives often go unheard. One of the most significant characteristics of a synodal Church is its sincere desire to provide space for minorities and those without a voice.

---

[20] Pope Francis, address to the International Symposium, October 2016.

They too are part of the community of disciples. The addresses of the Holy Father on this subject are sufficiently eloquent: "The Church is called to become increasingly inclusive, recognizing and valuing the contribution of everyone, particularly those who find themselves on the peripheries of our communities."[21] He was even more explicit in a homily: "No one must be excluded; no one can feel distant or removed from this journey of discipleship. The Church is a family where all are welcomed and loved."[22] The Synod on Synodality represents this idea of a radical inclusion, especially of the poor and marginalized, with the metaphor of a home: "The relation between place and space leads us also to reflect on the Church as 'home.' When it is not thought of as a closed space, inaccessible, to be defended at all costs, the image of home evokes the possibility of welcome, hospitality, and inclusion" (FD 115).

Conclusion:
Synodality as a Path to Renew the Church

Avery Dulles's *Models of the Church* offers a framework for understanding the Church's complexity through six key dimensions: institution, mystical communion, sacrament, herald, servant, and the community of disciples. While insightful, each model has limitations when taken alone. Dulles's most significant contribution is his insistence on bringing these models into dialogue to reflect the Church as a dynamic and multifaceted reality.

In our time, the emerging process of synodality revitalizes Dulles's models, breathing new life into each dimension. Synodality transforms the institutional model into one of shared authority, emphasizing participation and accountability.

---

[21] Pope Francis, apostolic exhortation *Gaudete et exsultate* on the call to holiness in today's world, n. 26.

[22] Homily, World Meeting of Families, September 27, 2015.

It deepens the mystical communion model through mutual listening and spiritual discernment in the Body of Christ. The sacramental model finds renewed communal significance as the Church gathers to celebrate God's grace. The herald model is invigorated as evangelization becomes collaborative and rooted in diverse contexts, while the servant model reflects a Church committed to justice, solidarity, and care for the poor. Finally, synodality enhances the community of disciples by including marginalized voices and fostering a sense of belonging.

Pope Francis's call for a "Church that walks together" ensures that ecclesiology remains dynamic and relational, preventing the models from becoming rigid. Synodality embodies *ecclesia semper reformanda*, a Church in constant renewal, attentive to the Holy Spirit and the lived experiences of all God's people. This approach resonates deeply with African ecclesiology, especially the Church as the Family of God model, which emphasizes relationality and inclusion. The African proverb "If you want to go far, go together" aptly reflects this synodal spirit; the Church's journey must involve everyone walking in unity and discernment.

The concept of synodality does not replace Dulles's models but activates and revitalizes them, ensuring the Church remains faithful to its mission while responding to contemporary challenges. It calls for a Church that listens, dialogues, discerns, and acts prophetically, fostering communion, participation, and mission in an ever-changing world. Synodality is the path forward for creatively reimagining or remodeling the Church as a living, inclusive, and vibrant community of God's people.

6

DIALOGUE, DISCERNMENT, AND TRUST

An Ethic for Synodality in a Global, Divided Church

ANTHONY EGAN

This essay explores the question of the ethics of synodality and the possibility of creating a genuine synodal ethic based on themes discerned from the many documents (*Vademecum, Instrumentum Laboris*, regional reports, guidebooks, etc.)[1] and processes that have led up to the Final Document of the Synod on Synodality.[2] It starts by exploring the context of the synod—a global but divided Catholic Church and the real divisions among those who participated.

Next, the essay will explore aspects of synodal ethics, focusing on a few theological explorations that seem to point to dialogue, discernment, and trust as keys to a successful ethic of synodality.

Following that, the essay summarizes all too briefly the key themes of the Final Document, concluding that it reflects an

---

[1] Most of these can be found at the Synod on Synodality website, www.synod.va/en.html. For the history of the synod yet to be written, one fervently hopes that it will be preserved!

[2] Sixteenth Ordinary General Assembly of the Synod of Bishops, *For a Synodal Church: Communion, Participation, Mission*, Final Document (October 26, 2024).

albeit imperfect expression of dialogue and discernment and expresses deep hope that trust between bishops, clergy, religious, and laity will be strengthened by and in turn strengthen the synodal process—particularly as it is to come.

Finally, I explore more deeply what a synodal ethic of dialogue, discernment, and trust might mean in practice.

A Global, Divided Church

The starting point for our ethic of synodality must be the state of the Catholic Church struggling over how such beliefs and practices are interpreted and lived. This tension is highlighted by models of church that appear contradictory—hierarchical centralism around the papacy and Vatican and a more conciliar approach. Local churches (dioceses and episcopal conferences) lean either way (and sometimes both ways), creating a tension in local churches between so-called conservatives and progressives over doctrinal issues such as women's roles (including possible ordination), authority, and many moral questions.

The clergy sex abuse crisis has damaged the Church's institutional credibility, particularly in the Global North but also in parts of the South (e.g., Chile and South Africa), suggesting a universal problem that has yet to surface elsewhere for various possible reasons. These may include collective denial in areas where the Church serves social functions (e.g., education, welfare, and health care) in politically dysfunctional states, societies where investigative media is weak or easily controlled (including by the Church), or simply where it has been more successfully covered up.

Doctrinal disputes and clergy abuse share certain features. Where there are high levels of education outside the ambit of the Church (including lay theological education, particularly that of lay women), where there is press freedom, rule of law, and moderately to high-functioning democratic governance, Catholic dissent and exposure of clergy abuse is high. Trust in the Church has also declined not only over the scandals but out of a sense that Rome and its local (Roman-appointed and loyal) representatives are simply unwilling to engage in dialogue. Active church membership has also declined, sometimes dramatically, particularly among young people who have grown up in environments where democracy and freedom of speech are the norm and where tolerance and acceptance of cultural, religious, and sexual differences are taken for granted.

Where the Church is a key service provider, often an alternative to corrupt, incompetent, and authoritarian governments, and where theological education tends to be more seminary-based, geared toward training loyal clergy, with few women studying (and fewer teaching) theology, levels of dissent are lower. These societies often tend to social conservatism, even where popular discontent with the established order is growing.

A Global, Divided Vision of Synodality

Given Pope Francis's vision of journeying together in a spirit of dialogue and listening, conversion, hospitality, compassion, and reform, it is unsettling to see the emergence of three distinct understandings of synodality based on two different and potentially incompatible visions of the Catholic Church.

The first sees synodality as much-needed institutional reform. Epitomized by the German synodal process, it emerges from societies that take democracy seriously and that are disturbed by the lack of representation lay Catholics have in the Church, particularly in addressing doctrinal and moral matters. Their moral, pastoral, and theological concerns revolve around church reform, devolved authority structures, renewed involvement of women at all levels of leadership, and rethinking of moral teachings on sexuality.

The second sees synodality as a primarily pastoral renewal. This group is generally in the South, where the Church enjoys considerable respect for the many services (including development, health, education, and in many places human rights advocacy) it provides, often in contexts of authoritarian, dysfunctional, and corrupt governments. Many such societies are patriarchal, culturally conservative, less offended by hierarchical structures (which mirror their societies), and more well-disposed to official Catholic teachings on matters such as sexuality and gender. They are the Church's numerical majority. Deeper inculturation and the Church's ongoing sociopolitical witness are their intellectual, pastoral, and moral preoccupations.

A third bloc, a minority whom I call the Rejectionists, straddles these communities. On the religious right, they see synodality as a threat to doctrinal and institutional purity (and implicitly to established hierarchical structures). On the left, they see the process as window dressing, a publicity stunt that has been manipulated from the start. There seems to be no single understanding of synodality.

Who has final authority to determine doctrine and morals? The answer is, historically, less clear than one might imagine. Edmund Hill[3] has noted that the history of ecclesial authority is one of the tensions between what he calls Magisterial Papalists (MPs) and Ministerial Collegialists (MCs). The former stand for hierarchical centralism rooted in a strong papacy, while the latter embrace conciliarism: synodal, united yet diverse leadership centered on the local church, episcopal conferences, and collegial governance. Historically, Hill argues, until 1870, the MCs have been more prominent, with MPs emerging during crises, with mixed outcomes. At Vatican I, MPs gained ground, although moderated by MC qualifications of papal primacy; Vatican II embraced a more

---

[3] Edmund Hill, *Ministry and Authority in the Catholic Church* (London: Geoffrey Chapman, 1988).

MC church, but it was challenged by a reassertion of MP after the council, classically expressed in the encyclical *Humanae vitae*.[4] The pontificate of Pope Francis and the Synod on Synodality suggest an attempted, uneven, and in many places resisted return to MC. But even here, it is more complex.

At the opening of the second session of the synod in October 2024, Cardinal Mario Grech affirmed the synod as a "school of discernment: . . . the Church gathered together with Peter to discern together," but he added that it was not a direct means to collectively create reform but "aims to help Peter in his discernment for the whole Church."[5] Earlier in the year, Grech argued that the purpose of the synod was not parliamentary (i.e., deliberative—as one might describe a council of the Church); it was to create a new synodal culture, one that envisioned a church united in diversity rather than in uniformity.[6]

Developing an Ethics of Synodality

First Step: Some Recent Ethical Approaches to Synodality

Before exploring an ethic of synodality, let us consider three recent Catholic ethical perspectives[7] from Malta, the United

---

[4] See Robert Blair Kaiser, *The Encyclical That Never Was: The Story of the Pontifical Commission on Population, Family and Birth, 1964–1966*, rev. ed. (London: Bloomsbury/T&T Clark, 1987).

[5] "Synod: Cardinal Grech's Opening Address. Full Text," *Vatican News*, October 2, 2024, www.vaticannews.va/en/vatican-city/news/2024-10/synod-cardinal-mario-grech-opening-address-full-text.html.

[6] "Cardinal Grech Sets Out Vision for 'Rainbow' Synodal Church," *The Pillar*, March 25, 2024, www.pillarcatholic.com/p/cardinal-grech-sets-out-vision-for.

[7] Emmanuel Agius, "Ethical Perspectives on Synodality," in *Towards a Synodal Church: Moving Forward, Vol. 1*, ed. Shaji George Kochuthara and Joby Jose Kochumuttom (Bengaluru: Dharmaram Publications, 2023), 132–47; Xavier M. Montecel, "Eucharist, Synodality, and Ethics: Making

States, and India that have much in common: that synodality is an inclusive, dialogical, participatory process rooted in collective discernment by the whole Church aimed at renewal and reform of entrenched power structures with a view to improving the Church's credibility, mission, and impact in the world. They see synodality as a virtue, posing the question, what should we be like as a Church?[8] and focusing on it as the virtue of listening together to the guidance of the Holy Spirit in an inclusive spirit of collaboration between laity, clergy, and bishops in order to discern the will of God for the Church.[9]

Their emphases also differ. Emmanuel Agius, drawing on the synod's metaphor of journeying together, sees synodality as embracing personal and collective moral conversion, based on cultivation and practice of virtues (notably inclusivity, tolerance, respect, trust, patience, compassion, and accountability among others)[10] that generate institutional and structural conversion through genuine communication. He notes,

> The People of God, including the clergy, is called to . . . learn a new grammar, semantics, syntax and vocabulary of synodality. The entry requirements for a successful process of learning at the school of synodality are the attitudes of docility, humility and openness of heart to the Holy Spirit.[11]

Connections," *Religions* 14, no. 11 (November 2023): 1379, https://doi.org/10.3390/rel14111379; Carlos Luis, "Synodality: Ethical Perspectives," *Asian Horizons* 18, no. 2 (June 2024): 328–40.

[8] Or as Agius puts it, "What kind of Church are we now? What kind of Church do we want to become? How do we get there?": Agius, "Ethical Perspectives," 132.

[9] Luis, "Synodality," 329–32; Montecel, "Eucharist," 1379:6–9 of 11; Agius, "Ethical Perspectives," 136–40.

[10] Agius, "Ethical Perspectives," 136–37.

[11] Agius, "Ethical Perspectives," 144.

And he adds that the Church needs, following Habermas's insights, to distance itself from a strategic rationality (that seeks goals and self-interests) and to embrace a communicative rationality that pursues mutual understanding and agreement. Dialogue, discernment, and trust are essential to the latter; they have been part of the synodal process at its best, and they are essential for the synod to truly be implemented.

Drawing on the 2018 document of the International Theological Commission[12] and the work of liturgist Joris Geldhof,[13] Xavier Montecel argues that synodality should be grounded in the Eucharist as a focus of unity for all, "the ground of communion . . . the essential identity of the church and the goal of its being in the world,"[14] with particular emphasis on eucharistic devotion. My concern with this otherwise commendable proposal is that while it is a source of unity, the Eucharist in certain instances has become a source of disunity. These instances range from what constitutes acceptable understanding of its nature, who may or may not preside at it, and who among those present—notably people in so-called irregular relationships (of types ranging from same-sex unions, through divorced and remarried, to non-Catholics)—may be excluded from full participation. In short, the Eucharist as a sign of synodality (outside great celebrations such as we saw at the synod) is itself something to be put on a synodal reform agenda, resolving tensions around the sign that will become the sign par excellence of synodality, as part of a postsynod synodal ethics. As the Final Document notes, "There is

---

[12] International Theological Commission, *Synodality in the Life and Mission of the Church* (2018).

[13] Joris Geldhof, "Spirituality of Communion in a Synodal Church: A Liturgical Approach," in *Towards a Synodal Church: Moving Forward, Vol. 1*, ed. Shaji George Kochuthara and Joby Jose Kochumuttom (Bengaluru: Dharmaram Publications, 2023), 236–46.

[14] Montecel, "Eucharist," 1379: 3 of 11.

a close link between *synaxis* and *synodos*, between the eucharistic assembly and the synodal assembly" (27).

Carlos Luis's approach emphasizes synodality as shared responsibility for evangelization and social witness, a task shared by all the baptized, rooted in collaborative decision-making and shared power.[15] His concern is that, through this virtuous process of what I have called dialogue and discernment, attitudes such as the hitherto "rigid and exclusionary"[16] official stance on the LGBTQ+ question can be transformed into something more inclusive. Living a synodal praxis *within* the Church, he further implies, would also give Catholic social teaching added credibility: the Church practicing what it preaches.

A voice from Africa that echoes much of this is Stan Chu Ilo, who in his essays and books[17] sees the synodal process as inherently dialogical, akin to the African cultural understanding of palaver, a process of collective discussion seeking consensus. Several essays in this volume attest to the importance of this approach. It is deeply connected to the African notion of Ubuntu, which emphasizes shared humanity, community, and interdependence. Both these concepts offer strong potential for discernment and the building of trust, but they are also subject to certain problems—groupthink and/or conformity for the sake of (possibly false) harmony, sometimes risking being manipulated by authoritarians[18]—points Chu Ilo readily acknowledges.

---

[15] Luis, "Synodality," 334–36.

[16] Luis, "Synodality," 333.

[17] See Stan Chu Ilo, "The African Palaver Method: A Model Synodal Process for Today's Church," *Concilium* 2021, no. 2: 68–76; Stan Chu Ilo, "Exploring the Possible Contributions of the African Palaver towards a Participatory Synodal Church," *Exchange* 50 (2021) 209–37; and Ikenna U. Okafor, Josée Ngalula, Nicholaus Segeja, and Stan Chu Ilo, eds., *Toward a Synodal Church in Africa: Echoes from an African Christian Palaver* (Maryknoll, NY: Orbis Books, 2024).

[18] Michael O. Eze, "What Is African Communitarianism? Against

There is also a potential tension for Ubuntu to fail to resonate with more individualistic cultures, as in many parts of the North, and for its potential to preserve patriarchy.[19] At the very least, it is a contested term[20] that can be seen as analogous when read from a palaver perspective to a combination of dialogue and discernment—but with trust assumed or expected as a given.

While sharing much in common with these fine scholars, my proposal is that the sources for an ethic of synodality (and the practical synodal ethics that this synod will hopefully produce) need to be simpler and based on dialogue, discernment, and trust.

Second Step: Dialogue, Discernment—And above All, Trust

How then do we understand these virtuous concepts that I would suggest more universally articulate an ethic of synodality?

First, consider dialogue, above all, negotiation, as any good play will tell you. Dialogue is a negotiation between two or more characters over something. Karl Popper, the great defender of a free society, defined rationalism as "an attitude of readiness to listen to critical arguments and to learn from experience."[21] He embraced the idea of a society rooted in respectful conversation aimed at serving the good. He noted,

> We demand a government that rules according to the principles of equalitarianism and protectionism;[22] that

---

Consensus as a Regulative Ideal," *South African Journal of Philosophy* 27, no. 4: 386–99, doi.10.4314/sajpem.v27i4.31526.

[19] See Precious Simba, "A Feminist Critique of Ubuntu: Implications for Citizenship Education in Zimbabwe" PhD diss., University of Stellenbosch, 2021.

[20] Nyasha Mboti, "May the Real Ubuntu Please Stand Up?" *Journal of Media Ethics* 30, no. 2: 125–47, doi.10.1080/23736992.2015.1020380.

[21] Karl Popper, *The Open Society and Its Enemies*, vol. 2, 5th ed. (London: Routledge & Kegan Paul, 1966), 225.

[22] Not in any Marxist sense; more equality of opportunity and protection of personal rights.

tolerates all who are prepared to reciprocate, i.e., who are tolerant; that is, controlled by and accountable to the public. And we may add that some form of majority vote, together with institutions for keeping the public well informed, is the best, though not infallible, means of controlling a government.[23]

For Popper, polite, informed conversation that gave everyone opportunities to speak rationally and be heard was essential to good governance and law, the rule of just law. While different in many aspects, Popper's views blend in with a dialogical, discourse ethics[24] and with a process called in political philosophy deliberative democracy.[25] These theories suggest that dialogue over issues by the community should be integral to governance and politics, particularly electoral politics. In a spirit of freedom, disposed to believe that all participants genuinely believe one another's good intentions and integrity, participants present and discuss their positions without being silenced or excluded. The only criterion is that speakers are properly informed, substantiate claims, and freely engage with opposing views. This does not mean endless claims and counterclaims; it means informed debate.

Naturally, it is unfair to set unequally knowledgeable discussants against each other. This is particularly problematic in a Church where access to theological education, particularly for the laity, is limited. Should we, in the name of dialogical ethics, exclude such folk from the conversation? No, but there is an alternative.

---

[23] Popper, *The Open Society and Its Enemies*, 265–66.

[24] Here I draw loosely on the thinking of Jürgen Habermas, *Theory of Communicative Action*, 2 vols. (Cambridge: Polity Press, 1984, 1987), *Moral Consciousness and Communicative Action* (Cambridge: Polity Press, 1990).

[25] For an outline of the theory, see Jon Elster, ed., *Deliberative Democracy* (Cambridge: Cambridge University Press, 1998); Amy Gutmann and Dennis Thompson, *Democracy and Disagreement* (Princeton, NJ: Princeton University Press, 1996).

The classical sources[26] of moral theology—scripture, tradition, reason, and experience—engage with problems at different levels. Each offers insights into a moral problem, though sometimes contradictorily. What in the scripture seems obvious may be contradicted by the evidence of science—or personal experience may call into question a supposedly universal principle. This suggests that in discussions between more or less theologically informed people, so long as there is a genuine openness and desire to learn from each other, something fruitful can occur and even add depth to the conversation. Instead of tying us up in knots (of dogmatism and calls of relativism, of accusations that the Church does not understand reality), it offers us an opportunity for deeper, broader truth.[27]

One of the gaps I perceive in these sources of Christian ethics is the missing (possibly implied, possibly overlooked) dimension of prayer: *discernment.* Prayerful discernment—the "art of choosing well"[28]—is a mixture of head work and heart work, careful exploration of possibilities, options, and consequences, and the opening of one's mind and heart to the will of the Holy Spirit. This has been a part of the synodal process through the exercise of spiritual conversations at every stage. The Final Document expressly links discernment with the nature of the Church.

> Ecclesial discernment is not an organizational technique but rather a spiritual practice grounded in a living faith. It calls for interior freedom, humility, prayer, mutual

---

[26] Charles E. Curran, *History and Contemporary Issues: Studies in Moral Theology* (London: Bloomsbury Academic, 1996), 13–27.

[27] Jesus's praxis of open dialogue with the Samaritan or Syro-Phoenician woman (Mark 7:24–30; Matthew 15.21–28; John 4.4–42), historical "enemies" of his fellow Jews, is an example ripe for reflection in this regard.

[28] Pierre Wolff, *Discernment: The Art of Choosing Well* (Ligouri, MO: Ligouri Publications, 2003). Much of the spirituality of the synod seems to draw implicitly if not explicitly on processes associated with Ignatian (and Jesuit) discernment.

trust, an openness to the new and a surrender to the will of God. It is never just a setting out of one's own personal or group point of view or a summing up of differing individual opinions. Each person, speaking according to their conscience, is called to open themselves to the other who shares according to their conscience. In this sharing, they seek to recognize together "what the Spirit is saying to the churches" (*Rev* 2:7). As this discernment entails the contribution of everyone, ecclesial discernment is both the condition and a privileged expression of synodality, in which communion, mission and participation are lived. The more everyone is heard, the greater the discernment. Therefore, it is essential that we promote the broadest participation possible in the discernment process, particularly involving those who are at the margins of the Christian community and society. (81)

Another, distinctly Ignatian, dimension is not only discerning good from bad choices, but also the discernment of spirits.[29] In discernment, our choices may be influenced by social, cultural, emotional, and even economic forces, sometimes unduly. St. Ignatius of Loyola recognized the need for a further discernment—of what he calls the good spirit (inspired by the Holy Spirit) that leads us to the right choice, or the evil spirit (whether seen as the devil or our capacity for self-deception, confusion, and self-destruction) that undermines decision-making and leads to wrong decisions.

If dialogue offers the synodal process a means of seeking truth by evidence or reason, and discernment firmly puts prayer and awareness of the Holy Spirit at the core of decision-making, the

---

[29] For an excellent account of this, see Jules J. Toner, *A Commentary on Saint Ignatius' Rules for the Discernment of Spirits* (St. Louis: Institute of Jesuit Sources, 1981).

third element—trust—is what can move synodal processes into the synodal church Pope Francis and many of us seek. It is the moral foundation of synodality: "Wherever the Church enjoys trust, the practices of transparency, accountability and evaluation help to strengthen its credibility" (FD 97).

Trust is often associated with faith, which Paul Tillich defined as basic trust and ultimate concern.[30] Faith is the act of putting basic trust in the source of ultimate concern—God. Philosophers sometimes see it as reliance, but reliance "plus some extra factor."[31] It is characterized by a willingness to being vulnerable to another (who may or may not use one's vulnerability against you), reliance on others to do what one wishes them to do, and on them to be willing to do it, often unconsciously.[32] The trust relationship occurs on many levels: personal (trust in myself), interpersonal (trust in another or a few), communal (trust in a community, organization, or tribe), national (in country or government), or international (including organizations such as the universal Church). Political theorists who write about trust in public life[33] call trust social capital, "connections among individuals—social networks and the norms of reciprocity and trustworthiness that arise from them."[34]

Trust sometimes entails the trustor and trustee in relationships of partnership, or of patronage and clientage.[35] Partnership is

---

[30] Paul Tillich, *Dynamics of Faith* (New York: Harper, 1957), 1.

[31] Katherine Hawley, "Trust, Distrust and Commitment," *Noûs* 48, no. 1 (2014): 4, doi.10.1111/nous.12000.

[32] Olli Lagerspetz, *Trust: The Tacit Demand* (Dordrecht: Springer Netherlands, 1998).

[33] E.g., Robert D. Putnam, *Bowling Alone: The Collapse and Revival of American Community* (New York: Simon and Schuster, 2001); Francis Fukuyama, *Trust: The Social Virtues and the Creation of Prosperity* (New York: Free Press, 1995); Pete Buttigieg, *Trust: America's Best Chance* (New York: Liveright, 2020).

[34] Putnam, *Bowling Alone,* 19.

[35] Cf. S. N. Eisenstadt and L. Roniger, *Patrons, Clients and Friends:*

mutual trust among equals, give and take, a willing exchange of reliance and vulnerability that is mutual. These forms of trust are based on a kind of social contract: Insofar as partners (whether individuals, communities, or societies) maintain the relationship based on mutuality and shared vulnerability, the relationship holds. But if this is broken, the relationship is renegotiated. In democratic governance, when a government loses the people's trust, it is voted out and replaced with a new government based on a new set of relationships seeking to establish once again social capital. The process is continuous and deeply rooted in a mixture of evidence-based perceptions of the good and subject to revision based on further evidence. This model, strongest in the North, is how many parts of the Catholic Church (mostly laity) perceive things. Authority to govern or define doctrines and practices is given but can be revoked if trust is perceived to be violated.

Patronage-clientage is an exchange (whether willing or unwilling) of reliance and vulnerability, normally an exchange of favors or gifts for loyalty. We see this to varying degrees in cultures that are hierarchical (monarchies, linear chiefdoms, etc.) and often marked by religious legitimation of the relationship. Classic Judeo-Christian examples are the Mosaic covenant and the relationship of bishops, clergy, and laity in the Catholic Church. There is a classical trade-off—divine protection or promise of salvation in return for faith, worship, and conformity to certain divinely ordained commandments mediated to the faithful through a clerical caste. The authority in such a relationship privileges the trustee or patron; dissent and disobedience become acts of disloyalty, violations of covenant or divinely sanctioned social order, often with dire real or potential consequences. This problem may help us understand why fear or hostility toward the synodal process can

---

Interpersonal Relations and the Structure of Trust in Society (Cambridge: Cambridge University Press, 1984).

be found among many clergy: the honor, prestige, and patronage relationship seems to them to be threatened.

Space prevents a more detailed exploration of the claim that patronage-clientage is at the heart of traditional Catholicism (and many other religions), but it serves as an interesting tool in mapping how synodality has been variedly received. The most conservative, synodally hostile responses occurred in societies where patronage-clientage relationships are strong (i.e., where the Church offers material as well as spiritual incentives for loyalty), often where democracy/social capital is low. The most radical responses—those who hope that synodality is a step toward a democratic church—occur in places where material incentives are less significant, where spiritual plurality (including nonreligiousness) is normal, and where democracy and/or social capital is high. In particular, the varied attitudes of bishops, priests, and religious is informative: The mind-set of clericalism, we found, is still strong, still in many places operating out of a patron-client notion of trust.

Trust is complex. It is also, as we have noted earlier, in short supply. It is also the linchpin for an ethic (indeed, following Agius, Luis, and Montecel, a virtue) of synodality. Without trust in the relationships among bishops, clergy, religious, and laity, dialogue and discernment become re-hierarchicalized. Institutional *position* holds more weight than content in a dialogue, and the supposed correctness of a discernment is based less on a deep sense of God speaking than on *who* is controlling the discernment process. This is particularly acute among those (particularly clergy) who see synodality as a diminishment of their positional privilege, a privilege often linked in their minds to a nondisambiguated sense of doctrinal, moral, and institutional truths. Here, too, lies a challenge. Trust should be based on—and in turn expressed through—mutual accountability, transparency, and evaluation of all members of the Church. But these features can equally be read by (particularly but not exclusively clergy) skeptics and rejectors as mistrust and even hostility.

Exploring the Final Document

Despite the differences and tensions in implementation, the synod happened. The Synod on Synodality, more precisely, the second session of the Sixteenth Ordinary General Assembly of the Synod of Bishops, is over.[36] The Final Document,[37] situating synodality as an ancient and constant practice of Eastern and Western churches, defined synodality as

> the walking together of Christians with Christ and towards God's Kingdom, in union with all humanity. Orientated towards mission, synodality involves gathering at all levels of the Church for mutual listening, dialogue, and communal discernment. It also involves reaching consensus as an expression of Christ rendering Himself present, He who is alive in the Spirit. Furthermore, it consists in reaching decisions according to differentiated co-responsibilities. (28)

It added that it was "primarily a spiritual disposition . . . that flows from the action of the Holy Spirit and requires listening to the Word of God, contemplation, silence and conversion of heart" as well as "asceticism, humility, patience and a willingness to forgive and be forgiven" (43). It facilitates better, more-consultative governance in the Church and serves the Church's wider mission. Noting that "we have experienced that it is relationships that sustain the Church's vitality, animating its structures" (49), the Final Document called for greater nurturing of relationships—particularly with those who feel excluded or judged because of things such as sexuality or complex

---

[36] See Austen Ivereigh, "The Church at a Turning Point," *The Tablet*, November 2, 2024, 4–6.

[37] Sixteenth Ordinary General Assembly of the Synod of Bishops, *For a Synodal Church: Communion, Participation, Mission*, Final Document.

relationships, or who are the most socially marginalized. The point here was that

> to be a synodal Church, we are required to open ourselves to a genuine relational conversion that redirects each person's priorities, and we must once again learn from the Gospel that attending to relationships is not merely a strategy or a tool for greater organizational effectiveness. Relationships and bonds are the means by which God the Father has revealed Himself in Jesus and the Spirit. When our relationships, even in their fragility, allow the grace of Christ, the love of the Father, and the communion of the Spirit to shine through, we confess with our lives our faith in God the Trinity. (50)

Above all, dialogue over controversies in the Church (such as women deacons) should remain open (60). Women should be brought into new ministries (66). Laity should have a much greater role in the appointment of bishops, and greater effort should be taken to build co-responsibility and supportiveness between clerical and lay ministries.

In Part 3, a "conversion of process" in how the Church makes decisions, the call is strong for discernment rooted in transparency, and accountability is encouraged. A large section (81–94) deals with such discernment in matters of mission, noting that among other things, there must be formation opportunities for leaders (86). Crucially, existing structures that facilitate synodal processes should be strengthened, even expanded, and canon law should clarify the difference between consultation and deliberation. The theme of transparency and accountability is continued in trying to see how such structures might promote the more synodal, consultative vision of church (95–101). Above all, a point made earlier in Part 3 is worth noting.

Decision-making processes need ecclesial discernment, which requires listening in a climate of trust that is supported by transparency and accountability. Trust must be mutual: decision-makers need to be able to trust and listen to the People of God. The latter, in turn, need to be able to trust those in authority. (80)

Part 4 focuses on "bonds of communion that unite us and with space for all peoples and all cultures" and the need to "cultivate new forms of the exchange of gifts and the network of bonds that unite us" (109). The discussion explores places where this can happen, how opportunities and challenges meet, and how some institutions like bishops' conferences need to be strengthened while others like parishes may need to be reconfigured.

After stressing that formation (including in discernment) for the new missionary discipleship envisioned (Part 5) needs to be integral, ongoing, and shared between men and women, lay and ordained, and needs to safeguard minors and vulnerable adults (143, 150), the document ends with a hopeful vision of an eschatological banquet that includes especially the marginalized: "She knows She cannot forget the poorest, the last, the excluded, those who do not know love and are without hope, nor those who do not believe in God or do not recognize themselves in any established religion" (153). In that sense, too, "the Church's synodality, thus, becomes a social prophecy, inspiring new paths in the political and economic spheres, as well as collaborating with all those who believe in fellowship and peace in an exchange of gifts with the world" (153).

What then are we to make of the fundamental ethic/s of the Final Document? The underlying ethos it seems to embrace is one of dialogue, discernment, and trust, but what exactly does such an ethic mean, how far does it play out, and how might such an ethic be formulated not simply to capture what has happened but provide a groundwork for the future—for the implementation of synodality, and in particular for the ten[38] issues reserved by Pope Francis for Synod study groups to explore?

Beyond the Synod: Building Synodal Ethics

How, then, should the Final Document be assessed under my proposed ethic of synodality? Prima facie, it rates quite well. It makes important statements about working together, dialogue, and good discernment through spiritual conversation; it emphasizes the need to reform church structures, placing bishops in a more collegial, consultative role both horizontally (between bishops, within bishops' conferences, with the bishop of Rome) and vertically (with clergy, religious, and laity); it acknowledges differences in culture (to some degree, perhaps less than many in the South might like); and it recognizes and commits the Church to more open, honest dialogue over contentious issues.

---

[38] These include the relationship of the Western Latin Church with Eastern Catholic Churches; listening to the cry of the poor; mission in the digital environment; revision of the *Ratio Fundamentalis Institutionis Sacerdotalis*; theological and canonical matters regarding specific ministerial forms; relationship between bishops, consecrated life, and ecclesial associations; aspects of the person and ministry of the bishop (criteria for selecting candidates to episcopacy, judicial function of the bishops, nature and course of *ad limina apostolorum* visits) from a missionary synodal perspective; role of papal representatives; theological criteria and synodal methodologies for shared discernment of controversial doctrinal, pastoral, and ethical issues; reception of the fruits of the ecumenical journey in ecclesial practices. Cited in Matthew Santucci, "Pope Francis: Study Groups to Examine 10 Synod on Synodality Themes through June 2025," *Catholic News Agency*, March 14, 2024, www.catholicnewsagency.com/news/257097/pope-francis-study-groups-to-examine-10-synod-on-synodality-themes-through-june-2025. In this Vatican-speak, we find such hot-button issues as sexuality and sexual orientation, ordination of women as deacons, and broader questions of lay collaboration in church governance—a blow for the progressives, and a challenge in terms of how far genuine dialogue, discernment, and trust may prevail.

But it was also frustrating—to many observers and participants—that the synod was not employed to explore such issues. While from a professional, academic view, these issues need close academic and pastoral study, there is a real fear that they will be buried in a committee, perhaps in the hopes of some conservatives that they will be forgotten. This is unhelpful, particularly as the Catholic Church continues to hemorrhage members in many countries, and not least in that it suggests to some that the promise of transparency (and trust in the process) of synodality might have been compromised.

On a more positive note, in his closing speech, Pope Francis declared,

> I do not intend to publish an Apostolic Exhortation, what we have approved is sufficient. There are already highly concrete indications in the Document that can be a guide for the mission of the Churches, in their specific continents and contexts. This is why I am making it immediately available to everyone; it is the reason I said that it should be published. In this way, I wish to recognize the value the synodal journey accomplished, which by means of this Document I hand over to the holy faithful people of God.[39]

This unprecedented decision is in effect a statement that in regard to the outcome, the Final Document has the mind of the pope fully behind it. This is a clear indication that Francis has committed himself unreservedly to the move to a more synodal Church, that synodality (at least under his pontificate) is here to stay.[40] Francis trusts the synod! Yet the challenge, particularly as and when the committees of experts explore the ten reserved

---

[39] Pope Francis, "The Spirit Whispers Words of Love into the Heart of Each Person," *L'Osservatore Romano*, November 1, 2024, 4.

[40] It confirms what he said in Pope Francis, *Walking Together: The Way of Synodality* (Maryknoll, NY: Orbis Books, 2023).

issues of the synod, is that a spirit of dialogue, discernment, and trust will continue. Building trust as the foundation for real and fruitful dialogue and discernment, particular among those (clergy and laity) who are mistrustful and even opposed to the process, is essential. For these people, the challenge will be to help educate them (akin to post–Vatican II theological renewal programs) in the longer, broader, and deeper traditions of the Church—something I see implicit in Francis's recent letter encouraging better clergy formation in church history.[41] If we see a genuine change in how local churches operate more consultatively, and how ideally the Catholic Church becomes a communion of communions, then perhaps we may see the Church actually operating under synodal ethics. When, *how*,[42] and if the committees explore these topics, present their findings, and perhaps see them presented to the wider faithful for consultation before implementation, we may see the emergence of a genuine synodal ethics.

---

[41] Pope Francis, "Letter of the Holy Father Francis on the Renewal of the Study of Church History," November 21, 2024. While I heartily agree with him, I believe church history "literacy" needs to be extended to the whole Church for this to be effective.

[42] And the *how* should, in the spirit of an ethic of synodality, include wide consultation with the faithful, careful and broad research, and actual discernment!

7

RELIGIOUS WOMEN TEACHERS OF SYNODALITY

The "Abundant Catch" of the Peripheries

LÉOCADIE LUSHOMBO

> What would the Church be without religious sisters and consecrated laywomen? The Church cannot be understood without them.[1]

Women's synodality teaching skills and methodologies are rooted in their deep search for understanding the tradition of the Church and experiences of faith of the first communities of believers and the living base ecclesial communities, also known as Small Christian Communities (SCCs) in the twenty-first-century world context. This essay focuses on the voices of African women religious, showing how they teach synodality by drawing on the Christian tradition, taking seriously the claim that "Listening to

---

[1] Pope Francis, "For Religious Sisters and Consecrated Women," February 2022, https://thepopevideo.org/february-for-religious-sisters-and-consecrated-women/#:~:text=What%20would%20the%20Church%20be,challenges%20that%20we're%20experiencing.

the Word of God is the starting point and criterion for all ecclesial discernment" (Final Document [FD] 83).

This essay also explores women's synodal processes through their ministry to those at the peripheries, ministering in a participatory manner, and fostering SCCs, small schools, small jobs, and a "smaller share" of their resources.[2] Women's participation in SCCs exemplifies the synodal ecclesiology par excellence. As Veronica Rop mentions in her essay, they participate in large numbers in the activities of SCCs. Their ministries help understand the claim that "All baptized are called to model Christ, putting their freely given gifts at the service of all God's people wherever they happen to be planted in God's vineyard."[3]

The Working Document (WD) for the Continental Stage of the synodal process affirms that "women, especially women religious, are already at the forefront of synodal practices in some of the most challenging social situations we face.... [They] seek collaborators and can be teachers of synodality within wider Church processes" (WD 65). Indeed, they are teachers of synodality in several ways. They teach the biblical elements that undergird the full participation of women based on our "common baptismal dignity" (WD 60), for "All Christians participate in the *sensus fidei* through baptism" (FD 23). Women's teaching is also grounded in the early Church's gifts of women who already were "the backbone of Church communities" (WD 61), taking active roles, including the diaconate (WD 64). Their giftedness and wisdom are seen throughout their many associations and

---

[2] Catherine Sexton and Maria Calderón Muñoz, "Religious Life for Women in East and Central Africa: A Sustainable Future: Report of a Research Project on Sisters' Understandings of the Essence of Religious Life for Women in East and Central Africa 2017–2020 Institute" (Durham University and Margaret Beaufort Institute of Theology, February 2020), 124.

[3] Maureen O'Connell, "'Just Church' Is the Definitive Book on Women and Synodality," *National Catholic Reporter*, September 15, 2023, 11.

ministries with many small groups of Christians. They call on both men and women to cultivate intellectual virtues, a pursuit of cognitive excellence, the "innate ability or acquired habit that enables one to consistently achieve some intellectual good, such as truth in a relevant matter."[4] This pursuit of truth, in turn, facilitates the attainment of knowledge. Women religious theologians highlight that accessing truth requires epistemic humility, which summons us to recognize our limited understanding and maintain an openness to new perspectives. S. J. Harrington argues that epistemic humility "[is that] form of humility [that] allows us to enter into discourse rather than to tower above it. By relinquishing the power of certitude, it discovers a new authority, an authority in which the admission of ignorance might actually be a way to truth. If truth is found, then, not by me but by us, then there must be certain virtues that aid us in our pursuit of truth."[5] This humility is "the basic condition for communal as well as individual moral discernment."[6] It is a bedrock of synodal virtue that provides grounds for genuine dialogue and empathetic listening.

The task of synodality, "A fruitful dialogue between the charisms and ministries at the service of the Kingdom" (Synthesis Report 3), can take place only if the partners are willing to listen authentically. There is no listening without an attitude of learning. The gifts of women as teachers of synodality are, first

---

[4] John Greco, "Virtue Epistemology," *Stanford Encyclopedia of Philosophy*, Winter 2009.

[5] S. J. Harrington, *Paul and Virtue Ethics: Building Bridges between New Testament Studies and Moral Theology*, 1st ed. (Lanham, MD: Rowman & Littlefield, 2010), 146.

[6] Margaret Farley, "Ethics, Ecclesiology, and the Grace of Self-Doubt," quoted in Christopher Alt, "The Dynamic of Humility and Wisdom: The Syrophoenician Woman and Jesus in Mark 7:24–30," *Lumen et Vita* 2, no. 1 (July 25, 2012): 9.

of all, their theological teachings that call on the Church to be open to learning to allow for a shared understanding about what "common baptismal dignity" (FD 60) and being "the backbone of Church communities" entail. As Bernadette Mbuy-Beya, a Catholic religious woman from the Democratic Republic of Congo (DRC), suggests, despite all the efforts and advancements of inculturation theology, there will be no hope of experiencing the freedom of Jesus Christ without considering women's gifts.[7] If synodality is to be "an expression of the dynamic and living Tradition" and the Church is to "enhance the differentiated co-responsibility in the mission of all the members of the People of God,"[8] they are to pay attention to the theological elements that underscore the critical participation and integral presence of women as leaders and protagonists of a truly synodal Church. These elements, along with women's many services to the Church, are the root gifts of women to synodality. These gifts are deeply grounded in Christian scripture and traditions.

For the African continent, women draw on a cultural hermeneutical approach and the historical women figures that allow women to consider the cultures that shape women in the Church and society. I will draw on biblical scholars and commentaries on a few women's theological messages in the Deuterocanonical books (Ruth, Judith, Esther)[9] and the New Testament, showing how they inspire women teachers of synodality.

---

[7] Carrie Pemberton, "Circle Thinking: African Women Theologians in Dialogue with the West," *Studies of Religion in Africa* 25 (Boston: Brill, 2003), 100.

[8] General Secretariat of the Synod, "XVI Ordinary General Assembly of the Synod of Bishops—Towards October 2024," December 11, 2023, 2.

[9] Toni Craven, "Judith," in *The Jerome Biblical Commentary for the Twenty-First Century*, ed. John J. Collins et al., 3rd, fully rev. ed. (London: T&T Clark, 2022), 556.

Religious Women's Teaching Gifts as Informed by Scripture

Religious women theologians' gifts are, first, their faith conviction that women who longed for the God of the Hebrews have something to teach us all, and their discipleship as followers of Christ dedicated to his ministry. They take seriously the claim that not only have "we heard the invitation of Peter's successor, and we accepted it; we set out with him and followed his lead" (FD 49); we have also heard the testimony of Mary Magdalene, who "was given the first proclamation of the Resurrection,"[10] becoming the first witness of the risen Christ and a believer in the resurrection (John 20:8). Avoiding biblical proof-texting, women learn scripture and do exegesis to discover the moral coherence within the canon, which distinguishes the "core, context, and coherence" within biblical texts to apply the Bible's core messages on moral issues.[11]

Biblical scholar Gina Hens-Piazza suggests that the story of Ruth, disclosing "the legal, religious, familial, moral, and national complexities reflective of ancient Israelite society,"[12] teaches us that God affirms women's roles and agency in "the broader vision of what it means to be the people of God ... care and responsibility for one another."[13]

Hens-Piazza highlights two pivotal moments in the story: God provides relief from famine (Ruth 1:6) and addresses the threat to the family's future (4:13). In both cases, Ruth serves as a central figure, acting as a "divine channel" through the grain she gleans and in the birth of a child. She exemplifies God's extraordinary

---

[10] Ibid., 60.

[11] James T. Bretzke, "Scripture and Ethics: Moving along the Sacred Claim Axis," in *A Morally Complex World: Engaging Contemporary Moral Theology* (Collegeville, MN: Liturgical Press, 2004), 79–108.

[12] Gina Hens-Piazza, "Ruth," in *The Jerome Biblical Commentary for the Twenty-First Century*, 422.

[13] Hens-Piazza, "Ruth," 424.

kindness (*hesed*) toward Naomi and Boaz, helping those in need while surpassing cultural and legal norms. Hens-Piazza underscores that the actions of Ruth, Naomi, and Boaz reflect "the realm of the divine *hesed* which knows no boundaries."[14]

Women theologians highlight and teach the lessons of divine hesed in the story of Ruth. Her virtues exemplify compassion for orphans, foreigners, and widows, showing that these groups are essential to God's plan (Ruth 2:1–3). They are "already included in the care of Israel's God."[15] This divine hesed calls us to adopt an inclusive vision of God that welcomes everyone regardless of gender. Ruth's story empowers women to teach us the true meaning of being part of God's community[16] and "the inclusive Character of God's people (4:18–22)."[17] Being a People of God is ground for becoming and embodying a synodal Church.

The story of Judith was written in a period in which "there seems to have been an intensified concern for purity."[18] Among other significant theological conceptions pointed out by biblical scholar Toni Craven, Judith's narrative emphasizes a God who cares for the weak, is merciful (16:15), and uses the female agency, including widows, to face enemies (9:10, 13:15, 16:5), and leads the people to victory, survival, and continuance of the cult. Despite the violence of the story, Judith's figure defies conventional norms (13:8), reverses the theology that stresses male leadership in the community (8:9–34), "delegates the management of her household to another woman (8:10), and refuses to marry (16:22)."[19] Judith exemplifies how faith can inspire decisive action. As a childless widow, she rises to achieve

---

[14] Hens-Piazza, "Ruth," 424.
[15] Hens-Piazza, "Ruth," 426.
[16] Hens-Piazza, "Ruth," 424.
[17] Hens-Piazza, "Ruth," 429.
[18] Craven, "Judith," 556.
[19] Craven, "Judith," 556.

Yahweh's triumph over Assyria (8:1–16:25), demonstrating the power of unwavering belief.[20]

Esther, in turn, "dares to challenge the king"[21] to save her people, prays for courage to overcome her fears, and risks her life (4:16). This illustrates that God empowers us all—men and women.

Barbara Reid[22] teaches that, besides Mary, mother of Jesus, there were women who followed Jesus and ministered to the Gospel, and many others who did what the opening line of *Dei verbum* urges: "Hearing the Word of God with reverence, and proclaiming it with faith."[23] Reid adds this:

> The Bible itself gives us many examples of women in the Old Testament, women such as Miriam (Ex 15:20–21), Judith (Jdt 16:1–17), Deborah (Judges 5), and Hannah (1 Sam 2:1–10), who hear God's word and utter prophetic proclamations extolling God's saving deeds. In the New Testament, women who hear the word and proclaim it include Jesus' mother (Lk 1:46–55), Elizabeth (Lk 1:25, 39–45, 57–66), Anna (Lk 2:36–38), the woman evangelist of Samaria (Jn 4:4–42), Mary Magdalene and the other Galilean women (Mt 28:1–10; Lk 24:1–12; Jn 20:1–2, 11–18), to name only a few.[24]

These examples are vital for creating a listening Church that values women's gifts and reflects Jesus's care for the marginalized.

---

[20] Craven, "Judith," 560.

[21] Irene Nowell, "Esther," in *The Jerome Biblical Commentary for the Twenty-First Century*, 563.

[22] Barbara Reid is a religious woman, biblical scholar, Dominican sister, and Distinguished Professor of New Testament Studies.

[23] Barbara Reid, "Using Scripture to Further Gender Equality," *America, the National Catholic Review*, Women Proclaiming the Word, November 16, 2015.

[24] Reid, "Using Scripture to Further Gender Equality."

Religious women's teachings are inspired by Prisca, Aquila, Junia, and Phoebe, among other women who co-discipled with Paul in the early Christian missionary movement. Whereas Junia was arrested for her preaching activity, Phoebe exercised the authoritative function as Paul's ambassador in Rome, where she was accepted as such. Paul named her as a sister and deacon of the church of Cenchreae (Romans 16:1–2). In Romans 16:7, Paul highlights Junia as a relative and fellow prisoner who was prominent among the apostles, and someone who was in Christ before him. For women biblical scholars, this recognition reflects the significant roles women played in the early Church. He also refers to Prisca and Aquila as "co-workers in Christ Jesus," showing that they too contributed meaningfully and faced persecution alongside him. Galatians 3:28 asserts that distinctions between people are irrelevant in Christ. This message is reinforced in 1 Corinthians 12:13, reminding us that we are all vital parts of one body—the Body of Christ.

The early Church discerned and embraced a progressive view of women's roles. A listening synodal Church actively learns from this history, which inspires religious women today and promotes their full participation. It illustrates women's equal authority. Mary and Martha, who welcomed Jesus with their brother Lazarus, showed diverse ways of following him—one by listening attentively and the other by serving (Luke 10:38–42). This diversity reflects God's inclusive calling, urging us to honor and empower all women in our communities.

Women learn from the Bible's powerful women whose encounters with Jesus transformed their lives and those of others. Anna, the prophetess, expressed gratitude and proclaimed Jesus to those awaiting redemption in Jerusalem (Luke 2:36–38). The Samaritan woman at the well shared her life-changing experience, revealing that Jesus might be the Messiah (John 4:1–42). Jesus also publicly addressed the woman with a hemorrhagic condition as "daughter," affirming her faith and healing her (Mark 5:22–29).

He recognized the woman crippled for eighteen years as a "daughter of Abraham," restoring her dignity (Luke 13:10–13). These accounts highlight Jesus's commitment to uplifting women from all backgrounds, empowering them as teachers and leaders in the Church while embodying the virtues seen in these stories.

Anne Arabome reinforces the above points by explaining that scripture confirms that our common baptism makes us all sharers in equal dignity. Romans 8:14–17 and Galatians 4:4–6 argue that we all become the Body of Christ once baptized and share equal dignity in Christ (Hebrews 12:23), enjoying "God's free gift of sonship and daughtership."[25] Since God has already incorporated women by making them part of the one Body of Christ, the Church must also welcome the gifts given to women by God. To waste these gifts is not only alienating women; it is also obstructing God's "reconciliation, justice, and peace for all."[26]

Arabome notes how God makes men and women share the discipleship of equals, stating that, without discrimination, "the 120 disciples, including many women, received the Holy Spirit as tongues of fire since they were to be the speakers."[27] Religious women call on the Church to listen to these disciples' experiences. They affirm that the synodal process is an opportunity to affirm and act according to women's roles in the Church from its early days to the present. The Church cannot continue ignoring women's voices and roles as they appear in scripture, roles taken forward by lay and religious women. If it does, it fails to listen "to the voice of the Spirit enacted by the People of God, [not] allowing its *sensus fidei* to emerge" (Working Document for the Continental Stage 8).

---

[25] Anne Arabome, "Woman, You Are Set Free! Women and Discipleship in the Church," in *Reconciliation, Justice, and Peace. The Second African Synod*, ed. Agbonkhianmeghe E. Orobator (Maryknoll, NY: Orbis Books, 2011), 19.

[26] Arabome, "Woman, You Are Set Free!" 23.

[27] Arabome, "Woman, You Are Set Free!" 18.

The Church historian Gusto González has argued that the early Church gave responsibilities to its widows for different reasons, including caring for themselves, avoiding remarrying with pagans out of financial need, and losing their faith. Some widows were in charge of catechism, and others were ministers leading other groups. There even came to exist several unmarried widows in the early Church, and the practice eventually gave rise to "feminine monasticism."[28] González suggests that it was only in the effort to fight heresies in the second century that the Church centralized its teaching and ended up excluding women from leadership.[29] Women religious and lay women biblical scholars have been recovering the early Church's tradition, making it a living one. A listening Church needs to pay attention to this process of recovery. The overwhelming evidence of female teachers, co-workers with Paul, and disciples of Jesus indicates that Christian scriptures foreground women's participation in a synodal Church.

Josée Ngalula, drawing on the tradition of the Church, echoes Jesuit Father Federico Lombardi, who asserted in 2013 that appointing women as cardinals is "theologically and theoretically possible." Grounded in Church canon law and scripture, she points out a troubling trend: Many laypeople and priests overlook biblical affirmations of women's dignity due to cultural biases. Many African pastoral agents advise women against challenging their husbands, citing that Eve was taken from Adam's side. She affirms that this projection is the result of theological illiteracy affecting many faithful Catholics, including clerics.[30] It is time to challenge these narratives and promote a more inclusive Church leadership[31] if the Church wants to be synodal.

---

[28] Justo L. González, *The Story of Christianity,* vol. 1: *The Early Church to the Reformation,* rev. and updated, 2nd ed. (New York: Harper One, 2010), 114.

[29] González, *The Story of Christianity,* 114.

[30] González, *The Story of Christianity,* 181.

[31] Josée Ngalula, "Milestones in Achieving a More Incisive Feminine

It is even more liberating for women to know that, long before the United Nations and NGOs, God regarded women with respect and dignity, as biblical texts attest.[32] A synodal Church is essential for addressing the cultural alienation of women, moving beyond mere biblical interpretations. Ngalula highlights the necessity of including women and youth, as their representation is fundamental to the essence of a synodal Church. Women, laypeople, and young people—all majorities in the Church, especially in Africa—are absent among those surrounding and advising the pope.[33]

The idea of women teachers of synodality challenges a hierarchical Church and clericalism. As Chin Ngoinso of Cameroon notes, "Hierarchies have often treated competent women religious as 'placeholders, spare tires' waiting to be ejected when a male counterpart is available."[34]

Religious Women's Gifts of Cultural Hermeneutics

A significant contribution religious women as teachers of synodality make is their culturally informed theological perspective. African women theologians use cultural hermeneutics to explore the relationship between religion and culture, demonstrating their deep interconnection. Referring to African traditions and

---

Presence in the Church of Pope Francis," in *The Church We Want: Foundations, Theology, and Mission of the Church in Africa—Conversations on Ecclesiology*, ed. A. E. Orobator (Nairobi, Kenya: Paulines Publications Africa, 2015), 180.

[32] Marguerite Akossi-Mvongo, "The Church We Want: Ecclesia of Women in Africa?" in *The Church We Want: African Catholics Look to Vatican III*, ed. A. E. Orobator (Maryknoll, NY: Orbis Books, 2016), 182.

[33] Ngala Killian Chimtom, "African Women Push for Greater Representation in the Church Management: Africa Correspondent with Sr. Josée Ngalula," *Crux*, March 25, 2024.

[34] Chimtom, "African Women Push for Greater Representation in the Church Management."

historical figures such as Kimpa Vita, a pioneer of inculturation theology, they promote a decolonizing and enculturated approach that is vital for what the Synthesis Report of the Synod of Bishops calls "the renewal of the Christian community" (2c, p. 6). Women religious recognize that the Church is the sign of the Kingdom of God. Still, this sign is also structured in response to formulas deeply ingrained in rigid imperialist or colonial structures, cultures, and traditions. Women religious take on the task of retrieving the Christian message to "walk together with all the peoples of the earth, in dialogue with their religions and their cultures, recognizing in them the seeds of the Word, journeying towards the Kingdom" (FD 17). Women, as advocates for synodality, emphasize that the contradictions in the Church should not be ignored to maintain the status quo but instead be engaged in a dialogue that respects the diverse realities of the People of God, fostering empathy and understanding.

A hermeneutic of cultures acknowledges the negative impact of colonialism on cultures, making it essential to examine its effects on women's lives. This critique empowers African women theologians to recognize and appreciate the resilient aspects of indigenous cultures, uncovering both the empowering gifts and disempowering practices in African and Christian traditions.

Gifts of Space for Dialogue and Mutual Listening

Another set of gifts of women religious has to do with the place where women come together to experience solidarity, support each other, and listen to the grassroots. The Circle of Concerned African Women Theologians (the Circle) is a space where women "gather together in solidarity to deal with and decide matters vital to the community" (Synthesis Report 7). The Circle is a place for thinking and teaching in a spirit of "mutual activity and aid" (cf. *Gaudium et spes* 40), justice, solidarity, peace, and interreligious dialogue, as it regularly brings together African women of all religions and their collaborators from other continents. The Circle includes women from different Christian denominations and other religions, affirming that "Christian communities are to enter into solidarity with those of other religions, convictions, and cultures" to embrace "mutual learning and journeying together" (Synthesis Report 7). It builds upon the legacy of African women's traditions and inculturation theology. The Circle is synodality in action. It is one of "the many expressions of synodal life in cultural contexts" (Synthesis Report 5) where women walk together as a community.

The Circle was launched at the Accra Conference in 1989, which was attended by seventy African women theologians; it has been meeting every five years since. The issues African women suffer and seek to redress are brought to the fore at the Circle meetings. The Circle provides space where women and men can encounter one another, listen to each other as a Church, and dialogue, discern, and communicate with God. The Circle's distinctiveness is that it speaks to different and particular cultural contexts of Africa and Christianity in Africa. Through the Circle, religious views and cultural dimensions of the life of African women are represented. Thus, one of the Circle's tasks is rewriting women's stories.

Furthermore, the Circle's theological agenda aims to uncover African women's moral agency and their contributions to the task of enhancing, flourishing, and liberating Christianity. Thus, women joined groups of theologians such as the Circle, where younger theologians are trained to write and do theology in the multicultural contexts of Africa. They gather, listen to each other, and plan to work together to include and help those left on the peripheries.

Since one of the distinct aspects of the Church designated by synodality is the Church's ordinary *modus vivendi et operandi* (FD 30), I illustrate women as teachers of synodality by examples of their synodal ways of living and operating as well as their prophetic way of listening and accompanying the community. Women's examples of "missionary creativity explore new forms of pastoral care and identify concrete processes of care" (Synthesis Report 111). The next section looks at their gifts of "communion, mission, and participation—the three cornerstones of synodality" (Synthesis Report 142) through their culture of care.

Sharing the Gift of the Culture of Care by Addressing Poverty, Violence, and Oppression

Religious women's gifts for synodality materialize through their projects whereby they work for peace, justice, ecology, solidarity, and social change on behalf of vulnerable populations. Women religious and lay consecrated work as shepherds and healers, handmaids of Christ, facing daily marginalization and the factors that kill life on the continent. Thus, they consider that the first step for any theological engagement with women on the continent is to consider their daily struggles for "the necessities of daily life, for food, shelter, work, and health" and their resilience, nurturing life in the shadow of men, in the constant presence of violence.[35] Through this embodiment of Jesus's characteristics, they affirm motherhood, an important African theological concept affirming abundant life.

Motherhood is a gift and a joy. The motherhood of women religious goes well beyond biological fecundity and must remain associated with women's agency. Teresa Okure explains that the commitment to reproduction in African anthropology reflects the views of "the human person as a unity and human community

---

[35] Bernadette Mbuy-Beya, "Women in the Church in Africa: Possibilities for Presence and Promises"; Mbuy-Beya, "Faire La Théologie Dans La Perspective Des Femmes Africaines," cited in Pemberton, *Circle Thinking*, 99–100.

as an inter-generational project."³⁶ It is shaped by distinctive theological and philosophical teachings: women as givers and protectors of life and their identities are not to be reduced to their societies' views of sexuality, which are deeply informed by religion and sexism.

Motherhood is lived from a very spiritual dimension for religious and lay-consecrated women in Africa. Motherhood, therefore, becomes the key to agency and social transformation, which Bernadette Mbuy-Beya affirms as "social motherhood." In this, she echoes John Paul II, who argued, "At the same time, motherhood in its personal-ethical sense expresses a very important creativity on the part of the woman, upon whom the very humanity of the new human being mainly depends" (*Mulieris dignitatem* 19). Mbuy-Beya sees motherhood as a means for "the humanization of the world" and the Church, which she believes "lies in the hands of women."³⁷ This search for humanization inspired her commitment to serve and protect women commercial sex workers and many others who are vulnerable in their society. This same approach should inspire the Church to let women be who they are—creators of life in its fullness and all roles. The Final Document reminds us,

> The local Churches are asked to continue their daily journey with a synodal methodology of consultation and discernment, identifying concrete ways and formation pathways to bring about a tangible synodal conversion

---

[36] Teresa Okure, "A New Testament Perspective on Evangelisation and Human Promotion," in *Evangelization in Africa in the Third Millennium: Challenges and Prospects*, ed. J. Ukpong and Teresa Okure (Port Harcourt, Nigeria: CIWA Publications, 1992), 86.

[37] Bernadette Mbuy-Beya, "Stand Up and Walk, Daughter of My People: Consecrated Sisters of the Circle," in *African Women, Religion, and Health: Essays in Honor of Mercy Amba Ewudziwa Oduyoye*, ed. Mercy Amba Oduyoye, Isabel Apawo Phiri, and Sarojini Nadar, Women from the Margins Series (Maryknoll, NY: Orbis Books, 2006), 208.

in the various ecclesial contexts (parishes, Institutes of Consecrated Life and Societies of Apostolic Life, movements of the faithful, dioceses, episcopal conferences, groupings of Churches, etc.). (9)

Women religious, through their ministries and commitment to the vulnerable, have shown many ways that local churches can adopt the synodal methodology of consultation and discernment.

Women Teachers of Synodality in Action

The second session of the synod invites the whole People of God to move beyond expressions of concern and to take concrete steps in response. Women's movements, particularly those of Catholic women, teach synodality through concrete actions. The following are examples of religious women and Catholic women's best practices of humanization at the peripheries, in Small Christian Communities (SCCs), and in inclusive, diverse associations.

Humanization is an important characteristic of Jesus and a task taken up by religious women and lay consecrated through their commitment to reduce poverty and oppression. As the president of the International Union of Superiors General (UISG), Sr. Mary Barron, OLA, claims, religious life, with its sense of community and discernment, can significantly support the Church in achieving synodal conversion. The many gifts the UISG brings to synodality include their projects against oppression, including the Talitha Kum project. This international initiative was formally established in 2009 to fight human trafficking and exploitation. It operates through sixty local networks, spread across almost ninety countries, and actively supports victims, survivors, and at-risk people. Each network of Talitha Kum operates within its region or country, maintains its unique identity, and is very much present on the peripheries.

Women are vital in breaking cultural barriers and connecting with those on the peripheries of life. Their unique insights reveal realities often missed by those in centers of power, where important decisions are made (*Fratelli tutti* 215). These peripheries represent segments of society "that call the baptized to solidarity,"[38] learning from listening "to those living along the various social and ecclesial margins."[39] The peripheries principle encourages "de-centering," which involves expanding our perspectives to engage with marginalized communities. The synodal tradition will be expanded if it can learn from this principle and its process of "both testimonial and hermeneutic inclusion."[40] Women exemplify this approach, offering valuable lessons in synodality by seeking to understand social realities through their engagement at various peripheries. This principle serves as "An Abundant Catch" (FD 11), opening "space for all peoples and all cultures" (FD 109), and building "intercultural communities" (FD 112). "Increased mobility and interconnectedness make the boundaries between churches fluid, requiring ministry across a 'vast socio-cultural territory'" (FD 119) with the Small Christian Communities.

The SCCs are the foundations of Catholic Christian life in some African countries. In the "Eastern African region [they] counted over 180,000 SCCs in the 2010s."[41] I agree with J. J.

---

[38] Patricia Jones, "Catholic Social Teaching and the Peripheries: The Case for Addressing Prostitution," *International Journal for the Study of the Christian Church* 23, no. 1 (January 2, 2023): 5.

[39] Anna Rowlands, "Listening Practices in a Synodal Church: Interim Reflections from a Symposium in Rome," *Journal of Moral Theology* 13, no. 2 (2024): 1.

[40] Jones, "Catholic Social Teaching and the Peripheries," 6, 15.

[41] J. J. Carney, "The People Who Do All Things Together: Living Base Ecclesial Communities in the Democratic Republic of the Congo," *Theological Studies* 85, no. 2 (June 2024): 263.

Carney: "In the DRC, base communities compose the church's foundation in both urban and rural areas, integrating faith formation with community and family life."[42] However, this integration is met more in rural than urban areas, leaving much to be desired. In the DRC, for example, there is a need to integrate faith with family and community life. Besides, the integration of faith and community life could improve if there would be more integration among SCCs and between the SCCs and the hierarchy at the local and diocesan levels. Still, this disintegration does not diminish the relevance of SCCs in the local communities, nor does it question the idea that SCCs are an "original manner of being church."[43] Religious women and synodal processes play a crucial role in building more integration of Christian faith and life, especially in SCCs.

Women's roles as faith formators across SCCs, parishes, and dioceses are often underrepresented despite having a significant teaching impact. Still, "Faith formation at any level, especially with adults, is essentially a training in the art of synodality."[44] Besides, its synodal art integrates the victims of violence, giving them space and voice. Ngalula argues that despite theological circles expressing concern for these individuals, they often neglect to truly engage with the victims' perspectives. Victims of human cruelty should be seen as active interlocutors, offering valuable insights rather than mere subjects needing representation. To promote dialogue and healing, we must empower victims of abuse as peacemakers through genuine engagement. Empathetic listening, rooted in openness and humility, enhances human connections and fosters recognition

---

[42] Carney, "The People Who Do All Things Together," 263–64.

[43] Healey, "Small Christian Communities," 176; quoted in Carney, "The People Who Do All Things Together," 67.

[44] O'Connell, "'Just Church' Is the Definitive Book on Women and Synodality," 11.

of our shared humanity. This approach can heal wounds and encourage enduring peace.

A listening Church is vital in appreciating the diverse voices filled with lament, protest, and hope that shape our world, often marked by violence. Prioritizing these voices is essential for building a community grounded in understanding and compassion,[45] including those of religious and consecrated women—those of the victims of violence of nonrecognition and noninclusion. Women religious include these voices in many associations that aim to work together and bring everyone on board against the abuses.

The Association of Consecrated Women in Eastern and Central Africa (ACWECA), which Veronica Rop describes in her essay, is crucial in amplifying the often overlooked voices of religious women in the region. Representing nine English-speaking countries—Eritrea, Ethiopia, Kenya, Malawi, Sudan, South Sudan, Tanzania, Uganda, and Zambia—ACWECA unites over 30,000 sisters committed to empowering each other for effective evangelization. Through sharing regional resources, ACWECA equips consecrated women to advance their missions effectively. The organization emphasizes its members' formation and leadership development, starting with essential training in formation houses. This approach is vital for cultivating leaders who can advocate for their communities and become teachers of synodality. ACWECA prioritizes listening and open dialogue, promoting an environment where every voice is valued. The Final Document highlights the need for "openness to the Spirit and mutual trust in search of a consensus that could, possibly, be unanimous" (90)—allowing a collaborative implementation process that encourages ongoing engagement and innovation. ACWECA is a dynamic synodal movement

---

[45] José Ngalula, "African Women Theologians Conference: Celebrating Decades of Women's Theological Empowerment," March 7–10, 2024, Hekima College University.

that empowers women to unite, elevate their voices, and drive transformative change through shared faith and action.

Women are leading in advancing synodal gatherings through powerful initiatives. Examples include these.

1. Catholic Sisters' Initiatives, which transform entrenched cultural practices for the common good, harnessing cultural richness to promote virtues essential for society.
2. Justice and Peace Commissions in which religious and lay-consecrated women play a crucial role in peacemaking and opposing violence perpetrated by the exploitation of natural resources, working tirelessly for societal change, children, and elderly care.
3. Nigerian Conference of Women Religious Against Human Trafficking, which actively combats human trafficking, supports survivors, and raises community awareness.
4. The Catholic Women's Association, prominent in the Democratic Republic of the Congo. This association highlights that women are the majority of churchgoers. Their involvement in SCCs allows them to run schools, hospitals, and shelters while leading initiatives for reconciliation and social justice.
5. The "Nyumba Kumi" (Ten Houses) Initiative entails a community policing strategy implemented in countries such as Kenya and the DRC, encouraging families to collaborate on local safety and security, enhancing community well-being. Nyumba Kumi highlights the essential role of African women in SCCs, where their participation often exceeds that of men.

These initiatives show how women lead in promoting social justice and community welfare, integrating faith into their daily lives. These women are leaders, teaching synodal methodology through managing schools, hospitals, and shelters, enhancing the

Church's mission. Their contributions go beyond traditional roles; they lead initiatives for reconciliation, human dignity, and social justice. They foster spiritual growth by organizing community prayers, coordinating charitable actions, and conducting catechism, "feeding the hungry . . . providing dispensary services, [and] involvement in community development."[46] Through this involvement, they teach as silent teachers. As a woman religious puts it, "Our presence is very much appreciated, even without [being] given a chance to be a fixed teacher, but our presence, silent presence is there."[47] Women teach through action and stand with the vulnerable on the peripheries.

Synodality summons us to go beyond charity to meet the persons where they are and empathetically communicate with them from the deepness of the heart. One woman religious responded to the question of how many people have passed through the congregation's schools with this.

> Very many. Very many. Big or small, ministers' wives, presidents' wives.... And you will always find the greater section of the country wanting their children to be educated by the sister, by the religious, because they know there is some moral output there, input to their children.[48]

These moral inputs create environments for meaningful relationships between the religious women and the local communities built on closeness and reciprocity. They offer a key

---

[46] Sexton and Muñoz, "Religious Life for Women in East and Central Africa: A Sustainable Future: Report of a Research Project on Sisters' Understandings of the Essence of Religious Life for Women in East and Central Africa 2017–2020," 74.

[47] Sexton and Muñoz, "Religious Life for Women in East and Central Africa," 65.

[48] Sexton and Muñoz, "Religious Life for Women in East and Central Africa," 88.

opportunity to engage with synodality meaningfully, integrate the Christian faith into our lives, and summon us to embrace epistemic humility, without which our ability to engage in empathetic listening will be hindered.

In light of the foregoing, the assertion that women are teachers of synodality is not mere rhetoric. There is ample evidence that demonstrates the teaching roles of women through concrete actions and practices in the Church and in society.

8

THE GIFT OF AUTHORITY IN A SYNODAL CHURCH

Ludovic Lado

> The authority of pastors is a gift to the Church, bound to the sacrament of order, for the service of the People of God. (Final Document 33)

Political anthropology teaches that no community exists without authority, understood as the legitimate exercise of power. Authority, as a means of resolving conflicts and maintaining order in a group, takes different forms across cultures worldwide. No community, including the Catholic Church, can sustain itself without some structured exercise of authority. The Catholic Church, however, is unique as a community characterized by a dual nature: both human and divine, earthly and heavenly, temporal and spiritual, social and mystical. Ecclesiology, the most sociological branch of theology, is tasked with articulating this dual dimension, explaining how the Church as an organized community is governed from earth and heaven by human and divine authorities.

Another insight from the social sciences relevant to the dynamics of authority is political sociology's distinction between power and authority through the concept of legitimacy. Power becomes authority only when it is legitimately acquired and exercised. Max Weber identifies three sources of legitimacy: charisma, tradition, and law.[1] The Catholic Church uniquely encompasses all three forms of legitimacy because of its dual nature: on one hand, charisma aligns with direct divine inspiration, and on the other, tradition and law provide an enduring framework for authority exercised over time.

Within this dual nature, the Church's spiritual authority often takes precedence over its temporal authority. In the Gospels, Jesus, the spiritual head of the Church, distinguishes between worldly power and Gospel-inspired power (Matthew 20:25–28). Synodality, by emphasizing communion, mission, and participation, seeks to promote a shared exercise of authority in fulfilling the Church's common mission. This essay will show that, prior to Pope Francis's pontificate, authority in the Church was primarily shaped by the concepts of primacy and collegiality centered on the figure of the bishop. Under Pope Francis, synodality introduces an additional dimension aimed at de-clericalizing authority in the Church. For this shift to take root, however, the Church may need to reevaluate the doctrinal and legal provisions that shape the distribution of roles and positions between clergy and laypeople.

This essay begins by revisiting the three key concepts of primacy, collegiality, and synodality—drawing extensively on *Lumen gentium*—which together shape the gift and exercise of authority in the Church. I then turn to the African context, examining its historical and present predominantly patriarchal approach to power and authority. Following this, I address the

---

[1] Max Weber, *Economy and Society: An Outline of Interpretive Sociology*, ed. G. Roth and C. Wittich (Berkeley: University of California Press, 1978); see also Max Weber, "Les trois types purs de la domination légitime," *Sociologie* 5 (2014): 291–302, https://doi.org/10.3917/socio.053.0291.

gender question as a recent societal shift that is challenging and reshaping the dynamics of authority in both society and the Church on a global scale. Drawing extensively on the final document of the recent Synod on Synodality (2021–2024), I conclude with a prospective and critical reflection on reimagining the gift and reception of authority in a more synodal Church in Africa.

Lumen Gentium and the Centrality of Episcopal Authority

In this section, I argue that *Lumen gentium* (LG) presents authority in the Catholic Church as fundamentally episcopal. LG describes the Church as "the people of God" with "Christ as its head."[2] It underscores the Church's dual nature as "a society structured with hierarchical organs and the Mystical Body of Christ," which is "one complex reality coalescing from both a divine and a human element" (LG 8).

This dual nature of the Church shapes its approach to authority, illustrated by various images such as flock, vineyard, family home, heavenly Jerusalem, mystical Body of Christ, and bride. Given the Church's hierarchical structure, the exercise of authority within it is also organized hierarchically. At the top is Christ, the eternal shepherd, who guides the Church "through the Supreme Pontiff and the bishops." This authority is embodied in the episcopal order, which draws legitimacy from apostolic succession: "Among those various ministries which, according to tradition, were exercised in the Church from the earliest times, the chief place belongs to the office of those who, appointed to the episcopate, by a succession running from the beginning, are passers-on of the apostolic seed" (LG 20).

---

[2] Vatican II, "Dogmatic Constitution on the Church, *Lumen gentium*," November 21, 1964, §9 (hereafter, LG).

The pope, as Saint Peter's successor, holds a unique status as "the Vicar of Christ, the visible Head of the whole Church" (LG 18). Thus, the primacy of the pope is affirmed: "And in order that the episcopate itself might be one and undivided, He placed Blessed Peter over the other apostles, and instituted in him a permanent and visible source and foundation of unity of faith and communion ... firmly believed by all the faithful" (LG 18, 22).

Nevertheless, even though *Lumen gentium* states that "the Roman Pontiff has full, supreme and universal power over the Church and is always free to exercise this power" (LG 22), the pope is not an absolute monarch. The principle of primacy is balanced by collegiality, where bishops—together with the pope, the Vicar of Christ—share in the governance of the Church. This collegiality is most clearly expressed during ecumenical councils, when bishops gather with the pope to discern God's will for the Church (LG 22).[3]

Bishops exercise their episcopal authority with the assistance of priests and deacons, who share in the sacrament of Holy Orders to varying extents. Thus, "Bishops, with their helpers, the priests and deacons, have taken up the service of the community, presiding in place of God over the flock, whose shepherds they are, as teachers for doctrine, priests for sacred worship, and ministers for governing" (LG 20). This highlights the "collegiate character" of episcopal authority. While the pope's authority is "full, supreme, and universal" (LG 22), that of bishops—though also supreme and plenary—requires the consent of the pope. Each bishop's authority is limited to his diocese: "The individual bishops, who are placed in charge of particular churches, exercise their pastoral government over the portion of the People of God

---

[3] On collegiality, see Vatican II, *Christus dominus: Decree on the Pastoral Office of Bishops in the Church*, October 28, 1965.

committed to their care, and not over other churches nor over the universal Church" (LG 23).

In describing the hierarchy, *Lumen gentium* places deacons at the lowest level, suggesting an exclusion of the laity from hierarchical authority and thus promoting an essentially clericalist vision of power. This notion is reinforced by the following lines.

> Having set forth the functions of the hierarchy, the Sacred Council gladly turns its attention to the state of those faithful called the laity.... There are certain things which pertain in a special way to the laity, both men and women, by reason of their condition and mission. (LG 30)

However, *Lumen gentium* does provide a space for lay involvement, observing that

> besides this apostolate which pertains to all Christians, the laity can also be called to a more direct form of cooperation in the apostolate of the Hierarchy. This was the way certain men and women assisted Paul the Apostle in the Gospel, laboring much in the Lord. Further, they have the capacity to assume from the Hierarchy certain ecclesiastical functions, which are to be performed for a spiritual purpose. (LG 33)

By contrast, those in religious orders are described as contributing to the Church's life and holiness though they are not part of its hierarchical structure: "Thus, the state constituted by the profession of the evangelical counsels, though not the hierarchical structure of the Church, undeniably belongs to its life and holiness" (LG 44).

Overall, *Lumen gentium* suggests that authority in the Church remains predominantly male-centered and clerical and fundamentally episcopal.

The Mainstreaming of Inclusive Governance

The concept of synodality, beyond its spiritual and theological dimensions, reflects the Church's efforts to embrace inclusive or participative governance, which has become common practice in many organizations around the world. Participative or inclusive leadership involves all stakeholders in decision-making processes with the aim of attending to the needs and interests of all. This approach to governance is based on two assumptions: The first is that people are quicker to take ownership of and implement decisions in which they have participated. The second is that perspectives vary according to stakeholders: Women, men, youth, the disabled, the poor, and the rich do not see the world or appreciate situations in the same way.

Regarding the greater inclusion of women in the sharing of authority, the twentieth century witnessed the emergence and rise of gender theories that have repercussions in all areas of social life worldwide. One of the major contributions of gender studies has been to distinguish gender from sex by describing gender as a historical, social, and cultural construction or production, meaning that the differentiation of the social roles and positions of men and women are not given but defined by society and particularly by those who hold power. "Gender" also refers to the social production of sexual categories that in recent decades have challenged the dominant heterosexual norm to make room for other sexual identities. The promotion of gender equity has been on the agenda of the United Nations since the 1970s. Indeed, the last thirty years have been marked by a number of world conferences aimed at sensitizing policymakers to the need to factor gender equity into development policies to provide equal opportunities for both men and women. The Church is no exception to the influence of gender theories and policies aimed at establishing equality between men and women. The political dimension of such an evolution is obvious, since it is a question of redistributing power between men and women in all spheres of social life.

Pope Francis wanted the Synod on Synodality to be as inclusive as possible, extending participation to the laity, including forty women who had the right to vote. This is unprecedented in the history of the Church, which is clearly seeking to break with a long tradition of male-only clerical authority. This inclusion has the advantage of bringing us back to an essential truth of the human condition: According to God's design, humanity takes masculine and feminine forms, and ecclesiology in its dynamic should embody this truth. Veronica Rop and Léocadie Lushombo provide an extensive and deeper discussion of women's voices and unique gifts in lived synodality in their essays.

The growing participation of the laity, and especially that of women, in the government and discernment of the Church raises the question of the appropriateness of designating the synodal gathering of the universal Church as the Synod of Bishops. If Pope Francis wants to follow through on his logic of breaking with clericalism in favor of a more synodal Church, it would be appropriate to rename this assembly the Synod of the Church, the Church being understood here as a community of Christ's disciples who journey and discern together. Indeed, in his address at the general congregation of the Synod of Bishops on October 25, 2023, Pope Francis described the Church as the "holy, faithful people of God" comprising both saints and sinners journeying together in the Lord's presence. He emphasized that this community embodies an "infallibility in believing" (*in credendo*), highlighting the profound faith inherent within the laity. The pope also underscored the significant role of women in transmitting faith, reflecting the Church's maternal and feminine nature. He cautioned against clericalism, warning that it distorts the Church's true essence by imposing hierarchical dominance over the faithful.[4]

Indeed, by retaining the name Synod of Bishops, there is a great risk of perpetuating the idea that this assembly, and consequently the Church, is first and foremost a matter for the bishops and that nonbishops and nonclerics would participate only by accident. The fact that laypeople, and moreover women, take part in such an assembly in Rome should become normal for three main reasons: first, laypeople make up the majority of the members of the Body of Christ; second, among those laypeople who take an active part in the life of the Church, as witnessed by the life of parishes, women are the most numerous; and third, the clergy do not have a monopoly on the Holy Spirit and discernment. If the Synod on Synodality is to follow through on its logic of inclusion of all components of the church, inclusion must indeed inform the way we are and function as a Church.

Power and Authority in Africa Yesterday and Today

Africa's diverse cultural landscape is reflected in its varied forms and practices of power and authority.[5] Despite the imposition of the modern state as the primary framework for governance since colonization, precolonial systems of authority have shown resilience, adapting alongside colonial structures. This adaptation has resulted in a form of political hybridity in modern Africa, where traditional and modern power structures coexist and often intertwine.[6] What are the main forms of traditional

---

[4] Francis, "Intervention at the 18th General Congregation of the 16th Ordinary General Assembly of the Synod of Bishops," speech, October 25, 2023.

[5] George Ayittey, *Indigenous African Institutions* (Leiden, The Netherlands: Brill | Nijhoff, 2006), https://doi.org/10.1163/ej.9781571053374.i-586.

[6] Bernard Salvaing, *Pouvoirs anciens, pouvoirs modernes dans l'Afrique d'Aujourd'hui* (Rennes: Presses Universitaires de Rennes, 2015).

authority in Africa, and how have they evolved in response to modernity?

Political anthropology categorizes African social and political systems into two main types: societies with centralized power and societies with decentralized power. Centralized societies are typically governed by a monarch, whose authority may be absolute or checked by advisory structures. Examples of absolute centralized power include the precolonial kingdoms of Abyssinia, Rwanda, and Swaziland, where the monarch had complete control over his community. In other cases, monarchs ruled with constraints from advisory councils, ensuring accountability. Societies such as the Zulu of southern Africa, the Nupe and Yoruba of Nigeria, the Baganda of Uganda, and the Bamileké of Cameroon exemplify this form of centralized power, where the king is seen as embodying both the people and the kingdom.[7] The king is accountable to the people, for he owes them good governance, and failure in this duty could lead to his removal.

In contrast, decentralized societies vary widely in their distribution of authority. For example, among the Oromo and Kikuyu of East Africa, authority is exercised by rotating age groups, while among the Igbo and Tiv of Nigeria, village councils hold primary governing power. Among the Oromo, the Gadaa system demonstrates an egalitarian, democratic form of governance in which elected age groups (*luba*) assume leadership in eight-year cycles, taking on political, military, judicial, legislative, and ritual responsibilities.[8]

Both centralized and decentralized societies derive legitimacy from tradition, which is transmitted orally across generations.

---

[7] Jean-Pierre Warnier, *Régner au Cameroun* (Paris: Karthala, 2009), 173–200.

[8] Tesema Ta'a, "The Gadaa System and Some of Its Institutions among the Booranaa: A Historical Perspective," *Ethiopian Journal of the Social Sciences and Humanities* 12, no. 2 (2016): 82–97, www.ajol.info/index.php/ejossah/article/view/159459.

Authority is generally male-centered, though women hold important roles in certain contexts. Among the Akan of Côte d'Ivoire and Ghana, for example, the queen mother plays a key role in legitimizing a new king as she holds the royal court's genealogical knowledge.

Consensus-building is central to decision-making in many traditional African societies. Among the Akan, for instance,

> Decisions taken after deliberation are always presented to the public as emanating from the entire community. When both sides have put forward their arguments, a small group of notables break away from the assembly to consult in secret (*be ko asule*). On their return, they inform the assembly of the decision they have reached together, without anyone being able to tell who among them supported or opposed it.[9]

This process, often symbolized by the palaver tree, ensures that decisions are fair and accepted by all parties. This consensus-based model contrasts with democratic systems that favor majority rule. It also aligns closely with the synodal approach in the Church, which prioritizes collective discernment for the common good through a process of listening and dialogue. However, consensus societies do not suppress dissent; often, groups that disagree relocate to form new communities.

The persistence of precolonial institutions in modern governance and Church structures illustrates the resilience of traditional forms of authority. According to the "institutional persistence" theory, colonialism failed to eliminate traditional power structures entirely, with survival depending on the colonial approach

---

[9] Claude-Hélène Perrot, "Le Pouvoir du roi et ses limitations dans un royaume Akan de Côte d'Ivoire," in *Pouvoirs anciens, pouvoirs modernes dans l'Afrique d'Aujourd'hui*, ed. Bernard Salvaing (Rennes: Presses Universitaires de Rennes, 2015), 77–81.

to domination.[10] Missionaries, for example, attempted mass conversion strategies by appealing to the authority of local chiefs, yet many chiefs, particularly in chieftaincy societies, resisted that due to their traditional responsibilities. In West Cameroon, missionaries found success by aligning with land chiefs, but conversion rates among traditional leaders were low because chiefs, as guardians of custom, faced conflicts of loyalty. They were expected to uphold both traditional values and fulfill colonial expectations, making conversion to Catholicism complex. In West Cameroon, for example, many missionaries

> sought the support of the traditional authorities and the sympathy of the people. Thanks to their power as land chiefs, their action is much more effective than that of a simple catechist. It should be noted, however, that the traditional chief is in a highly ambiguous position. He is the guardian of the ancestors' skulls, and therefore their representative. According to custom, he embodies traditional values. At the same time, he must serve the colonial administration and the religious authority on which his prestige and authority depend. This situation explains the reluctance of the majority of traditional chiefs and the fact that very few convert to Catholicism.[11]

Nowadays, traditional, state, and religious authorities coexist in most African societies, reflecting this historical layering.

---

[10] Clara Neupert-Wentz and C. Müller-Crepon, "Traditional Institutions in Africa: Past and Present," *Political Science Research and Methods* 12, no. 2 (2024): 267–84, https://doi.org/10.1017/psrm.2023.50.

[11] Célestine Colette Fouellefak KanaDongmo, "Acteurs locaux de l'implantation du catholicisme dans le pays Bamiléké au Cameroun," *Chrétiens et sociétés* [En ligne], 13 (2006), mis en ligne le 15 septembre 2009, http://journals.openedition.org/chretienssocietes/2145; DOI: https://doi.org/10.4000/chretienssocietes.2145; see also Augustin Sagne, *Cameroun: L'Évangile à la rencontre des chefferies. 1917–1964* (Saint-Maurice [CH]: Saint-Augustin, 1997).

As in the Church, power and authority in African societies remain male-centered. Africa, like many other regions, faces challenges in closing the gender gap. Though the LGBTQ+ community's visibility is growing, heterosexuality remains institutionally dominant.[12] The concept of gender offers a lens to examine male-female power relations, but African scholars caution against imposing Western gender frameworks uncritically. As Oyeronke Oyewumi notes, "If gender is socially constructed, then gender cannot behave in the same way across time and space."[13] African gender studies must avoid theoretical mimicry and respect cultural specificities.

African societies remain predominantly patriarchal, whether structured by matrilineal or patrilineal kinship systems. Social norms expect women to submit to men, who are in turn required to provide for them. Women often internalize these expectations, leading to persistent inequalities in education, employment, and political engagement. However, attitudes are gradually shifting toward inclusive governance, as reflected in the Church's concept of synodality, which emphasizes not only shared authority but also discerned governance and mutual accountability. This evolving model of synodality challenges patriarchal structures and promotes a discernment-based approach to governance, which is slowly reshaping African societies toward a more inclusive future.

---

[12] Ludovic Lado, *The Politics of Gender Reform in West Africa: Family, Religion, and the State* (Notre Dame, IN: University of Notre Dame Press, 2023), 11–16; Christophe Broqua, "L'émergence des minorités sexuelles dans l'Espace public en Afrique," *Politique Africaine* 126, no. 2 (2012): 5–23; Ashley Currier, "Political Homophobia in Postcolonial Namibia," *Gender and Society* 24 (2010): 110–29.

[13] Oyewumi Oyeronko, "Visualizing the Body: Western Theories and African Subjects," in *African Studies of Gender: A Reader*, ed. O. Oyewumi (New York: Palgrave Macmillan, 2005), 11.

Insights from the Synod: Toward the Authority of the Community

The final document of the Synod of Bishops[14] underscores the idea that authority, when exercised in a synodal style, becomes a gift entrusted to the community and shared in service. Synodal authority is distinct from a hierarchical or top-down approach; it acknowledges the community as the true bearer of authority, entrusting it to specific leaders—bishops, priests, and lay leaders—who exercise it on the community's behalf. This entrusted authority is not self-referential but is inherently accountable to the community, reinforcing the concept of co-responsibility in the Church.

The synod's model for governance embraces three interconnected practices: ecclesial discernment, meticulous decision-making processes, and accountability, all essential to renewing how authority is exercised. As the document states, "Decision-making processes need ecclesial discernment, which requires listening in a climate of trust that is supported by transparency and accountability" (FD 79–80). This model seeks to balance the Church's hierarchical structure, ensuring that authority respects both unity and diversity. Synodality, as the synod suggests, necessitates consultation, deliberation, and shared responsibility, underlining the importance of participatory bodies at all Church levels—parish, diocesan, and national—for effective governance.

Emphasis on the Discerning Community

In our current context, synodality emerges as a counterpoint to societal crises marked by alienation and individualism, where people often feel disconnected from collective destinies. The

---

[14] *Final Document of the Sixteenth Ordinary General Assembly of the Synod of Bishops: For a Synodal Church: Communion, Participation, Mission* (2024) (hereafter, Final Document or FD).

Final Document states that the Church's mission is to witness to God's plan to unite humanity "in freedom and communion" (20), offering synodality as a response to the challenges of modern life. Synodality, therefore, reflects the Church's prophetic call to foster participation and co-responsibility among all members, bridging gaps and nurturing a sense of belonging in the Body of Christ.

Indeed, one foundational element is the Church's nature as a "community of disciples of Jesus Christ sent out to their brothers and sisters to witness the good news of resurrection." This communal orientation affirms that the exercise of authority in the Church is not about dominion but about service to a shared mission guided by discernment and consensus. The document stresses the "importance of community discernment as a tool of governance through the practice of conversation in the spirit," reflecting the collective, dialogical nature of the Church's authority. Accordingly, "The People of God is never the simple sum of the baptized but the communitarian and historical subject of synodality and mission, still on pilgrimage through time and already in communion with the Church in heaven" (FD 17).

A key aspect of synodality is the concept of *sensus fidei*—the "anointing by the Holy Spirit received at Baptism" (cf. 1 John 2:20, 27)—which enables believers to possess an instinct for the Gospel's truth. Marcel Uwineza explores this concept in his essay. This shared "instinct," also called *consensus fidelium*, is fundamental to a discerning Church. The document clarifies that this is not mere public opinion but a profound participation in the communion of the Church: "The *sensus fidei* aims at reaching a consensus of the faithful (*consensus fidelium*), which constitutes a sure criterion for determining whether a particular doctrine or practice belongs to the apostolic faith" (FD 22). This underscores the Church's belief that the People of God, under the guidance of pastors, cannot err in matters of faith—a truth that requires integrating the *sensus fidei* into decision-making processes.[15]

The document articulates the Church as a "community of disciples of Jesus Christ" (FD 17) in which authority is a collective gift from God. Faithful to the intuition of *Lumen gentium*, the Church as a People of God is viewed as the primary holder and subject of authority, not individual leaders. This communal dimension aligns with the document's emphasis on synodality as a form of governance that prioritizes dialogue and discernment in the community, allowing the exercise of authority to emerge from a communal understanding of God's will.

Authority Accountable to the Community

The Final Document specifically states, "The authority of pastors is a gift to the Church, bound to the sacrament of order, for the service of the People of God" (33). This description reflects the notion that authority is not a privilege, but a responsibility granted to specific members for the welfare of the entire community. When exercised in a synodal style, authority takes the shape of service and guidance rather than control, emphasizing the responsibility of pastors and leaders to serve the mission of the whole Church rather than their personal agendas. The concept of synodality places the Church community at the heart of authority's function. The Final Document makes it clear that authority exercised in a synodal manner is both relational and participatory. It calls for "conversation in the Spirit" and community discernment as tools of governance (20), creating a model where decisions are taken in consultation with and in response to the voices of all Church members.

---

[15] Joseph Famerée, "*Sensus fidei, sensus fidelium:* Histoire d'une notion théologique discutée," *Recherches de Science Religieuse* 104, no. 2 (2016): 167–85.

Because authority in a synodal Church is entrusted to specific leaders for the community's benefit, it naturally demands accountability. This principle is underscored in the document's call for transparency and evaluation, where authority must be exercised with an ongoing sense of responsibility to the Church community: "The dimension of authority's being accountable to the community is in need of restoration" (FD 99). This appeal aligns with synodality's core commitment to a shared, participatory exercise of authority that holds leaders accountable for their decisions and actions. Accountability is a hallmark of a synodal Church, where authority must continually engage with the voices of the People of God. In practice, this requires leaders to engage in regular dialogue with the faithful, inviting feedback, guidance, and discernment from those they serve. Synodality thereby transforms the exercise of authority from a position of unilateral decision-making to one of collaborative stewardship, where leaders are answerable to the communities they represent.

Theological and Pastoral Implications for the African Context

The synod's call for a "conversion to a more synodal way of exercising authority" is especially challenging and transformative in the African context, where—as other contributors to this volume emphasize—authority is often shaped by patriarchy, clericalism, and cultural norms that tend to justify exclusion, particularly of women and laypeople. For African communities, this conversion requires a shift not just in structure but also in the attitude toward authority, moving from a dominion-centered to a service-centered model that reflects Christ's mission. Participation, therefore, is not about sharing clerical power but about inviting all members of the Church to share in the mission of Christ, emphasizing that true authority serves the community rather than consolidates control.

This synodal approach calls for a "pedagogy of listening and silence" in which those in power—often bishops, priests, and male leaders—humbly listen to voices previously marginalized or silenced, such as those of women and youth. In Africa, this means recognizing how authority has often borrowed from cultural practices, which sometimes perpetuate oppressive norms. Thus, synodality requires a critical engagement with culture, discerning which elements align with gospel values and which need transformation.

Furthermore, the historical tension between *Lumen gentium*'s communal vision of the Church and Vatican I's approach of centralized authority reflects a larger challenge in African churches: how to respect hierarchical structures while fostering inclusive and participatory decision-making. African bishops must navigate this tension, shifting authority toward co-responsibility without undermining ecclesial unity. This requires leaders to regard synodality not as a threat to their power but as a space of shared responsibility or co-responsibility.

Addressing cultural authority, the Final Document warns of the potential harm caused when cultural norms, including those tied to patriarchy, justify the exclusion of voices. Cultural hermeneutics, along with anthropology, can play a vital role in critiquing and reshaping these norms to prevent the abuse of authority. Cultural adaptation in African Christianity should not become an excuse to reinforce social hierarchies that exclude women, youth, or marginalized groups from Church participation. Instead, the Church is challenged to cultivate "new cultures" of inclusion, drawing on the wisdom and creativity of young people, who are already forming cultural expressions that challenge traditional boundaries.

The synod's emphasis on co-responsibility and de-clericalization is essential in Africa, where clericalism often centralizes authority in the hands of ordained men, limiting the laity's role. This transformation includes expanding lay participation in governance, decision-making, and leadership roles. The Final Document calls for increased access for laypersons—both men and women—to positions of responsibility, including those in diocesan and educational institutions such as seminaries and theological faculties. This shift is essential to avoid an oppressive version of inclusion, where lay involvement is symbolic rather than substantial. Instead, it calls for shared decision-making that genuinely incorporates diverse voices.

Additionally, the synod's view that authority should be accountable to the community addresses the often-unquestioned power of Church leaders in African contexts. Many African churches suffer from a lack of transparency, as leaders may dismiss challenges and questions from lay members. In the synodal Church envisioned by the synod, accountability becomes a hallmark of genuine authority, as leaders are called to act transparently and responsibly before the communities they serve. This model resembles the palaver tree tradition, where decisions are made through communal deliberation and authority is subject to the community's judgment. Anne Arabome identifies and discusses the social and cultural practice of palaver in relation to the spirituality of synodality nourished by insights from African spirituality.

In African churches, where authority is often paternalistic, this transformation calls for leaders to adopt a model of authority as "conversion and reform," learning from families where love, shared responsibility, and accountability create a nurturing space (FD 33). Embracing a model of synodality that is dialogical and participatory aligns with a broader African communal worldview but challenges patriarchal norms by redefining authority as life-giving rather than dominating.

Finally, the synod's insights urge African churches to view authority as a tool for healing and accompaniment, especially given the continent's deep struggles with poverty, conflict, and social exclusion. Authority exercised in the spirit of synodality can address suffering by integrating a pastoral approach that seeks not control but communal healing. The African Church is thus invited to not only embrace this model but also to embody it by walking together with the People of God, ensuring that all voices contribute to the Church's journey toward a more inclusive and authentic expression of Christ's mission.

Conclusion

The Final Document of the Synod of Bishops (2021–2024) represents a significant paradigm shift in the understanding and exercise of authority within the Church, especially when contrasted with the models of Vatican I (1869–1870) and Vatican II (1962–1965). Vatican I emphasized papal primacy and infallibility, reinforcing a highly centralized model of authority. Here, authority was largely unilateral, centered on the pope as the ultimate decision-maker, and underscoring a top-down structure with minimal lay involvement. The focus was on the pope's unique role, creating a model in which authority flowed directly from him downward, with limited input from other bishops or the laity.

Vatican II expanded this vision by affirming the Church as the People of God and recognizing the collegial nature of the episcopate. It introduced a more balanced view, where bishops, in communion with the pope, were seen as co-responsible for guiding the Church. It acknowledged the Church as a communal body rather than a purely hierarchical institution, thus softening Vatican I's rigid centralism and opening the door for greater collegiality among bishops.

In contrast, the Synod on Synodality embraces a synodal approach, which further decentralizes authority and incorporates the whole People of God in decision-making processes. Authority here is seen as a communal gift, entrusted to leaders for service and exercised in dialogue and discernment with the faithful. It advocates for co-responsibility and participation at all levels, aiming to make governance more inclusive by involving laypeople, particularly women, and enhancing transparency and accountability. This approach marks a profound shift toward a model where authority is relational and dialogical, grounded in the spiritual gifts and insights of the entire community, thus transforming the Church's governance into a more participatory and responsive structure.

Because of this shift, the Synod on Synodality calls for a "conversion to a more synodal way of exercising authority" (FD 33). This conversion is both personal and structural, communal and institutional, inviting leaders at all levels to adopt a mind-set of humility, openness, and receptivity to the voice of the faithful. Such reform underscores the necessity of moving away from clericalism and adopting a declericalized approach to governance that acknowledges the gifts and insights of laypeople as essential to the Church's mission.

9

Consecrated Women Religious Journeying Together for a Missionary Synodal Church in Africa

Veronica Jemanyur Rop

The Synod on Synodality (2021–2024) convoked by Pope Francis was a journey characterized by reflection and pastoral conversion that breathed a new spirit and dynamism into the life of the Church, from the Small Christian Communities to the universal Church. This was a unique synodal journey that saw the bishops, clergy, consecrated persons, laity, women, men, and young and old members of the Family of God come together to reflect, dialogue, and discern about the meaning of communion, participation, and mission in the Church and in the world. All members of the Church by virtue of their baptism were accorded the opportunity to listen to what the Spirit is saying to each and every one of us as well as through our sisters and brothers of other religious traditions. Reflections from the whole Church in various contexts and cultures contributed to and shaped the discussions about a shared mission of making the reign of God a reality in our times.

My essay discusses the experiences and contributions of consecrated women religious under the Association of Consecrated

Women in Eastern and Central Africa (ACWECA) serving in the Association of Member Episcopal Conferences in Eastern Africa (AMECEA). I introduce the concept of synodality by relating it to Small Christian Communities (SCCs) and consecrated life, namely, consecrated religious life. I then discuss the collaboration between consecrated women religious and bishops and clergy on their shared mission toward evangelization and development of people in Africa. I will emphasize the importance of leadership and ministries, authority and hierarchy, and voice and agency in relation to the role of women in the Church and the participation of consecrated women religious in decision-making processes and how this is shaped by a hermeneutics of culture.

I conclude by showing how young women religious are part of a wider youth population. When they are valued and supported, they could use their enthusiasm, education, and technological knowledge to make a positive impact in their institutes and to advance a synodal missionary Church.

Consecrated Women Religious

The Final Document (FD) of the Synod on Synodality offers consecrated women religious the opportunity to deepen and evaluate some of the praxis and processes in regard to their charisms in a synodal missionary Church. "Synodality is the walking together of Christians with Christ and towards God's Kingdom, in union with all humanity" (FD 28). The Synod on Synodality brings a freshness to the practice of SCCs, which have existed in Eastern Africa for at least fifty years. One phenomenon to note about SCCs is the reality that women are the majority and the heart of parish activities[1] that the dioceses depend on to mobilize

---

[1] Veronica J. Rop, *Human Dignity—Participation of Women in Integral Human Development: A Study among the Kalenjin in the Catholic Diocese of Eldoret, Kenya* (Hamburg: Verlag Dr. Kovac, 2020), 144.

their members.² Sharing leadership and management activities between the ordained ministers and nonordained ministers that include consecrated women religious is an important subject. Through their way of life, a life modeled after Jesus Christ and some aspects of the early Christian communities, the consecrated women religious live a life akin to synodality.³ For this reason, as Léocadie Lushombo demonstrates in her essay, they justly qualify to bear the title of "teachers of synodality."

Moreover, Can. 207 §2 of *The Code of Canon Law* states that through the profession of the evangelical counsels, consecrated women religious are consecrated to God in their own special way, and though they do not belong to the hierarchical structure of the Church, they participate in its life and holiness.⁴ Yet the majority of common folk view religious women as part of the hierarchy, something that creates a barrier between them. To help the people see religious as part of the People of God, the consecrated need to remain faithful to their nature, purpose, spirit, and character in a way that brings out their charisms in a shared mission.⁵

Understanding the differences and similarities between consecrated and religious life is crucial to appreciating the work done by these groups in the synodal Church. Much of my reflection in this essay, however, focuses on consecrated women religious whose experiences are not that much divorced or different from the experiences of other women. The consecrated

---

[2] Joseph G. Healy, *Building the Church as Family of God: Evaluation of Small Christian Communities in Eastern Africa* (Nairobi: AMECEA Gaba Publications—CUEA Press, 2012), 134–35.

[3] "Theological Basis and Canonical Implications of Involvement of Religious in the Local Church," www.canonlawsocietyofindia.org/wp-content/uploads/2019/11/Theological-basis-and-Canonical-implications-of-Involvement-of-Religious-in-the-Local-Church.pdf.

[4] Canon Law Society, *The Code of Canon Law* (Vatican: Liberia Editrice Vaticana, 1983), Can. 207 §2.

[5] *Code of Canon Law*, 1983, Can. 578.

life is made up of societies of apostolic life, secular institutes, and religious institutes. Societies of apostolic life are those consecrated to the mission of Christ, but their lives are not characterized by the taking of vows but rather by their dedication to their apostolates and missions. Their ways of life are adapted to the demands and requirements of mission contexts.[6]

In contrast, members of secular institutes do not live in community and do not profess public vows, but they live the evangelical counsels voluntarily. Their main focus is to live the Christian life in the midst of the society to transform it from within. Therefore, consecrated life is an all-embracing term that includes all other forms of ecclesial life focused on mission and ministry but not necessarily on community or vows.[7]

Finally, members of religious institutes described as consecrated women religious include congregations of sisters serving within the AMECEA region. These congregations are either of pontifical or diocesan status.[8] Their religious life is characterized by the public profession of the vows of chastity, evangelical poverty, and apostolic obedience as well as prayer and life in community. Those who embrace religious life voluntarily dedicate themselves to God and to Christ's service in the Church "to the exclusion of all other primary commitments through perpetual commitment of celibacy in community and mission."[9] In other words, the ultimate goal of religious life is to follow Christ as portrayed in the Gospels.[10] Their apostolic life springs from their

---

[6] *Code of Canon Law*, 1983, Can. 731 §§1 and 2.

[7] *Code of Canon Law*, 1983, Can. 571 §1.

[8] *Code of Canon Law*, 1983, Can. 589.

[9] M. Sandra Schneiders, *Selling All: Commitment, Consecrated Celibacy, and Community, Catholic Religious Life*, Religious Life in a New Millennium, vol. 2 (New York/Mahwah, NJ: Paulist Press, 2001), xxi.

[10] Paul VI, Decree on the Adaptation and Renewal of Religious Life, *Perfectae caritatis* (1965).

intimate union with Christ, which in turn makes them love God and neighbor.[11] Hence, religious life is a state of life dedicated exclusively to God and God's service through the public profession of vows lived within the Church and in community and expressed through various charisms and ministries. The ultimate goal of the consecrated women religious is the evangelization of the people through a wholehearted response to the love and service of God in and through the Church.

Consecrated women religious within the AMECEA region are under the ACWECA, a regional religious body made of National Associations of Sisters (Conference of Women Superior Generals) from nine English-speaking countries in Eastern Africa—Eritrea, Ethiopia, Kenya, Malawi, Sudan, South Sudan, Tanzania, Uganda, and Zambia. The mission of ACWECA is "to promote the spirit of collaboration and sharing of spiritual, human and economic resources among member conferences, to enhance religious formation and strengthen leadership capacity for deeper evangelization."[12]

Essentially, the call for fuller recognition of women highlights the achievement of the consecrated women religious in the entire Church. In their various ministries, consecrated women religious have always participated in the evangelization and integral human development of people, alongside their brother bishops, priests, and men religious. Initially, a number of missionary women religious worked in various parts of Africa. Currently, many local congregations of diocesan status and pontifical rights serve in the region. In the spirit of synodality, missionary congregations

---

[11] Paul VI, Decree on the Adaptation and Renewal of Religious Life, *Perfectae caritatis*, 8.

[12] ACWECA Secretariat, "Rooted in Christ: Called to an Identity of Rootedness in the Person of Jesus Christ as Consecrated Women: A Challenge for Mission and Formation Today," ACWECA General Assembly 15 (2011): 15.

opened their communities to African women who shared the purpose and charism of these institutes. These African women religious belonging to missionary congregations, like those in local congregations, come from diverse communities, languages, and cultures where positive traditional African religious beliefs and values are embedded in their lives.[13] In turn, these women enrich their religious communities with African values such as relationality, hospitality, and celebration and respect for life.[14] Respect for life and human dignity is accorded not only to the elderly members but also to the unborn, the living-dead, and extended to all creation. These consecrated women religious also bring their communitarian spirit that understands the family as going beyond a nuclear family or a particular congregation to welcoming their extended families and working hand in hand with other consecrated persons as well as the clergy. Through this communitarian spirit, a belief and practice that embraces various members of the community including those who are not religious, Catholic, or Christian, the consecrated women religious understand and demonstrate what inclusion is in a synodal missionary Church.[15] Their spirit of solidarity reaches out to various members of society who in turn embrace the Gospel of Jesus Christ. As Lushombo points out, their commitment to the promotion of human dignity, development, justice, reconciliation, and peace demonstrates synodality in action.

The Final Document acknowledges that over the centuries, consecrated women religious, by following the path of Christ and

---

[13] ACWECA Secretariat, "Rooted in Christ," 17.

[14] Elizabeth Isingi and Dominic Byarugaba, "Shaping Future Values: The Relics of Today Began Yesterday in Africa," in *African Culture in the 21st Century: Persistence, Opportunities, Challenges and Prospects*, ed. Mary N. Getui (Eldoret: AMECEA Gaba Publications—CUEA Press, 2024), 6–7; see also ACWECA General Assembly 15 (2011): 34–35.

[15] Sixteenth Ordinary General Assembly of the Synod of Bishops, second session, 43.

evangelical counsels and by their consecration to the service of the Church either as contemplatives or other forms of service, have enriched the Church. "Over the centuries, the Church has also been enriched spiritually by the many different forms of consecrated life" through their communal discernment and harmonization of individual gifts for a common mission to manifest for the whole Church what synodal living means (65).

Leadership and Ministries in the Church

The Final Document points out that the task of the bishop "is to preside over a local Church as a visible principle of unity within it and a bond of communion with all the Churches" (69). Hence, the bishop plays a leadership role in the Church. However, to the question of sharing of responsibility, namely co-responsibility, the Synod on Synodality prioritizes a Church that is closer to the lives of the people and that is less bureaucratic and more relational. Though not confined only to the African continent, male dominance in various places of authority, both in society and places of worship, is an issue that the Final Document rightly challenges (60).

In light of the approach of the Synod on Synodality concerning the role of women in the mission of the Church, the Church in Africa is challenged to promote a Church in which men and women walk and work together without subordination, exclusion, or competition. The sacrament of baptism gives women and men equal dignity as members of the Family of God. Consequently, any organization or body that denies women fuller appreciation and participation in various activities of the Church and by extension society is doing a disservice to the entire concept of synodality and shared mission (60).

Collaboration between episcopal conferences and the Conferences of Superiors and Major Superiors of Institutes of Consecrated Life and Societies of Apostolic Life is an area where the practice of co-responsibility and shared mission ought to be renewed and strengthened. In their way of life, the consecrated women religious offer a vision of living and working together that is closely aligned with the understanding and practice of synodality. This vision is the antithesis of an exaggerated notion of authority and hierarchy.

Authority and Hierarchy

As Anne Arabome points out in her essay, synodality is a path of spiritual renewal and structural reform that involves all members of the Church. The synod opened the space for a fuller participation and inclusion of various lay members including women. To demonstrate the spirit of synodality, Pope Francis adopted the Final Document and called for its implementation. Francis's action shows that a synod convened in order to reflect and deliberate on matters touching the universal Church is a place where all members of the Church are represented, participate, and have their voices heard (56). Authority and hierarchy are ordered toward the service of the entire Christian community. In fact, the Final Document asserts, "As with all ministries in the Church, the episcopate, priesthood and diaconate are at the service of proclaiming the Gospel and building up the ecclesial community" (68). The authority of pastors "is a specific gift of the Spirit of Christ the Head for the up-building of the entire Body" (33).

Moreover, consecrated women religious in ACWECA are cognizant of the fact that the Church is not only hierarchical; it also belongs to the entire People of God. ACWECA observes that when too much power is vested in the hierarchy, there is a possibility that this may be challenging.[16] Therefore, they concur

---

[16] ACWECA, "A Life-Giving Vision of Synodality from African Consecrated Women, ACWECA Leadership Listening and Discernment Retreat on Synodality Nairobi, Kenya, May 2022.

with the teaching of the Church that authority exists in order to serve the Family of God and that those who exercise this authority should do so as a service.[17] The power to govern the Church is meant to provide leadership, and those in authority are to identify themselves with the sheep.[18] Authority, according to Pope Francis, is a service and should be exercised for the good of all and for the proclamation of the Gospel. It should be understood as rooted in service rather than in power modeled by the world. Authority is the capacity to enable others to grow by encouraging and supporting them in their journey of faith.[19]

The Synod on Synodality reiterates that baptism gives all members of the Family of God equal dignity from which proceeds all other rights and privileges. The Final Document acknowledges that women have not been accorded a fuller recognition, which they deserve in regard to their charisms, vocations, and places in various spheres of the Church. These actions are contrary to how Jesus in his life, words, and praxis treated women in the Gospels. It fails to reflect how the early Christian community treated women as attested and narrated in the Gospels and the Acts of the Apostles. Lushombo explores some of these instances in her essay. The synod powerfully declared, "There is no reason or impediment that should prevent women from carrying out leadership roles in the Church: what

---

ACWECA Leadership Listening and Discernment Retreat on Synodality, Nairobi, Kenya, May 2022, www.jesuits.africa/wp-content/uploads/2022/09/ASI-A-Life-Giving-Vision-of-Synodality-from-African-Consecrated-Women.pdf.

[17] *The Catechism of the Catholic Church: Compendium* (Nairobi: Paulines Publications Africa, 2010), 2235.

[18] Francis, apostolic exhortation *Evangelii gaudium* (Nairobi: Paulines Publications Africa, 2013), 24.

[19] Sixteenth Ordinary General Assembly of the Synod of Bishops, *Instrumentum Laboris*, For a Synodal Church: Communion, Participation, Mission, first session (Nairobi: Paulines Publications Africa, 2023), 57.

comes from the Holy Spirit cannot be stopped" (60). It is worth noting that the Final Document kept open the discussion about women's access to diaconal ministry as a matter for ecclesial discernment. The Church in Africa bears responsibility for full participation in this discernment process in collaboration with consecrated women religious.

Voice, Urgency, and Role of Women in the Church

The Final Document affirms that "the synodal style enables the Church to be a prophetic voice in today's world" (47). Religious life is primarily a prophetic call. By embracing the evangelical counsels of chastity, poverty, and obedience, vows that form the basis for living a life of radical consecration to God for the good of the Church, consecrated women religious share in the prophetic office of Christ.[20]

Speaking of consecrated women religious, Vatican II attests, "Their vocations are like so many rays of the one light of Christ, whose radiance brightens the countenance of the Church."[21] The document further asserts that it is the duty of the consecrated women religious to show that the "Incarnate Son of God is the eschatological goal toward which all things tend, the splendor before which every other light pales, and the infinite beauty which alone can fully satisfy the human heart."[22] Following the example of the Virgin Mary, their model and patroness, consecrated women religious learn to listen, remain attentive to God's will, and obey God's Word in readiness to hear and serve all humanity (FD 29).

---

[20] John Paul II, postsynodal apostolic exhortation *Vita consecrata* (Nairobi: Paulines Publications Africa, 1996), 84.

[21] Vatican II, Dogmatic Constitution on the Church, *Lumen gentium* (Nairobi: Paulines Publications Africa, 1965), 1.

[22] *Lumen gentium*, 44.

To be prophetic means being able to take roles similar to those of prophets in ancient Israel. Most of these prophets were ordinary people called by God; they responded to the call by risking their lives, speaking truth, and challenging the powers of the day in regard to the plight of the poor and the suffering in society. Consecrated women religious remain prophetic in their mission by engaging in ministries and apostolates that advocate for and promote the dignity and development of the human person. Living prophetic lives means engaging in actions that promote social justice and cohesion in society. It translates to taking an active part in pastoral social work, education, health, advocacy, empowerment, accompaniment, and care of creation. It is an invitation to be a voice for the vulnerable, marginalized, and the poor.[23] This exemplifies synodality in action.

Consecrated women religious engage in matters related to social justice, a constitutive dimension of preaching the Gospel.[24] In fact, their ministry goes beyond the mere material needs of the people[25] to recognizing a person's spiritual and transcendent nature.[26] Their participation in the world of today extends to addressing contemporary issues such as human trafficking, corruption, and practices that undermine the integrity of family, creation, and religion.[27]

---

[23] Clement Njoroge and Agnes Wamuyu, *Reaching the Most Vulnerable: Catholic Sisters Serving Communities through Health, Education, Home Care and Social Service* (Nairobi: AOSK, 2016), xvi.

[24] Synod of Bishops, *Justitia in Mundo* (Nairobi: Paulines Publications Africa, 1971), 6.

[25] Paul VI, *Populorum progressio* (Nairobi: Paulines Publications Africa, 1971), 14; see also Vatican Council II, Pastoral Constitution on the Church in the Modern World, *Gaudium et spes* (Nairobi: Paulines Publications Africa, 1966), 86.

[26] John Paul II, *Sollicitudo rei socialis* (Nairobi: Paulines Publications Africa, 1988), 29.

[27] John Paul II, postsynodal apostolic exhortation *Ecclesia in Africa* (Nairobi: Paulines Publications Africa, 1996), 68.

The synod has summoned the Church in Africa to unite, dialogue, discern, collaborate, and model Christ in its members' shared mission of being salt and the light of the world (Matthew 5:13–16). Walking together makes the words of the psalmist come true: "How very good and pleasant it is when kindred live together in unity" (Psalm 133:1). This moral integrity presupposes fidelity to the moral teaching of the Gospel as prescribed in the golden rule: "Do to others what you want done to you" (Matthew 7:12; Luke 6:31), as well as in the Beatitudes (Matthew 5:3–12). Therefore, the call for a fuller recognition of women in the mission aims at the integration of women in formation and training of those seeking ordained ministries. Greater involvement of women in the formation of clergy enhances the understanding of religious life and fosters mutual relations and communion and the eradication of clericalism in favor of synodality.[28]

Consecrated Women Religious and Decision-Making Processes

According to the Final Document, decision-making processes are not reserved for certain members of the Church. Decision-making is a shared responsibility in which the bishop, presbyters, and other baptized members have full participation based on differentiated co-responsibilities. The Final Document states, "The whole community, in the free and rich diversity of its members, is called together to pray, listen, analyse, dialogue, discern and offer advice on taking pastoral decisions" for mission (87–89).

However, decision-taking processes in a synodal Church observe the hierarchal order of the Church in which the authority of the bishop, the episcopal college, and the bishop of Rome takes effect after factoring in directions that emerged from consultative

---

[28] ACWECA, "A Life-Giving Vision of Synodality."

process as deemed possible. The implementation processes as well take on a synodal style (90–94). The Final Document states that in any stage of a synodal activity such as a decision-making process, discernment plays a crucial role and goes hand in hand with practices of accountability and evaluation (95). Hence, there is a call for a culture of responsibility, openness, and accountability in all endeavors.

While consecrated women religious find decision-making and decision-taking processes something akin to their way of life, accountability and evaluation are practices that can be made open to others. Decision-making processes are the responsibility of all the baptized and are rights that come with duties and obligations. Each consecrated and religious woman brings her originality and genius, that is, her unique qualities, to the processes, just like in all other services.[29] John Paul II points out that the personal resources of femininity are certainly no less than the resources of masculinity but that they are merely different.[30] Participation of consecrated women religious in the discernment and consultation processes adds a feminine touch and enriches the ultimate decision taken by the competent authority. Moreover, women's patience and great capacity to adapt to the unexpected demands of real life can be transformative.[31] The synod stresses that "each member of the community must be respected, with value placed upon their gifts and abilities in light of the goal of shared decision-making processes" (89).

---

[29] Anne Arabome, "Women, You Are Set Free! Women and Discipleship in the Church," in *Reconciliation, Justice, and Peace, 2nd African Synod*, ed. A. E. Orobator (Nairobi: Action Publishers, 2011), 120.

[30] John Paul II, apostolic letter *Mulieris dignitatem* (Nairobi: Paulines Publications Africa, 1988), 10.

[31] Ghirmai Abraha, "An Overview on Religious Life, Its Motives and Strengths in the Past, Present and Future," in Empowerment of Women Religious in the Light of Our Past Heritage, Our Present Reality and Future Challenge, *ACWECA Plenary* 13 (2005): 166.

The need to put in place or improve the existing mechanisms, structures, systems, and procedures that ensure accountability, transparency, and evaluation in religious-run institutions, apostolates, and ministries benefits not only the particular institute but also serves as a witness and testimony to our collective, communitarian, and synodal stewardship (FD 94). "The way to promote a synodal Church is to foster as great a participation of all the People of God as possible in decision-making processes" (87). The implementation of the processes of decision-making are to be done in a synodal way while adhering to what is provided for in Canon Law (94).

Equally expected of consecrated women religious is the cultivation of a culture of accountability and transparency, a practice of responsibility and openness that is demonstrable and informs every activity at all levels (99). While the practice of accountability and transparency is in line with the evangelical vow of poverty, the call is for a deeper introspection, evaluation, and conversion within and beyond the religious institute. Therefore, the fuller participation and meaningful engagement of consecrated women religious or any woman in general in any synod or ecclesial process requires theological formation and education in fields such as theology and canon law.[32] Some organizations such as Catholic Theological Ethics in the World Church, African Sisters Education Collaborative, Higher Education for Sisters in Africa, and the Sisters Leadership Development Initiative have taken the lead in promoting education for women in theology and other fields, but much more is needed.

Hermeneutics of Culture

The Final Document encourages the Church to create a culture of synodality. Culture encompasses the whole life of a people, and while it distinguishes them from any other group, it has the

---

[32] Rop, *Human Dignity*, 149.

capacity to be influenced by the other. Hence, culture is dynamic in nature.

Culture is equally a transmitted pattern of meanings.[33] Therefore, while the culture of accountability and transparency presented by the synod holds true, the Final Document revisits the concept of culture from a relational perspective. Here, the synod acknowledges the different contexts and unique cultures in which the Church exists and flourishes. Cultures that are marked with relational structures and systems need conversion and transformation for them to remain true to Gospel values (53). Further, the synod highlights the important role that culture plays in the life of a people.

One such culture is made up of African traditional beliefs and practices that tend to relegate women to second place in society despite the equal dignity that comes from being created in the image and likeness of God and re-created in Christ Jesus through baptism.[34] Arabome, Lushombo, and Ngalula examine this phenomenon in their essays. Male dominance in various places of authority in society, with few exceptions of women in higher positions, promotes the superiority of men over women.[35] The majority of the people in such cultures have doubts when a woman performs extremely well in spheres exclusively believed to be male. Many women led resistance and social movements during the dark era of colonialism, while others wielded spiritual powers in the early years of evangelization.[36] Hence, the culture of ascribing authority and leadership roles solely to one gender, male, in the Church needs to be revisited and challenged if the Church is to challenge with credibility any practice or structure that discriminates against women, including consecrated women

---

[33] Rop, *Human Dignity*, 92.

[34] Rop, *Human Dignity*, 52.

[35] Rop, *Human Dignity*, 84–87.

[36] David Sweetman, *Women Leaders in African History: African Historical Biographies* (Oxford: Heinemann Educational Books, 1984), 51.

religious.[37] Speaking during the Fifteenth ACWECA General Assembly, Sr. Veronica Openibo noted, "We need to speak our truths in the presence of all peoples, especially the men, even in the Church, and not relent or be discouraged."[38] The Final Document of the synod underscores the dynamic interplay between the Gospel and oppressive cultures and calls for a closer look at how women in general are viewed or treated both in the Church and in society. The synod acknowledges, "Many of the evils that afflict our world are also visible in the Church" (55).

While the Church in Africa has contributed to the positive perception of women, their enhanced dignity, and their influence, mainly through education, there is more to be done. Indeed, status and participation of African women in various fields and levels in the Church and society remain paradoxical. On one hand, women have exalted roles as transmitters of human life, faith, and religious as well as family values. On the other hand, the majority of women are regarded unequal to men and their voices minimally heard in various domains including the Church.[39] The synod exemplified participation and inclusion of women in matters touching the whole Church. As such, listening to women or those who feel excluded "strengthens the Church's awareness that taking on the burden of wounded relationships is part of its mission" (56). Women are not the only people who need full participation in the Church; young people also do.

Young People in the Synodal Church

As Sheila Pires argues in her essay, youth and young adults are vitally important in the synodal journey and need accompaniment in the area of discernment (FD 62). Young people in the synodal

---

[37] ACWECA, "A Life-Giving Vision of Synodality."
[38] ACWECA General Assembly 15 (2011): 43.
[39] Rop, *Human Dignity*, 74.

Church include men and women religious and the laity. Youth are identified as individuals between ages fifteen and twenty-four.[40] Youth is best understood as a period of transition from the dependence of childhood to adulthood's independence. That is why, as a category, youth is more fluid than other fixed age groups.[41] Participation of young people in the synodal Church is a vital dimension of our shared participation, communion, and mission as baptized members of one Family of God that goes beyond one's age. The synod states, "Young people also make a contribution to the synodal renewal of the Church. They are acutely aware of the values of fellowship and sharing while rejecting paternalism or authoritarian attitudes" (62).

In fact, young people in our contemporary society are more inclusive, tolerant, empathic, and at home with people from other cultural, ethnic, gender, or religious backgrounds. They tend to be more critical and vocal in challenging unethical and oppressive systems and structures, calling for transparency, accountability, and individual responsibility in the way society and the Church conduct themselves. Some members of the consecrated women religious fall into the category of youth, and they are not different from other youths in their way of thinking. Young sisters want more dialogue and participation in matters touching them. They feel that with formal education and advanced knowledge in technology, they can utilize their talents, skills, and expertise to improve and advance various services provided by their institutes. Young religious women are the most vibrant, energetic, and dynamic members of religious life. They are eager to live like their role models and share their faith, and they are often frustrated and anxious when experiences of life prove otherwise.

---

[40] United Nations Department of Economic and Social Affairs, "Definition of Youth," www.un.org/esa/socdev/documents/youth/fact-sheets/youth-definition.pdf.

[41] United Nations, "Youth."

Young consecrated women religious are idealistic because they are taught from childhood and later in their years of religious formation to value ideals that are instilled in them. Values that are inculcated include family, ethics, social, cultural, and Christian moral formation. These ideals are enhanced as the consecrated women religious participate in the charism and spirituality of their institutes. Access to information through education and technology has enabled young people, religious included, to interact with others around the world. With global exposure, young people stand to be influenced by emerging and modern cultural perspectives, including religious traditions, values, beliefs, and ideas—some of which may be contrary to African traditional values and Catholic social teaching.[42] Hence, there is a need for accompaniment and a revision of formation syllabi that reflects reading the signs of the times and addressing challenging issues with Gospel values. In regard to young women religious, ACWECA notes that there is need for improved and transformative formation, training that integrates values and the actual needs of the candidates.[43]

While many young women who enter consecrated and religious life possess a lot of knowledge and expertise in new areas such as digital technology, including the use of social media, older members command respect. The older members are in turn challenged to appreciate and offer positive criticism while teaching the young members by way of example and witness of

---

[42] John Okoye, "Proclaiming the Word of God to Young People in a Synodal African Church," in *Journeying Together for a Synodal Church in Africa*, Pan-African Theology and Pastoral Studies Series 2, ed. Ikenna U. Ukafor, Josée Ngalula, Nicholaus Segeja, and Stan Chu Ilo (Nairobi: Paulines Publications Africa, 2023), 39.

[43] ACWECA, "ACWECA Needs Improved Formation Says Sr. Nnantamu," *ACWECA Plenary*, August 21, 2024, https://acweca.org/2024/08/21/acweca-needs-improved-formation-says-sr-nnantamu/.

life. The synod observes that at times, young people's attitude toward the Church can come across as negative criticism, yet it is often a personal commitment to the life of the institute and a desire to create a more objective, inclusive, and loving hospitable community for all (FD 62).

Digital knowledge is crucial in the world that is turning more toward social media and artificial intelligence. Young people have a lot to offer religious communities, the Church, and society at large in this area. The Pontifical Council for Culture notes, "The means of social communication have become so important as to be for many the chief means of information and education, of guidance and inspiration in their behavior as individuals, families not leaving behind consecrated and religious houses."[44]

The moral development of young people is significantly affected by social media, especially in terms of their choices, aspirations, and attitudes. This calls for sustained catechetical and creative initial religious formation programs. Equally important is the role of ongoing formation in religious life. Digital and social media have become the fora of social interaction and a means of evangelization among the youth, something that consecrated and religious institutes as well as the Church can take advantage of. Since social media use many tools to reach their audiences, such as Instagram, X-Space, YouTube, Facebook, Google Meet, Zoom, and WhatsApp, young consecrated women religious in particular can utilize these platforms for evangelization, education, and formation, and more important, to promote a culture of synodality. This is evident among some women religious institutes such as the Daughters of St. Paul, who have excelled in this digital space particularly in their evangelization through various media platforms.

---

[44] Pontifical Council for Culture: *Towards a Pastoral Approach to Culture* (Nairobi: Paulines Publications Africa, 1999).

Conclusion

Being of one heart, mind, and purpose in communion, participation, and mission with the universal Church, consecrated women religious are called to work in unity as members of one Family of God, where the culture of synodality is expressed by co-responsibility, listening, dialogue, discernment, inclusivity, transparency, and accountability. Walking and working together has enabled consecrated women religious to share their gifts of diverse backgrounds, languages, and cultures to make the reign of God a reality with a more renewed vigor. Over the years, the witnesses of the consecrated women religious through their charisms and ministries have contributed positively to building the Family of God in Africa. Through their diverse ministries, they continue to dedicate themselves to the mission of Jesus Christ.[45] Through their associations, religious women have worked in the spirit of synodality to contribute immensely to promoting the good of every person and of the whole person.[46]

The Synod on Synodality calls for the full and active participation of consecrated women religious as well as the laity in the overall mission of the Church. Their contributions will henceforth go beyond mere consultations and include the creation of the spirituality and culture of synodality needed for the proclamation of the Gospel and the flourishing of the Church in Africa.

---

[45] Sacred Congregation for Religious and Secular Institutes, *Religious Life: Essential Elements in the Church's Teaching on Religious Life as Applied to Institutes Dedicated to Works of the Apostolate* (London: Incorporated Catholic Truth Society, 1983), no. 24.

[46] Paul VI, *Populorum progressio*, 14.

10

THEOLOGICAL FOUNDATIONS OF CO-RESPONSIBILITY

David Kaulemu

> Proceeding from the love of the eternal Father, the Church was founded by Christ in time and gathered into one by the Holy Spirit.
>
> —*Gaudium et spes* 40

Co-responsibility in the Church rests on the foundations of its origin in the love shown in the Trinity. The Church, the Family of God whose members are created in God's image, is called to emulate the love that God radiates and how the Church has experienced, in history and in the day-to-day lives of its members, the love of the Father, the Son, and the Holy Spirit (Matthew 5:43–48).[1] *Lumen gentium* begins by showing the foundational relationships between God and humanity through Christ and the Church that is commissioned by Christ through the apostles: "Since the Church is in Christ like a sacrament or as a sign and instrument both of a very closely knit union with God and of the

---

[1] Subsequent texts are from *The African Bible* (Nairobi: Paulines Publications Africa, 1999).

unity of the whole human race" (1). As Marcel Uwineza, Josée Ngalula, and Veronica Rop believe, the Trinity is a model for the synodal Church. *The Compendium of the Social Doctrine of the Church* affirms the importance of this foundational reality for the Church as a communion: "This supreme *model of unity*, which is a reflection of the intimate life of God, one God in three Persons, is what we Christians mean by the word *communion*."[2]

The Final Document of the synod emphasizes, "The whole of Christian existence has its source and horizon in the mystery of the Trinity, which brings forth in us the dynamism of faith, hope and love" (15). Michael Himes[3] explains the importance of looking at God as a mystery that helps us express "faith, hope and love." This love is agape. It is more than self-love. Without neglecting the self, this love is oriented toward others. It is love that is altruistic in the sense of transcending the self to contribute to relationships with others and to the common good. It is "absolute unconditional self-gift."[4] This is the kind of love that Jesus talks about when he is asked, "Teacher, which commandment in the law is the greatest?" (Matthew 22:36). He answers,

> You shall love the Lord your God, with all your heart, with all your soul, and with all your mind. This is the greatest and the first commandment. The second is like it: You shall love your neighbor like yourself. The whole law and the prophets depend on these two commandments. (Matthew 22:37–40)

In a world that is individualistic and self-interested, love as agape is an imperative.

---

[2] Pontifical Council for Justice and Peace, *Compendium of the Social Doctrine of the Church* (Vatican: Libreria Editrice Vaticana, 2004), 19.

[3] Michael Himes, *Doing the Truth in Love: Conversations about God, Relationships, and Service* (New York/Mahwah, NJ: Paulist Press, 1995).

[4] Himes, *Doing the Truth in Love*.

The co-responsibility of all Christians entails working together in respect and love for the salvation of the world. The synodal call to journey together is a call to renew our response to Christ and the mission he gave us, following the example of his love manifested on the cross and Paul's insight that we "were baptised into his death" (Romans 6:3). The Final Document reminds us that when we contemplate the risen Christ, we see

> the mark of His wounds transfigured by a new life, yet engraved forever in His humanity. These are wounds that continue to bleed in the bodies of many brothers and sisters, including through our own faults. Looking upon the Lord does not distance us from the tragedies of history. Instead, it opens our eyes to the suffering of those around us and penetrates us: the faces of war-stricken terrorized children, weeping mothers, the shattered dreams of so many young people, refugees who face terrible journeys, the victims of climate change and social injustice. (2)

Thus, love as agape helps us transcend ourselves and reach out to become co-responsible for the welfare and well-being of others, just as Christ did for us.

Love as agape is not easy to realize because the Church and indeed the world are not places filled with like-minded people. Yet we are all called to walk together, although we come from different backgrounds, histories, and cultures. The synod acknowledges this reality as follows.

> Gathered from every tribe, language, people and nation and living in different contexts and cultures, the synodal process gave us "the spiritual taste" (EG [*Evangelii gaudium*] 268) of what it means to be the People of God. The People of God is never the simple sum of the Baptized but the communitarian and historical subject

of synodality and mission still on pilgrimage through time and already in communion with the Church in heaven. Within the plurality of contexts where the local Churches are rooted, the People of God proclaim and bear witness to the Good News of salvation. Being in the world and for the world, they walk together with all the peoples of the earth, in dialogue with their religions and their cultures, recognizing in them the seeds of the Word, journeying towards the Kingdom. (FD 17)

Himes emphasizes that God is revealed when we engage one another in communities and with love and respect.

For obviously we cannot talk about God meaningfully in the Christian tradition unless in some way we attempt to live in a community where genuine agape is realized. Only by participating in self-gift can one come to know what we are trying to designate by the word "God." If you want to know who God is, give yourself away.[5]

The Call to Co-Responsibility for Our Common Mission

The sharing of responsibility is at the center of the call to a synodal Church that recognizes the gifts we all have been given. To be in a synodal Church is essentially to be journeying together, in co-responsibility, inspired by the Holy Spirit. The call is for the People of God to renew and rediscover their baptismal commitment and dignity, which is the basis for their participation in the Church and the common mission of salvation of all humankind: "The missionary synodal Church springs from Baptism, in which Christ clothes us with Himself (cf. Gal 3:27) and enables us to be reborn of the Spirit (cf. Jn 3:5–6) as children of God" (FD 15).

---

[5] Himes, *Doing the Truth in Love*.

As Pope Francis made clear, the synodal journey on which the People of God are invited is the foundation of a long-term, renewed way of working and participating in the Church as equal, co-responsible members. It is a call to renew our encounter with Christ, with the Holy Spirit, with all of God's creation, with each other, and with the rest of humanity. This renewal is done in dialogue, prayer, and discernment. It creates space, time, and energy to participate and genuinely encounter one another: "In simple and concise terms, synodality is a path of spiritual renewal and structural reform that enables the Church to be more participatory and missionary so that it can walk with every man and woman, radiating the light of Christ" (FD 28). As Anne Arabome shows convincingly in her essay, the synodal process is first and foremost a spiritual process. An important expression of synodal spirituality that relates to co-responsibility is relationality.

The Final Document emphasizes this.

> To be a synodal Church, we are required to open ourselves to a genuine relational conversion that redirects each person's priorities, and we must once again learn from the Gospel that attending to relationships is not merely a strategy or a tool for greater organizational effectiveness. Relationships and bonds are the means by which God the Father has revealed Himself in Jesus and the Spirit. (50)

To be in relationship with one another is to take up an ethical and spiritual obligation of co-responsibility, of being our sister's and brother's keeper, hence the imperative to open ourselves to conversion that redirects our priorities in the light of our relationships and the ethical demands of the common good. In this way, synodal spirituality and morality provide ways of relating, engaging, and decision-making in the church structures and processes. The Final Document adds, "This ecclesiological framework shapes the commitment to promote participation based on differentiated co-responsibility. Each member of the community must be respected, with value placed upon their gifts and abilities in light of the goal of shared decision-making" (89). In reality, the principle of co-responsibility is founded upon a realization of mutuality as a community of faith. Whatever happens in the community affects all, and all should have a say in determining what happens in the community.

> The Fathers of the Church reflect on the communal nature of the mission of the People of God with a triple "nothing without": "nothing without the bishop" (St. Ignatius of Antioch, Letter to the Trallians 2,2), "nothing without the council of presbyters, nothing without the consent of the people" (St. Cyprian of Carthage, Letter 14,4). When this logic of "nothing without" is disregarded, the identity of the Church is obscured, and its mission is hindered. (FD 88)

Co-responsibility is placed at the center of the synodal relationships as an aspect of the identity of the Church; it has deep roots in the reality of baptism. "The identity of the People of God flows from baptism in the name of the Father and of the Son and of the Holy Spirit. This identity is lived out as a call to holiness and a sending out in mission, inviting all peoples to accept the gift of salvation (cf. Mt 28:18–19)" (FD 15). In this sense, the practice of co-responsibility as part of synodality is the practice of bearing witness in our day-to-day engagements and in our lives in general. "We bear witness to the Gospel when we seek to live in relationships that respect the equal dignity and reciprocity between men and women" (FD 52). This means being accountable in the Church and in the world at large. "The evangelical quality of relationships in a community is decisive for the witness that the People of God are called to make in history.

'By this everyone will know that you are my disciples, if you have love for one another' (Jn 13:35)" (FD 50). It also means sharing power and authority in the Church and in the world.

Learning from the Church's Teaching and Christian Tradition

The teaching of the Church and the values of the Christian tradition since Vatican II offer the foundation for the practice of co-responsibility in a synodal Church. Such a Church invites and welcomes the gifts of all the baptized—laity, consecrated, and ordained. The facilitation of all these gifts—commitment, charisms, abilities, professions, identities, cultures, and talents—allows the full participation of the whole congregation to realize and fulfill its mission in the world. Participation recognizes that all the faithful had opportunities to realize and fulfill their charism, and thus to activate the obligation to serve one another through the gifts they received from the Holy Spirit.

Co-responsibility also includes the relationship between churches. Pope John Paul II observed that Africa "is endowed with a wealth of cultural values and priceless human qualities which it can offer to the Churches and to humanity as a whole."[6] These values include love for life, a religious spiritual sense and commitment, respect for family and community life, and other values that prioritize solidarity, reconciliation, and forgiveness. Africans therefore are called by the Church's social teaching and tradition to co-responsibly contribute their values and traditions to the growth and deepening of the synodal encounter. While Vatican II highlighted the pertinence of cultures, it also

---

[6] Pope John Paul II, *Ecclesia in Africa* (1995), 42; see also Agbonkhianmeghe Orobator, *Religion and Faith in Africa: Confessions of an Animist* (Maryknoll, NY: Orbis Books, 2018).

emphasized the need to cultivate those cultures and traditions to uphold the dignity of each and every person and enhance universal integral human development. The Final Document expands and clarifies this point further.

> The call to renewed relationships in the Lord Jesus flourishes in the different contexts in which His disciples live and carry out the Church's mission. The plurality of cultures requires that the uniqueness of each cultural context is taken into account. However, all cultures are also marked by distorted relationships that are not in keeping with the Gospel. Throughout history, these relational failures have turned into structures of sin (cf. SRS 36), which in turn shape the way people think and act. In particular, structures of sin create obstacles and generate fear. We need to face these in order to set out on the road to the conversion of relationships in the light of the Gospel. (53)

While co-responsibility may be differentiated, it does not overlook demographic particularities. This is true in relation to the role of women in ministry and leadership. Vatican II underscored the importance of the participation of women: "It is up to everyone to see to it that women's specific and necessary participation in cultural life be acknowledged and fostered" (*Gaudium et spes* 60). Similarly, it specifically encouraged the Church to respect the role and contribution of young people, urging that "adults should be anxious to enter into friendly dialogue with the young, where ... they could get to know one another and share with one another their personal riches" (*Apostolicam actuositatem* 12). In the same spirit, the Final Document encourages the co-responsibility of everyone, especially those who are marginalized, impoverished, or living with disability, as "active agents of evangelization" (FD 63).

The principle of co-responsibility further allows participation in the mission of the Church in other spheres of secular activities, including ecology, global politics, economics, and culture. People of faith are encouraged to advocate for socioeconomic models that challenge and transform inequalities and poverty that undermine human dignity, especially those of the victims of global economic and political arrangements. In *Caritas in veritate,* Pope Benedict XVI emphasized, "The economy needs ethics in order to function correctly—not any ethics whatsoever, but an ethics which is people-centered."[7] The Christian tradition of always looking out for the welfare of the injured, the marginalized, the impoverished, "and the least of these" (Matthew 25:40) is a strong foundation of co-responsibility. In *Fratelli tutti*, Pope Francis uses the story of the good Samaritan to emphasize this point. Local and global economies are meant to work toward attainment of the common good and to uphold the dignity of human persons and the rest of God's creation.[8]

This theme is carried forward in the synod. The Final Document highlights the Church's concern for those who are made poor by economic, political, and social systems. And yet even they are equal in co-responsibility, for "God's heart has a special place for the poor" (EG 197), the marginalized, and the excluded. Therefore, they are at the heart of the Church. The whole Christian community is called to recognize in those made poor the face and flesh of Christ, who, though he was rich, became poor for us so that we might become rich through his poverty (cf. 2 Corinthians 8:9, FD 19).

Sharing Responsibility

The foundation of the synodal process is the fundamental interconnectedness of life that emanates from God. As *Vademecum* points out,

---

[7] Pope Benedict XVII, encyclical letter *Caritas in veritate* (2009), 42.
[8] Pope Francis, encyclical letter *Fratelli tutti* (2020).

> The entire People of God shares a common dignity and vocation through Baptism. All of us are called in virtue of our Baptism to be active participants in the life of the Church. In parishes, small Christian communities, lay movements, religious communities, and other forms of communion, women and men, young people and the elderly, we are all invited to listen to one another in order to hear the promptings of the Holy Spirit, who comes to guide our human efforts, breathing life and vitality into the Church and leading us into deeper communion for our mission in the world.[9]

The synodal process requires that as the People of God, we share the responsibility to bear witness to the love and communion of God. This witness offers to the Church and to humanity and the rest of creation the fullness of life in charity, reconciliation, justice, and peace. God's love is the source of the Church's mission of evangelization for salvation. Therefore, we are called to model ourselves on communion, mutual listening, and reconciled diversity. "Synodality expresses the nature of the church, its form, its style, its mission."[10] Thus, we are invited to "journey together, in order to experience a Church that receives and lives this gift of unity, and is open to the voice of the Spirit."[11]

---

[9] *Vademecum* for the Synod on Synodality (Vatican City: Secretary General of the Synod of Bishops, September 2021), 1.1.

[10] Pope Francis, "Address of His Holiness Pope Francis to the Faithful of the Diocese of Rome" (Paul VI Audience Hall, September 18, 2021), http://www.vatican.va/content/francesco/en/speeches/2021/september/documents/20210918-fedeli-diocesiroma.html.

[11] Pope Francis, "Address of the Holy Father Francis on the Occasion of the Moment of Reflection for the Beginning of the Synodal Journey" (New Synod Hall, Rome, October 9, 2021), https://press.vatican.va/content/salastampa/en/bollettino/pubblico/2021/10/09/211009a.html.

Our common mission[12] entails our responsibility to create space, time, structures, and encouragement for everyone to genuinely participate and express themselves, especially those who find themselves on the margins of the Church and society. It means recognizing "the wealth and variety of the gifts and charisms that the Spirit liberally bestows for the good of the community and the benefit of the entire human family."[13]

Reimagining the Synodal Church

Synodality is a call to renewal. The process is "intended to inspire people to dream about the Church we are called to be."[14] As the Preparatory Document points out, the purpose of the process is to reconceive and reimagine the nature of our ministries to allow all the baptized to participate in the realization of the mission of the Church.[15] The experience of reimagination extends to how we organize and run our parishes, Small Christian Communities, lay movements, religious communities, and other forms of communion.

Every baptized member of the People of God has a role to play. For the Church in Africa, this call is for the realization of the spirit of Ubuntu, as other contributors have discussed extensively. We are co-responsible for one another and for our common mission in the Church and in the world.

---

[12] Stephen Pope, *Common Calling: The Laity and Governance of the Catholic Church* (Maryknoll, NY: Orbis Books, 2004), 12.

[13] Preparatory Document for the Sixteenth Ordinary General Assembly of the Synod of Bishops (Vatican: Secretary General of the Synod of Bishops, September 7, 2021), 2.

[14] *Vademecum* for the Synod on Synodality, 1.3.

[15] Preparatory Document 32.

Our Synodal Responsibilities

The mission of the Church is to evangelize by proclaiming and sharing "the joy of the gospel [which] fills the hearts and lives of all who encounter Jesus."[16] The purpose of the synodal process is to prepare all of us as individuals, in our local communities and church structures, for the participation, communion, and mission that God is calling us to. By virtue of our baptismal dignity, we are all mandated to take up the responsibility to allow and encourage others to participate fully in the Church for the mission. Each group or church structure, from bishops, priests, laypeople, and church associations to church institutions, needs to reflect on how it can improve its way of organizing and working in order to facilitate others to participate in the mission of the Church. *Vademecum*[17] has identified some of the pitfalls that have affected us in the past. These should help us clarify our synodal responsibilities to ourselves and others. They should help us to be humble in listening to others in the spirit of dialogue and "leave behind prejudices and stereotypes" and "overcome the scourge of clericalism."[18] The call to journey together as the People of God and to be witnesses of God's love in the world bestows on all of us the following synodal co-responsibilities:

- To always be aware and remind each other of our history and tradition as children of a loving, triune God and how Christ redeemed us and how the Holy Spirit has guided and continues to guide us to be witnesses of God's love on earth.
- With the promptings of the Spirit, to work toward reconciling the form, structure, and style of the Church "so that

---

[16] Pope Francis, *Joy of the Gospel* (Nairobi: Paulines Publications, 2013), 7.

[17] *Vademecum* 2.4.

[18] *Vademecum* 2.3.

the Church's customs, ways of doing things, times and schedules, language and structures can be suitably channeled for the evangelization of today's world rather than for her self-preservation"[19] This involves "examining how responsibility and power are lived in the Church as well as the structures by which they are managed, bringing to light and trying to convert prejudices and distorted practices that are not rooted in the Gospel" (PD 2).

- To open up "a dynamism of mutual listening, conducted at all levels of the church, involving the whole people of God," allowing everyone to express themselves, especially those who for various reasons find themselves marginalized, discriminated against, devalued, ignored, neglected, or abused in one way or another.[20]
- To genuinely encourage, cultivate, recognize, and appreciate the richness of gifts and contributions from all members—women, men, young, old, lay, consecrated, ordained, and all those with "charisms that the Spirit liberally bestows for the good of the community and the benefit of the entire human family."[21]
- To actively encourage, prepare, and support our brothers and sisters committed to the common good, love, and service in society by promoting social justice, human rights, scientific research, teaching and learning, social and political commitment, and caring for our common home.[22]
- To listen with open hearts and open minds in order to regenerate relationships among members of Christian communities,

---

[19] *Vademecum* 27.

[20] Gerard O'Connell, "Pope Francis: Rigidity in the Church 'Is a Sin against the Patience of God,'" *America Magazine,* November 2021, www.americamagazine.org/faith/2021/09/20/pope-francis-synod-241467#:~:text=Francis%20noted%20that%20just%20as,against%20the%20patience%20of%20God.%E2%80%9D.

[21] Preparatory Document 2.

[22] Pope Francis, encyclical letter *Laudato si'* (2015), 30.

local and religious traditions, popular movements, civil society organizations, and other social groups in order to hear and collaborate on how God is prompting them to build a more beautiful and habitable world.
- To "break out of our routine in order to stop and listen, firstly to the Spirit in adoration and prayer, and then to our brothers and sisters, their hopes, the crises of faith around the world, the need for renewed pastoral life."[23] This means moving "structurally towards a synodal Church, where all can feel at home and participate."[24] It includes creating with courage and confidence space to listen to those who have been hurt in the church "in their flesh and in their spirit" and even listening to those who have left the church in order to strengthen "the Church's ability to accompany individuals and communities to reread experiences of mourning and suffering that have unmasked many false certainties, and to cultivate hope and faith in the goodness of the Creator and his creation."[25]

In light of the foregoing, it is also important to identify and name some pitfalls and attitudes that may distract us from the synodal path that leads to co-responsibility. The synod is an invitation to overcome, with the support and guidance of the Holy Spirit, some of the attitudes, opinions, prejudices, and ways of doing things that have prevented us from fully sharing and living the joy of the Gospel and "journeying together" with each other and with the rest of the world. "Many members of the Church, especially the lay faithful who participate in the structures of the Church as pastoral workers at parish and diocesan levels, feel frustrated and not listened to as they

---

[23] Pope Francis, "Address of the Holy Father Francis on the Occasion of the Moment of Reflection for the Beginning of the Synodal Journey."

[24] Pope Francis, "Address of the Holy Father Francis on the Occasion of the Moment of Reflection for the Beginning of the Synodal Journey."

[25] Preparatory Document 6.

frequently remain on the fringes."[26] The same can be said of many women and young people who feel that the Church is more concerned about self-preservation than witnessing to the Gospel; more comfortable with how things have been done in the past than facing the challenges of the new life demands that call for creativity, innovation, openness of hearts and minds, and new forms of pastoral care; reliance on "reforming structures, giving instructions, offering retreats and conferences, or by dint of directives and programmes," rather than "discern what are the ways of the Gospel in the present."[27]

As mentioned, the synod stressed the importance of baptism rather than ordination as the foundation of co-responsibility. To prioritize the latter is a manifestation of clericalism. The equality established through baptism must always be the basis of the call to co-responsibility. The Final Document reads,

> This call is based upon a shared baptismal identity. It is rooted in the diversity of contexts in which the Church is present and finds unity in the one Father, one Lord, and one Spirit. It challenges all the baptized, without exception: "The whole People of God is an agent of the proclamation of the Gospel. Every baptized person is called to be a protagonist of mission since we are all missionary disciples" (ITC 53). (FD 4)

This is an important issue for the Church in Africa. It has to be dealt with in order to confront the question of the abuse of power in religious contexts and of the influence of the Church in African societies. Clericalism, manifested in the ordained and

---

[26] Pope Francis, "Homily of His Holiness Pope Francis for the Opening of the Synodal Path" (St. Peter's Basilica, October 10, 2021), www.vatican.va/content/francesco/en/angelus/2021/documents/papa-francesco_angelus_20211010.html.

[27] Pope Francis, "Address of His Holiness Pope Francis to the Faithful of the Diocese of Rome."

in the practices of the laity, has sometimes erroneously given the impression that co-responsibility derives from ordained ministry and is the sole prerogative of the Church hierarchy. Also, it has propagated the false belief that co-responsibility is a form of participation in the power granted by virtue of being ordained or being a religious superior. It is worth reiterating that co-responsibility is based on the understanding that "there is nothing higher than this baptismal dignity, equally bestowed upon each person, through which we are invited to clothe ourselves with Christ and be grafted onto Him like branches of the one vine" (FD 21).

Conclusion: The Christian Tradition of Co-Responsibility in Africa

Given the history and tradition of co-responsibility, how then shall we renew and reimagine our roles and responsibilities in ways that will allow each and every member of the People of God to exercise and fulfill their charisms, gifts, talents, professional expertise, and cultural identity at the service of the Gospel and the promotion of the mission of the Church? *Vademecum* encourages us to take up "an innovative outlook" that will help us "develop new approaches, with creativity and a certain audacity."[28]

As we take up differentiated co-responsibility to reform the Church toward synodality, we must listen to those who have previously been marginalized rather than only those in power and authority. The Final Document identifies the co-responsibility not only of those in power but also of the laity, men and women, the young, children, the disabled, migrants, refugees, and people of other faiths and traditions. This rich diversity of backgrounds is what makes the Church a synodal community of rich harmony:

---

[28] *Vademecum* 2.3.

The synodal Church can be described using the image of the orchestra: the variety of instruments is necessary to give life to the beauty and harmony of music, within which the voice of each one retains its own distinctive features at the service of the common mission. Thus is manifested the harmony that the Spirit brings about in the Church, the One who is harmony in person (cf. St. Basil, *On Psalm* 29:1; *On the Holy Spirit,* XVI: 38). (42)

In Africa, many Christians in positions of power have sacrificed their lives and faced persecution to genuinely walk with the marginalized and the impoverished, especially the lay faithful. Several of these examples are worth recalling as creative and concrete realization of the principle of co-responsibility.

Bishop Kevin Dowling of Rustenberg (South Africa) demonstrated how bishops could act in co-responsibility with the People of God and other social and civil society groups. At the height of the scourge of HIV and AIDS, he brought hope to the sick and dying working collaboratively with hospitals established to serve people working in South African mines in Rustenberg, NGOs, and the government health department.

In Gulu in Uganda, Archbishop John Baptist Odama championed peacemaking efforts in the conflict zone, which accompanied and protected children from being recruited as child soldiers by the Lord's Resistance Army (LRA) and going into the jungles of South Sudan to talk to the LRA and to encourage peace talks with the Ugandan government. His work with other Christian traditions and of inspiring young people to take education seriously remains a great gift to the African Church on the way to synodality.

Bishop Patrick Kalilombe of Malawi courageously attempted to stimulate lay participation in the Church during the time of authoritarian president Kamuzu Banda and faced persecution for his efforts.

Many bishops, priests, and religious sisters and brothers have tried to live lives of synodality before the synod. In the spirit of differentiated co-responsibility, it is critical that we also learn from and listen to those who have been silent, invisible, and excluded from the structures of power.

11

A Synodal Church of the Young and the Young at Heart

Sheila Leocádia Pires

A synodal Church of the young and the young at heart is a vibrant, inclusive community where young people journey together in faith. This vision of a synodal Church—a Church that listens, dialogues, discerns, and collaborates—underscores the importance of youth as co-responsible for its mission. Inspired by the example of Jesus Christ, Pope Francis invites young people to embrace their roles with courage and creativity.

In *Christus vivit*,[1] Pope Francis reflects on the youthful years of Jesus, emphasizing his experiences of human joys and struggles. These years, lived with passion, openness, and service, resonate deeply with today's youth, highlighting that youthfulness is not just a stage of life but an attitude of the heart. As young people navigate the complexities of a globalized world, the Church seeks to provide space for dialogue, formation, and empowerment, recognizing them as agents of renewal and hope.

The call to build a synodal Church finds a powerful ally in the digital age. From local communities to online platforms, young

---

[1] *Christus vivit* (Christ is alive), post-synodal apostolic exhortation of Pope Francis on young people, faith, and vocational discernment, March 25, 2019.

Catholics are encouraged to be "digital missionaries," spreading the Gospel creatively and authentically. As the Church celebrates Jubilee Year 2025, it becomes an opportune moment to celebrate the energy and faith of young people, empowering them to lead and transform the Church and society.

In this essay, I explore the integral role of youth in a synodal Church and address their challenges, leadership opportunities, and mission in the digital age. I emphasize the Jubilee Year 2025 as a time for renewal, reconciliation, and active participation in building a synodal Church that is truly young at heart.

Jesus as a Model for Young People

In *Christus vivit*, Pope Francis outlines the significance of Jesus's youthful years for young people. Like all young people, Jesus lived fully as a human being; he experienced both the joys and struggles of youth, making him an inspiring role model for today's young Catholics. Quite significantly, Jesus's life reveals that youthfulness is not just a stage of life but an attitude of the heart, full of passion, openness, and a readiness to serve.[2] As Francis puts it,

> Jesus does not teach you from afar or from without; he does not love you only in words. He is the Word that became flesh. He is a Brother, a Friend, and a great Ideal. He is the true young man, who shares your journey and stays with you at every moment. He is a model for young people, who was deeply immersed in his people's life. He learned a trade from his father, Joseph, and worked with his hands. He was also part of a larger family, enjoyed celebrations, and was full of the Holy Spirit. He lived the everyday realities of life, but always in deep union with the Father.[3]

---

[2] *Christus vivit* 23.
[3] *Christus vivit* 31.

In this sense, Pope Francis presents Jesus as a relatable role model who fully embraced youth, work, friendships, and family life. As such, he models the struggles and joys of young people, becoming a source of hope for young people today.[4]

The call to build a synodal Church—a Church that journeys together—resonates deeply with young Catholics. Young people are not merely the future of the Church; they are its integral and vibrant present. This vision invites young people to embrace their faith courageously and actively participate in shaping the Church's mission and identity. Part 2 of the Final Document echoes this theme and emphasizes the significant role of young people in the Church's synodal renewal.

> Young people also contribute to the synodal renewal of the Church. They are acutely aware of the values of fellowship and sharing while rejecting paternalism or authoritarian attitudes. At times, their attitude toward the Church can come across as critical, yet often it manifests positively as a personal commitment to the creation of a welcoming community dedicated to fighting against social injustice and for the care of our common home. (62)

This observation resonates with an important point that Veronica Rop makes in her chapter on consecrated women religious. She makes the point that young people in our society tend to be more inclusive, tolerant, empathic, and at home with people from other cultural, ethnic, gender, or religious backgrounds. Also, they can be more critical and vocal in challenging unethical and oppressive systems and structures, calling for transparency, accountability, and individual responsibility in the way society and the Church conduct themselves.

---

[4] *Christus vivit* 23.

Formation:
Building a Strong Foundation in Faith

To create a truly synodal Church that includes the young and the young at heart, formation from an early age is essential. By formation, I mean the nurturing of an individual's spiritual, emotional, and intellectual growth in a Christian framework. This entails introducing them to the principles of faith and community life while ensuring that their spiritual, emotional, and intellectual growth aligns with Christian values. The Final Document emphasizes the importance of children and their formation in the Church's mission of synodality. There are several examples of formation programs dedicated to the nurturing of children and young people in the Church in Africa.

In the three countries (South Africa, Botswana, and Eswatini) that make up the Southern African Catholic Bishops Conference (SACBC), children—particularly in Black communities—often join movements like the Children of Mary and the Little Soldiers of Christ, known locally as *Amasolenyana*, to foster their spiritual development from a young age. These movements provide a foundation for lifelong engagement in the Church.[5]

Through these groups, the Church fosters environments in which children can grow spiritually and morally. Encouraging young people to be involved in the Church through liturgy, catechesis, and other activities helps them feel included and valued as active members of the Church, thus fulfilling a key dimension of a synodal Church. Formation includes fostering relationships between different age groups and emphasizing mutual learning and respect.

Furthermore, in some dioceses in the SACBC, bishops hold annual meetings with children's groups to listen, dialogue, and

---

[5] S'milo Mngadi, "Birds of a Feather: United under a Charism," *The Southern Cross* (April 14, 2021).

practice the call to promote intergenerational dialogue and ensure that young people are included in the Church's journey as active participants. Liturgical celebrations animated by children provide space for catechesis and education that are adapted to the realities of children and young people, fostering their spiritual growth and engagement with their faith. However, challenges such as limited access to resources in remote areas hinder participation in these activities. For children in such communities, the Church—along with families and local communities—is called to create accessible space for formation.

Initiatives like Small Christian Communities (SCCs)[6] offer young people opportunities to grow spiritually and to take on leadership roles. SCCs are especially crucial in supporting marginalized youth, including those in households headed by children, by creating environments of solidarity and care. They provide a space for the involvement of young people, fostering leadership skills and encouraging them to take active roles in the life of the Church, especially in rural or marginalized areas. In cases of child-headed homes due to various factors, SCCs are vital, as they create an environment in which members can grow spiritually while forming bonds of solidarity and support, especially with orphans and the marginalized.

A good foundation from early childhood shapes the youth. Children who are actively involved in the life of the Church often grow into responsible youth and young adults. They often assist in mentoring and assisting in the formation of peers and other young people.

Youth liturgies, catechetical programs, and mentorship from older members of the community ensure that young people feel

---

[6] Joseph G. Healey, MM, "Historical Development of Small Christian Communities / Basic Ecclesial Communities in Africa," 2013, https://smallchristiancommunities.org/historical-development-of-the-small-christian-communitiesbasic-ecclesial-communities-in-africa/.

included and valued. For this reason, Pope Francis urges older generations to view the youth not merely as recipients of the Church's mission but also as co-creators of its present and future.[7]

Youth: Africa's Challenges and Hope

Africa's demographic profile—a predominantly young population—positions its youth as a source of hope and transformation. As of recent data, the global youth population (individuals ages fifteen to twenty-four) stands at approximately 1.2 billion, accounting for about 16 percent of the world's total population.[8] Although the youth demographic in Africa is particularly promising, with over 60 percent under age twenty-five, the challenges they face cannot be overlooked. Africa's youthful segment is projected to grow, with estimates suggesting that by 2050, the continent's youth population could double to over 830 million.[9]

These statistics underline the significant role young people play both globally and in Africa, highlighting the importance of investing in education, employment opportunities, and health care to harness their potential for future development. However, high unemployment rates, political instability, and a lack of opportunities often compel young Africans to migrate, risking their lives in search of better prospects. Furthermore, societal issues such as substance abuse, mental health crises, and cultural pressures complicate their paths. African youth and young adults often seek better opportunities and livelihoods by migrating to urban centers or developing countries in the continent or by attempting dangerous journeys across the Sahara and the Mediterranean. Such situations have led to recent initiatives by

---

[7] *Christus vivit* 42.

[8] UNESCO, *World Report 2020*, www.unesco.org/en/youth?utm_source=chatgpt.com.

[9] Organisation for Economic Co-operation and Development, "Africa's Development Dynamics 2024: Skills, Jobs and Productivity," July 5, 2024.

the Catholic Church, such as the Mediterranean Meetings of September 2023, which brought together young people from various countries and religions to share experiences and discuss challenges in the region.[10]

Young people in Africa also face the challenges of addiction to drugs and alcohol, bullying, abuse, racial divides, religious persecution, and cultural and generational gaps as well as mental health issues, in some cases resulting in fatal outcomes. Besides, African youth trying to navigate the contours of a globalized world may struggle with the expectations of traditional culture. In some cases, Church leaders may be out of touch with the concerns of the youth, making it challenging to foster meaningful relationships or dialogue, hence the need for accompaniment and the creation of space for dialogue.

The accompaniment of young people as they navigate challenges is a central theme in the Church's pastoral approach, especially spiritual accompaniment for young people seeking better opportunities in new territories. In chapters 2, 3, and 5 of *Christus vivit*, Pope Francis emphasizes that young people need mentors who will walk alongside them, listening, guiding, and supporting them without imposing rigid structures. He encourages a model of synodal accompaniment whereby young people are not just passive recipients but active participants in shaping their faith journey. In this context, the Catholic Mental Health Ministry, for example, is one of the means of accompaniment provided by the Church in various dioceses worldwide including the Church in Southern Africa.[11]

Across the cultures of Africa, parents introduce children to their traditional culture before introducing them to the sacraments of initiation (Baptism, Confirmation, and First Communion).

---

[10] Delphine Allaire and Linda Bordoni, "Mediterranean Meetings: Young People Join Discussions and Plans," *Vatican News*, September 21, 2023.

[11] Catholic Mental Health Ministry, catholicmhm.org/.

Traditional African cultures in some cases offer a way of life that can be enriching for the formation and development of young people, but there are limitations and flaws as well. In some African countries, young Catholics face persecution or restrictions on their religious freedom, which can create a barrier to full participation in Church activities or cause a disconnect between faith and societal pressures. The Church recognizes these challenges and offers spiritual and practical support. Pope Francis's call to young people to find courage in their faith is especially relevant. Drawing from Jesus's life, he emphasizes that challenges are opportunities for growth and discernment.[12] For young Africans, this means embracing their unique roles as agents of change in their communities.

For the youth to truly be the strength and the hope for Africa, it is imperative that the Church develop and offer formation programs, social justice initiatives, empowerment in faith communities, and promote greater unity. In this way, young people are empowered to become co-creators of a synodal Church. As Pope Francis states in *Christus vivit*, just as Jesus's own youth was a preparation for his mission, the challenges of young people in Africa can also become an impetus for mission in a synodal, missionary Church.[13] Pope Francis uses Jesus's example to urge young people to take their faith seriously, seek authentic relationships, and embrace their unique mission in the Church and society. In this context, Luke 2:52 offers a powerful model for personal growth, describing Jesus growing "in wisdom and stature, and in favor with God and people," and highlighting Jesus's intellectual, spiritual, and physical development as a young man.[14]

---

[12] *Christus vivit* 31.
[13] *Christus vivit* 31.
[14] *Christus vivit* 31.

When Given Space, Youth Can Add Value

The Final Document highlights the Church's recognition of young people's desire for authentic community and their commitment to social justice and environmental stewardship. It calls for the Church to provide thoughtful and patient accompaniment, revisiting proposals that encourage shared experiences with educators, service to those in need, and a spirituality grounded in prayer and the sacraments.

> The request that they made at the 2018 Synod on Young People to "walk together in daily life" corresponds exactly to the vision of a synodal Church. For this reason, it is fundamental that we assure them of thoughtful and patient accompaniment; in particular, the proposal of "an experience of accompaniment given discernment," which arose thanks to their contribution, deserves to be revisited and taken up again. It foresees companionship shared with educators, an apostolic commitment lived at the service of the neediest, and the offer of a spirituality rooted in prayer and the sacramental life. (FD 62)

There are several examples of how young people can add value to and promote the mission of the Church when given the space and the opportunity to do so. During apartheid in South Africa, several Catholic youth movements played key roles in the struggle for social justice and human dignity. These movements empowered young people and served as platforms for social and political transformation. Movements such as the Catholic Youth Action, Young Christian Workers, and Catholic Students' Association encouraged young people to live their faith through action by organizing educational and social initiatives that highlighted the injustices of the apartheid regime, particularly the economic and social inequalities faced by Black South

Africans, who became increasingly engaged with the antiapartheid struggle. Young people organized and were involved in protests, strikes, and other forms of peaceful civil resistance, advocating for racial justice and equality.[15] Through these movements, the youth were encouraged to take active roles in improving their communities; they were also encouraged to read and reflect on pastoral statements issued by the SACBC leadership as part of their spiritual formation and involvement in social action.

The Catholic Church in South Africa, especially among youth groups, was also influenced by liberation theology, which emerged in Latin America and focused on the options for the poor and oppressed. Many young Catholics were inspired by liberation theology's call for solidarity with the marginalized and the oppressed. This perspective encouraged them to view the struggle against apartheid not just as a political issue but also as a moral and religious duty.

In one sense, the experience of young people in South Africa during the apartheid era prefigured the idea of co-responsibility in a synodal Church. Several Catholic priests, religious sisters, and lay leaders were instrumental in organizing youth movements and providing guidance during apartheid in South Africa. Prominent personalities such as Fr. Albert Nolan, OP, were actively involved in the antiapartheid struggle, as were Dominican Sisters, who ran schools and community centers and contributed to the educational and social empowerment of young people during this period.[16]

The foregoing examples show how synodality can be concretely lived in a Church that sees itself as an inclusive community of believers journeying together. This vision of the

---

[15] Stuart Bate, "The Catholic under Apartheid," in *The Catholic Church in Contemporary South Africa*, ed. Joy Brain and Philippe Denis (Pietermaritzburg: Cluster Publications, 1999), 151–86.

[16] Bate, "The Catholic under Apartheid."

Church fulfills the ecclesiological ideals of Vatican II pointed out by Marcel Uwineza and Ludovic Lado that emphasize the vital importance of the Church as the People of God and the shared responsibility of all for the Church's life and mission.

Building a Participatory Church

As I have already mentioned, the synod highlighted formation as a key priority for the emergence of a truly synodal Church. The Final Document offers principles and practical guidelines for implementing formation programs, especially for young people. Creating space for the youth means providing formation initiatives focused on empowering them to take leadership roles. Youth leadership programs in theology and pastoral care help equip them for active participation in synodal structures such as parish councils and diocesan assemblies. In the context of South Africa, there are ample examples of such leadership programs designed to foster the formation of young people.

In 1993, in post-apartheid South Africa, the Catholic Church established the Association of Catholic Tertiary Students (ACTS)—a unified body following the merger of the Catholic Students' Association and the National Catholic Federation of Students.[17] ACTS serves as a formative platform for young people to actively participate in Church life. Specific initiatives and activities include spiritual and human development through retreats, liturgical celebrations, and community service projects. Through ACTS, which operates as part of Catholic chaplaincies in universities focusing on the spiritual, human, doctrinal,

---

[17] Association of Catholic Tertiary Students (ACTS), https://sacbc.org.za/wp-content/uploads/2024/07/ACTS-Conference-2024.pdf. See also Fr. Mokesh K. Morar, "The Revival of the Young Christian Students Movement," *Worldwide* 33, no. 4, May 31, 2023, http://www.worldwidemagazine.org/vol-33-no-4/the-revival-of-the-young-christian-students-movement/.

and academic formation of its members, Catholic youth are encouraged to deepen their relationship with Christ through a variety of religious, spiritual, and social activities.

ACTS members are committed to principles of nonracialism, nonsexism, and ecumenism, reflecting the diverse and inclusive nature of the Church. Members are also helped with mental health awareness, academic challenges, and spiritual guidance through chaplains and leadership teams. Undoubtedly, movements like ACTS align with the principles of synodality, fostering dialogue and collaboration among young people, clergy, and Church structures to create a more participatory Church, as members are encouraged to hold regular engagements with chaplains, alumni, and Church leaders who in turn guide students navigating the challenges of tertiary education.

Similar platforms can be established using SCCs, especially for underprivileged youth who do not have access to tertiary education. As Jesus's interactions as a young man show—staying in the temple as a twelve-year-old (Luke 2:41–50), participating in community life, and searching for the truth with curiosity—through pastoral opportunities, young people can become active in their faith communities and ask profound questions.

While the synodal Church offers immense opportunities, it also acknowledges the challenges young people face. Cultural and generational gaps, limited resources, and societal pressures can create barriers to full participation. In the context of Africa, the Church's response is rooted in the principle of Ubuntu—"I am because you are"—emphasizing solidarity, mutual support, and collaboration.[18] Addressing these challenges requires

---

[18] Josée Ngalula explores the relationship between Ubuntu and synodality in her essay "Ubuntu and Synodality," in *Toward a Synodal Church in Africa: Echoes from an African Christian Palaver*, ed. Ikenna Okafor, Josée Ngalula, Nicholas Segeja, and Stan Chu Ilo (Maryknoll, NY: Orbis Books, 2024), 85–121.

collaboration between young people, Church leaders, and the wider community. Formation programs tailored to local contexts, pastoral care for marginalized groups, and inclusive policies are essential for building a truly synodal Church. In a synodal Church of the young and young at heart, space needs to be created to allow young people to fully express themselves and utilize their talents to promote the mission of the Church.

Digital Missionaries: Evangelization in the Digital Age

A key dimension of the role of young people in the creation of a synodal Church concerns the opportunities and challenges of digital platforms as a means of fostering a Church that is inclusive and responsive. A Church that is young at heart is not afraid to try new ways of evangelizing. Just as Jesus approached people in their particular contexts, the Church is also called to meet young people where they are. In Africa, young people are in many places—in both the digital and real world.

In an era dominated by technology, the Church calls young Catholics to become "digital missionaries." This invitation is an acknowledgment of young people's presence in digital spaces and the potential to use these platforms for evangelization. "The spread of digital culture, particularly evident among young people, is profoundly changing their experience of space and time; it influences their daily activities, communication and interpersonal relationships, including faith" (FD 113). The Synod on Synodality highlighted the importance of digital evangelization, recognizing it as a means to reach people who might feel disconnected from traditional Church structures.

Furthermore, the synod advocates for creativity in engaging with the digital environment as "a prophetic space for mission and proclamation" where all, particularly young people, "create bonds of belonging, promoting encounter and dialogue" (FD

113). Young people who grow up in a digital age can become evangelizers in online spaces, sharing the Gospel creatively and authentically. Also, the synod recognizes digital spaces as crucial for dialogue, catechesis, and forming deeper connections with those who might feel disconnected from traditional Church structures. Additionally, it highlights the role of young people in using technology for missionary activities, underscoring their unique ability to bring creativity and relevance to faith-based initiatives in a digital age.

It is important to note that while digital evangelization has great potential to improve people's lives, it can also cause harm and injury, intimidation, disinformation, sexual exploitation, and addiction. Therefore, the Church must provide adequate formation programs for young Catholics to integrate digital literacy and theological education and enable young Catholics to become effective digital missionaries and leaders in their communities.

Rop emphasizes how access to formation, education, and technology has enabled young people, religious included, to interact with others around the world. More important, she notes that young people's accessibility to the digital world challenges the older generation to appreciate and offer positive criticism while teaching the young by way of example and witness of life.

A Modern-Day Young Digital Evangelizer

Although access to the internet remains a challenge in some areas, the Church in Africa is actively engaging young people as digital missionaries through initiatives such as the Pan-African Catholic Theology and Pastoral Network.[19] Programs such as the Digital Faith Influencers Program, African Synodal Digital Youth Influencers, and African Synodality Initiative's Digital Synod Initiative

---

[19] Pan-African Catholic Theology and Pastoral Network, https://pactpan.org/.

with the Youth aim to equip young people with the skills needed for effective digital evangelization. These programs integrate digital literacy with theological education, enabling participants to navigate the digital sphere with confidence and purpose. Through these empowerment initiatives, youth are encouraged to use social media platforms to spread Gospel values by creating faith-based content, as did Italian teenager Blessed Carlo Acutis,[20] who is celebrated for his deep Catholic faith, particularly his devotion to the Eucharist, and his innovative approach to evangelization using modern technology.

The example of Carlo Acutis, also known as the Millennial Blessed, illustrates the power of digital evangelization. He used technology to create a website cataloguing eucharistic miracles, inspiring countless people to deepen their faith. As Pope Francis noted, Blessed Carlo's life shows how technology can serve as a tool for spreading the Gospel responsibly and creatively.[21] Blessed Carlo believed technology should be a tool for sharing the Gospel, and he used it responsibly, stating, "All people are born as originals, but many die as photocopies."[22] Young African digital missionaries can learn from Blessed Carlo's devotion to the Eucharist and remind their followers of the power of the Eucharist for enriching and transforming their lives and the lives of others.

In a synodal Church of the young and young at heart, the Church must embrace digital evangelization, offer formation to digital missionaries, and journey with young people. Part of becoming a synodal Church is committing to encouraging young Africans to use digital spaces to spread and understand their faith, promote conversations about the dimensions of faith, and become evangelists of other youth.

---

[20] Carlo Acutis, http://www.carloacutis.com/en/association/mostra-miracoli-eucaristici.

[21] *Christus vivit* 105.

[22] Eucharistic Miracles exhibition, http://www.carloacutis.com/en/association/mostra-miracoli-eucaristici.

The Jubilee Year 2025:
An Opportunity for a Synodal Church of the Young

The Jubilee Year (2025) is a powerful opportunity and invitation for young people to embrace their roles as catalysts of renewal, a time to celebrate their energy and creativity, nurture their faith, and inspire them to be missionaries of hope in the world.[23] The Jubilee Year has profound spiritual and social implications for youth, especially in the Catholic tradition. It is a time of renewal, hope, reconciliation, and transformation, offering unique opportunities for young people to deepen their faith, reflect on their mission in the world, and contribute meaningfully to their communities. The Jubilee Year emphasizes God's boundless mercy. For young people, it can be a moment to encounter God deeply, especially through the sacraments of Reconciliation and the Eucharist.

During the Jubilee Year, youth groups are encouraged to participate in pilgrimages to designated holy sites, fostering a sense of community and spiritual growth. Young people in Botswana, Eswatini, and South Africa make the annual youth pilgrimage to Tshitanini in the Tzaneen Diocese to promote devotion to South African Martyr Blessed Tshimangadzo Samuel Benedict Daswa.[24] Parishes and dioceses can organize retreats, catechesis, and workshops tailored to young people, helping them explore the jubilee themes of hope, renewal, and justice.

The jubilee invites young people to discern their unique vocation in the Church and society, be it in marriage, priesthood, religious life, or professional careers. Youth can be encouraged to take up leadership roles in the Church, embodying the jubilee

---

[23] Jubilee Year of Hope, www.iubilaeum2025.va/en/giubileo-2025.html.

[24] Blessed Tshimangadzo Samuel Benedict Daswa annual youth pilgrimage, https://sacbc.org.za/sr-munzhedzi-op-pilgrimages-are-meant-to-promote-devotion-to-blessed-daswa/.

spirit of renewal and service. Also, the Jubilee Year traditionally calls for acts of mercy. Youth groups can engage in community service projects such as helping the homeless, supporting migrants, and caring for the environment. Educational initiatives can focus on themes such as poverty alleviation, environmental stewardship, and human dignity, inspiring young people to become agents of change. In this way, the jubilee can be a time to connect with Catholic youth worldwide, promoting cross-cultural exchanges and solidarity. The jubilee offers an opportunity for diocesan and parish-level celebrations including music, art, and cultural festivals that resonate with young people.

Furthermore, by utilizing digital platforms, youth ministries can spread the jubilee message, share inspiring stories, and foster an online community of faith. The jubilee's focus on inclusion resonates with the synodal Church's mission to engage with young people on the peripheries—those who feel alienated, marginalized, or disillusioned. Special attention can be given to youth struggling with addiction, mental health issues, or family breakdowns, offering them hope and support. During the Jubilee Year, youth can lead jubilee-themed art, music, and drama projects that explore the themes of mercy, forgiveness, and renewal. The jubilee can inspire young people to start projects that address social challenges, emphasizing sustainable development and ethical practices.

As mentioned, the canonization of Blessed Carlo Acutis during the Jubilee Year carries profound significance, especially for the global youth population. As a millennial, Carlo Acutis is widely regarded as a role model for young Catholics, demonstrating that sanctity is achievable in today's digital age.[25]

---

[25] Jubilee of Teenagers, April 25–27, 2025, www.iubilaeum2025.va/en/pellegrinaggio/calendario-giubileo/GrandiEventi/Giubileo-degli-Adolescenti.html; Mass for the Canonization of Blessed Carlo Acutis, http://www.iubilaeum2025.va/en/pellegrinaggio/calendario-giubileo/Grandi-

Conclusion:
Youth at the Heart of the Church

"Young friends, don't wait until tomorrow to contribute your energy, your audacity and your creativity to changing our world. Your youth is not an 'in-between time.' You are the now of God, and he wants you to bear fruit."[26] With these words, Pope Francis reminds the Church that the journey of synodality is a path for young people, a journey to build a Church that is truly young at heart, where every member has a place, a voice, and a mission. In this Church, following the example of Jesus, young people are empowered to take up their roles as digital missionaries, community leaders, and advocates for justice, thus transforming both the Church and the world.

The Synod on Synodality and the apostolic exhortation *Christus vivit* remind us that young people are not just the future of the Church but also its vibrant present. Jesus, as a model for young people, shows us the values and opportunities of youthfulness in a synodal Church. The Church, in its synodal journey, is called to walk alongside young people, listening to their voices, addressing their challenges, and empowering them to take active roles in shaping the Church's mission and identity.

From the challenges of migration, economic hardship, digital culture, and social isolation to the opportunities for intergenerational dialogue, formation, and digital evangelization, the Church must create spaces where young people feel valued, heard, and equipped to live out their faith authentically. The Jubilee Year offers a unique moment for young people to embrace their role as catalysts of renewal, hope, and transformation within the Church and in the wider world.

Eventi/messa-canonizzazione-beato-carlo-acutis.html; Jubilee of Youth, July 28–August 3, 2025, www.iubilaeum2025.va/en/pellegrinaggio/calendario-giubileo/GrandiEventi/Giubileo-dei-Giovani.html.

[26] *Christus vivit*, 178.

As Pope Francis teaches, young people are the "now of God." They are called to be digital missionaries, community leaders, and advocates for justice, using their creativity and energy to spread the Gospel in ways that resonate with the needs and contexts of today's world. By fostering a culture of accompaniment, dialogue, and inclusion, the Church can truly become a synodal Church—one that is young at heart, where every member, regardless of age, has a place, a voice, and a mission. In this synodal journey, young people find inspiration and encouragement in the examples and witnesses of young saints including Blessed Carlo Acutis and South African Martyr Blessed Benedict Daswa. They are thus able to assume responsibility for building a Church that is not only responsive to the challenges of our time but also a beacon of hope, mercy, and love for all generations, young and old alike, reflecting the heart of Christ.

Afterword

Ubuntu, Dance, and Poetry of Synodality

William O'Neill

Lewis Carroll once wrote, "If you don't know where you are going, any road will take you there." Yet the Synod on Synodality has given us "a path of creative fidelity" in José Minaku's words, and the contributors to this remarkable volume are truly trailblazers. Their voices reflect the rich diversity of the African Church's reception of synodal theology. But in both form and substance, this work does far more: It offers us a truly *African* synodal theology for the Church in the third millennium, worthy of reception in its own right.

Several distinctive themes or leitmotifs are voiced throughout, revealing how African synodal wisdom both nourishes and is nourished by the *sensus fidei fidelium*. Let me note three: the underlying synodal theology of Ubuntu or familyhood, the role of Small Christian Communities in living Ubuntu synodality, and the rhetoric of synodal discernment as "palaver."

Ubuntu Synodality

We have no English word translating *Ubuntu*. At best, we may speak of "dignity in solidarity" in the words of Catholic social teaching. Humanity, says Archbishop Desmond Tutu, is never resolved into abstract relations of sovereign selves. "We belong in a bundle of life," says Tutu. "We say, 'a person is a person through other people.' It is not 'I think therefore I am.' It says rather: 'I am human because I belong.' I participate, I share." In his encyclical *Fratelli tutti*, Pope Francis acknowledges the inspiration of Tutu's African humanist philosophy—a philosophy, writes Agbonkhianmeghe E. Orobator, "based on a culture of sharing, openness, mutual dependence, dialogue and interpersonal encounter. In Ubuntu, human existence reaches fulfillment as part of whole, society thrives on a common humanity, and forgiveness and reconciliation are prerequisites for preserving social harmony."

Inspired by Ubuntu, the synodal Church emerges as a "we"—not a reified, collective entity like a class, race, or ethnicity but rather as a solidarity of solidarities extending not only across generations but also binding us to God and to "our common home." In Minaku's words, "The Church in Africa sees itself as 'the family of God joined in communion by the bonds of the Holy Spirit uniquely manifested in the experience of Ubuntu.'" Indeed, the Church is at once the sacrament of this communion and a countersign to the endemic violence, bias, and exclusion that have so riven our world today.

We may accordingly speak in Anthony Egan's words of a "synodal ethics" of "dialogue, discernment and trust," grounded in our "shared humanity, community and interdependence." Such an "inclusive and participatory" ethics, says Chijioke Azuawusiefe, will challenge patriarchal hierarchies "as well as gender and age biases that are deep-seated in the African sociocultural structures."

Ecclesiology from Below:
The Role of Small Chrisitan Communities

Mirroring the dance (*perichoresis*) of the Trinity, Ubuntu synodality reveals the dancer in the dance—a Church, writes Josée Ngalula, born in the "trinitarian dynamism" of divine love. And as Sheila Leocádia Pires and Léocadie Lushombo remind us, the dance begins at home, in vibrant Small Christian Communities (SCCs), base ecclesial communities, and Catholic youth movements. Here, the family of Church takes root, as it is incorporated in ever-larger structures—a "communion of communities," in Marcel Uwineza's words, fostering "listening, dialogue, and communal discernment" (Final Document 28).

The common good of synodality is realized in the complex solidarity of mediating ecclesial structures and roles. In discerning "differentiated co-responsibilities," writes David Kaulemu, each has a part in mission, each a voice in dialogue (Final Document 28). "Synodality," in Ludovic Lado's words, thus favors "inclusive and participative governance" in the Church. And as St. Paul reminds us, the Body suffers when any part is excluded, any voice suppressed.

Palaver as the Rhetoric of Synodality

As our authors observe, a living Church is a learning Church; only thus is it truly a teaching Church. And this is the tradition of palaver, the rhetoric and poetry of Ubuntu. Anne Arabome describes palaver as a rich "communicative practice that includes the voices of all members of the community in the discussion, discernment, and resolution of matters of consequence affecting the entire community." As synodal rhetoric, palaver underwrites an inclusive and "dynamic process of speaking and listening under the guidance and animation of the Spirit."

Where Western modernity bequeaths us rival rhetorics of abstract individual rights or ethnocentric communitarian ethics, palaver speaks of concrete universality—the universal solidarity of Ubuntu mediated concretely through overlapping solidarities, a differentiated unity. Just so, the Church's palaver, our authors insist, must remain open-textured and subject to criticism and renewal. And here the role of women in the Church is decisive. They are, in many ways, the weavers of tradition; there is no web of belief without them. Women, concludes Lushombo, are "teachers of synodality." Consecrated religious women, above all, writes Veronica J. Rop, have blazed our synodal path, showing us, "through their communal discernment and harmonization of individual gifts for a common mission" what "synodal living means."

Palaver is not only the rhetoric of synodality; it is also its enduring legacy. Indeed, this collected volume is itself the fruit of synodal palaver. The authors met on several occasions to discuss, revise, and deepen their respective analyses. The final draft is woven by a "we," African theologians inspired by Ubuntu synodality—a lesson, perhaps, for the Western academy still beholden to the ideal of individual scholarly achievement.

Conclusion

Our common call as Christians, the synod declares, "is based upon a shared baptismal identity" (FD 4). In preparation for the synod, the Missionary Sisters of Charles de Foucauld engaged Small Christian Communities in the Kakuma refugee camp of northwestern Kenya, home now to 350,000 refugees from many countries. Their faith is deep, a holy resilience amid sometimes unbearable suffering. Yet catechesis was often wanting in their war-torn homes and older, rigid practices imposed. One young refugee recalled being told that he must adopt a Western name in baptism. He asked, "Why can't my name be baptized with me? We need African saints." These voices of the synod testify that the baptism has indeed begun, an African synodal ecclesiology, in Elochukwu Uzukwu's words, that has "large ears." Large enough for the entire Church.

Contributors

Anne Arabome, SSS, is a member of the Sisters of Social Service of Los Angeles, California. She served as the associate director of the Faber Center for Ignatian Spirituality at Marquette University. She is the founding director of Sophia Institute of Theological Studies and Spiritual Formation and the Bakhita Initiative for African Women in Namibia, which aim to educate and empower both women religious and lay women and girls across Africa. She holds a PhD in systematic theology (University of Roehampton) and a doctor of ministry in spirituality (Catholic Theological Union), and she is the author of *Why Do You Trouble This Woman? Women and the Spiritual Exercises of St. Ignatius of Loyola* (2022).

Chijioke Azuawusiefe, SJ, a Jesuit from Nigeria, is the head of the Pastoral/Communication Studies Department at the Catholic Institute of West Africa, Port Harcourt, Nigeria. He researches the interplay of media, religion, and culture in local and transnational contexts, with emphasis on Nollywood, the cinema of Nigeria.

Anthony Egan, SJ, is a South African Jesuit currently teaching at Hekima University College in Nairobi, Kenya. He is a historian of church-state relations (BA Hons, MA [Cape Town], PhD [Witwatersrand]), who subsequently specialized in moral theology (MDiv, STL [Weston Jesuit School of Theology]). He has lectured at various universities and seminaries, was a founding member of the Jesuit Institute South Africa, and was on Witwatersrand University's Medical Human Research Ethics Board (2004–2021). He has published widely on politics, church history, and social ethics.

David Kaulemu is the dean of the School of Education and Leadership at Arrupe Jesuit University in Harare, Zimbabwe. He is the former chair of the Department of Religious Studies, Classics, and Philosophy at the University of Zimbabwe. He is the former regional coordinator for Eastern and Southern Africa of the African Forum for Catholic Social Teaching. He has published on leadership, social justice, ethics, and Christian social teaching.

Ludovic Lado, SJ, is a Jesuit priest and university lecturer specializing in social and cultural anthropology. His primary research and publications focus on the intersection of religion and society in Africa. He has worked at higher education institutions in Cameroon, Côte d'Ivoire, and Chad. His most recent book, *The Politics of Gender Reform in West Africa*, was published in 2023.

José Minaku Lukoli, SJ, a member of the Society of Jesus, is a Congolese national (Democratic Republic of Congo). He has held various roles in the Society, including serving as provincial of the Central Africa Province. He currently serves as the president of the Jesuit Conference of Africa and Madagascar. Father Minaku holds a master's degree in Latin philology from the Catholic University of Louvain (Belgium) and a licentiate in sacred theology (STL) in systematic theology from the Jesuit School of Theology at Berkeley (USA). His primary research interests are intercultural dialogue and ecclesiology.

Léocadie Lushombo, it, is a consecrated member of the Teresian Association. She earned a PhD in theological ethics from Boston College (USA) and a sacred theology licentiate degree from the School of Theology and Ministry/Boston College. She completed a master's degree in theological ethics at the Catholic Theological Union/Chicago, a master's degree in sustainable development at the Universidad Pontificio Comillas/Spain, and a master's degree in economics and development at the Catholic

University of Central Africa/Cameroon. Her fields of research and teaching expertise are fundamental moral theology and methods in Christian ethics, political theology, decolonial and liberation theology, economics and Catholic social thought, African theological ethics and inculturation, the theology of peacebuilding, and just peace ethics. She has worked extensively as a researcher and consultant-trainer in justice, peace, and gender issues in the Great Lakes Region in Central Africa and in Latin America. Her interdisciplinary experiences and studies inform her teachings and writings.

Josée Ngalula, RSA, from DR Congo, is a Sister of Saint Andrew. She was a voting member of the Synod on Synodality. She holds a doctorate in theology and teaches systematic theology at the Catholic University of Congo and other theological institutions in Africa. She is currently the director of the Observatory of Violence and Religious Fundamentalism in DR Congo at the Catholic University of Congo. She is a member of the following institutions and research groups: International Theological Commission, African Synodality Initiative, Pan-African Catholic Theology and Pastoral Network, Association of African Theologians (ATA), the ecumenical theological network Tsena Malàlaka, and the Association des théologiennes et femmes canonistes de Kinshasa. Her publications can be accessed at https://uccc.academia.edu/Jos%C3%A9eNGALULA.

William O'Neill, SJ, is professor emeritus of social ethics at the Jesuit School of Theology of Santa Clara University and a visiting professor of Hekima University College in Nairobi. He received an STL from the Jesuit School of Theology and a PhD from Yale University. His writings include *The Ethics of Our Climate: Hermeneutics and Ethical Theory; Reimagining Human Rights: Religion and the Common Good, Catholic Social Teaching: A User's*

Guide (Orbis Books), and book chapters and journal articles addressing questions of human rights, social reconciliation, restorative justice, refugee and immigration policy, race, mass incarceration, and the Church and public reason. He has worked with refugees in Tanzania and Malawi and has researched human rights in South Africa and Rwanda. Since 2019, he has been a member of the Mission and Identity team of the Jesuit Refugee Service while serving in the Kakuma refugee camp in northwestern Kenya.

Agbonkhianmeghe E. Orobator, SJ, is the dean of the Jesuit School of Theology of Santa Clara University, an international center for innovative theological education and formation of Jesuits and lay women and lay men for leadership and service in the global Catholic Church. He serves as the director of the African Synodality Initiative, and he participated in the Synod on Synodality (2021–2024) as a voting member.

Sheila Leocádia Pires, a Mozambican/South African journalist with over twenty years' experience in Catholic and secular media, was appointed by Pope Francis as the first woman secretary of the Commission for Information of the Synod of Bishops, and she represented Africa as a lay woman at the Synod on Synodality. She also serves as the Southern African Catholic Bishops Conference (SACBC) communications officer and Vatican News collaborator.

Veronica Jemanyur Rop, ASE, is a former superior general of the Assumption Sisters of Eldoret in Kenya. She is a member of Catholic Theological Ethics in the World Church. She is currently a lecturer at the Centre for Social Justice and Ethics of the Catholic University of Eastern Africa (CUEA), Nairobi, Kenya. Sr. Veronica is also a visiting lecturer at Hilton-Hekima Sisters Scholars Program and Theology for Laity, and a counselor at Tangaza University. She serves as a corresponding member for the Pontifical Academy for Life in Rome, Italy. She holds a PhD in theology with specialization in moral theology from CUEA. She has published several articles.

Marcel Uwineza, SJ, is a Jesuit priest from Rwanda and currently serves as the President of Hekima University College in Nairobi, Kenya. He is also the Associate Director of the Africa Synodality Initiative. He holds a PhD in Systematic Theology from Boston College (USA) and an MBA in Leadership and Management from York St. John University (UK). His recent publications include: *Risen from the Ashes: Theology as Autobiography* (2022); *Reinventing Theology in Post-Genocide Rwanda: Challenges and Hopes* (2023); and *Ressuscité de mes cendres: La théologie comme autobiographie dans le Rwanda post-génocide* (2025). His forthcoming book, *Healing a Wounded People: A Theology for a Divided World*, will be published in 2025. Among his notable public engagements are his address to the United Nations General Assembly on April 12, 2019, titled "*25 Years After the Genocide in Rwanda: A Testimony*," and his keynote address to global leaders of Jesuit universities and colleges in July 2024 at Loyola Chicago University.

Index

abashingantahe, 37
abuse scandals. *See* clergy abuse
accompaniment, xvi, 9, 21, 160, 173, 180, 207, 209
accountability
  and clergy, 84, 114
  and discernment, 114, 116–17, 154, 158, 175
  in ministry, 96
  political, 151
  in synod governance, 98, 105, 112, 116, 155, 158, 160, 162
  and women religious, 114, 154, 175–77, 182, 203
  and youth, 179
Accra Conference (1989), 133
Achebe, Chinua, 49
ACTS. *See* Association of Catholic Tertiary Students
Acutis, Carlo, 215, 217, 219
ACWECA. *See* Association of Consecrated Women in Eastern and Central Africa
Adam, 27–28, 69–70, 130
addiction, 207, 214, 217

Ad gentes, 41
ad limina apostolorum, 118
African Sisters Education Collaborative, 176
African Synodal Digital Youth Influencers, 214
African Synodality Initiative, 214
agapē, 24, 184–86
Agius, Emmanuel, 105, 114
AIDS, 199
Akan, 152
Amasolenyana, 204
Amazon, Synod on the (2019), 35
AMECEA. *See* Association of Member Episcopal Conferences in Eastern Africa
Amoris laetitia, 35
ancestors, 5–7, 38
apartheid, 209–11
apostles, 55, 81–82, 128
apostolate, 147, 166, 173, 176
apostolic exhortations, 35, 81, 96, 119, 218

artificial intelligence, 62, 181
ASI. *See* African Synodality Initiative
assembly, 19, 26–27
Association of Catholic Tertiary Students, 211–12
Association of Consecrated Women in Eastern and Central Africa, 139, 164, 167, 170, 178, 180
Association of Member Episcopal Conferences in Eastern Africa, 164, 166–67
authoritarianism, xvii, 102, 179, 203

Baganda, 151
Bamileké, 151
Banda, Kamuzu, 199
baptism
  and co-responsibility, 186, 188, 192, 197
  and early Church, 29
  and equality, xv, 33, 163
  and identity, 224
  and sensus fidei, 156
  and women, 122, 129, 169, 171, 177
baptismal dignity, xii, xv, xxii, 22, 29, 46, 64, 122, 124, 129, 186, 192, 194, 198
Baraza, 63
Barron, Mary, 136
Basil of Caesarea, 199

Beatitudes, 174
be ko asule, 152
Benedict XVI, 62, 191. *See also* Joseph Ratzinger
Bevans, Stephen, 7
Bitrus, Ibrahim S., 76
Boff, Leonardo, 87
Borras, Alphonse, 89
Botswana, 204, 216
Burundi, 37

Cameroon, 151
canon law, 116, 130, 176
Carey, James, 50–51
Caritas in veritate, 191
Carney, J.J., 137–38
catechesis, 204–5, 214, 216, 224
Catechism of the Catholic Church, 70
catholicity, xx, 41
Catholic Mental Health Ministry, 207
Catholic Sisters' Initiatives, 140
Catholic Students' Association, 209, 211
Catholic Theological Ethics in the World Church, 176
Catholic Women's Association, 140
Catholic Youth Action, 209
Catholic youth movements, 209, 212, 217, 223
celibacy, 35, 166
Central African Republic, 38

Index

centralization
  church, 36–37, 161
  political, 151
charisms, xiii–xiv, xix–xx, 66, 95, 164–65, 167–68, 171, 180, 182, 189, 198
Children of Mary, 204
child soldiers, 199
Chrism Mass (2013), 83
Christus vivit, 35, 201–2, 207–8, 218
clergy
  and church hierarchy, 30
  and church hierarchy, 60, 88
  and clericalism, 83, 144, 174
  and co-responsibility, xi, 34, 40
  and inclusivity, 16, 150
  need for accountability, 84, 105
  in patronage-client systems, 113–14
clergy abuse, 84, 101–2
clericalism
  and co-responsibility, 159, 197
  as obstacle to synodality, 43, 46, 86, 131, 158, 162
  overcoming, xix, 40, 174, 194
  and patronage-client systems, 114
  Pope Francis on, 83–84, 92, 149–50
climate change, 46, 60, 185
Code of Canon Law, The, 165

collegiality, xi, 27, 34, 92, 118, 144, 146, 161
colonialism
  and communal thought, 5–6
  influence on church structures, 152–53
  negative impact on cultures, 132
  and traditional power structures, 150, 152
  woman-led resistance to, 177
communal discernment, xix, 10–13, 15, 18, 91, 93, 115, 156–57, 169, 223–24
communication
  and active listening, 56–57, 60
  Church as, 54–55
  divine, 50, 52–53, 59
  importance to synodality, 45–47, 49, 63–64
  and modern technology, 61–62
  nonverbal, 58
  and palaver, 14, 17
  as symbolic process, 50–51
Communio et progressio, 57, 62, 64
communion
  central to synodality, 19, 24, 63–64, 66, 93–94, 106, 192–93
  Church as, 29, 86, 120, 184
  mystical, 85–86, 93, 98
  and ngiga, 48–49, 51

communion *(continued)*
  in scripture, 70–71
  and sensus fidei, 156
  Trinitarian view of, 24, 39, 54–55, 77–78
  and Ubuntu, 78, 222
  Vatican II on, 32–34, 86
Compendium of the Social Doctrine of the Church, The, 184
conciliarism, 101, 103
Conference of Women Superior Generals, 167
consecrated life, 118, 136, 164, 166, 169
consultation, xvii, 31, 93, 116, 118, 120, 135–36, 155, 175
conversation, xix, 12–16, 19, 21, 49–50, 59–60, 94, 109–10
conversion
  and conversation, 13
  and co-responsibility, 187
  and culture, 176–77
  importance in synodality, xi–xii, xvi, xxii, 1, 32, 42–44, 81, 158, 162
  missionary, 153
  and palaver, 17
  relational, 74, 116, 187
co-responsibility
  between churches, 189–90
  central to synodality, xi, xix, 65, 91, 155–56, 185–86, 196–97
  and civil society, 199, 210
  differentiated, 115, 124, 174, 188, 198, 200, 223
  ethics of, 191
  vs. hierarchical structures, 40, 42, 159, 169–70, 182
  and laity, 116, 162, 198
  and relationality, 187–88
  and Trinity, 183
  and Ubuntu, 193
  and Vatican II, 189–90, 211
  and women, 169–70, 182
co-responsibility and clericalism, 159, 197
Côte d'Ivoire, 152
Council of Jerusalem, 65
Craven, Toni, 126
Cyprian of Carthage, 188

Dar es Salaam, 6
Daswa, Tshimangadzo Samuel Benedict, 216, 219
Daughters of St. Paul, 181
deacons, 118, 128, 146–47
Declaration on Religious Liberty. See *Dignitatis humanae*
Decree on Means of Social Communications. See *Inter mirifica*
Dei verbum, 65, 82, 127
democracy, 62, 102, 114, 152
Democratic Republic of Congo (DRC), 124, 138, 140
descriptive approaches, 84–85

dialogue
  between God and humanity, 56, 80
  central to synodality, xvi, 55–56, 62–63, 100–102, 106–9, 111, 114–15, 222
  and conversation, 13, 15
  and discernment, xvii, 13, 40–41, 116–18, 120, 123, 222–23
  and listening, 57–59
  need for guidance in, 43–44
  and ngiga, 60
  and palaver, 18–20, 49–52, 54
  and reconciliation, 39
  Vatican II on, 57
  and women, 132–33, 162–63
Digital Faith Influencers Program, 214
digital missionaries, 202, 213–15, 218–19
digital spaces, 61, 181, 201–2, 213–15, 217
Digital Synod Initiative, 214
Dignitatis humanae, 57
dignity
  baptismal, xii, xv, xxii, 22, 29, 46, 64, 122, 124, 129, 186, 192, 194, 198
  in solidarity, 221
  women's, 70–71, 129–31, 169, 171, 173, 177–78
discernment
  and accompaniment, xvi
  and accountability, 114, 116–17, 154, 158, 175
  communal, xix, 10–13, 15, 18, 91, 93, 115, 156–57, 169, 223–24
  and dialogue, xvii, 13, 40–41, 116–18, 120, 123, 222–23
  and formation, 12, 19
  and Holy Spirit, 12–13, 110
  Ignatian, 110–11
  importance to synodality, xvii, 11, 19–21, 93, 96, 99–101, 104, 106–7, 120, 221
  and listening, xvi
  and palaver, 15–17, 107–8, 223
  and prayer, 110
  and resistance to change, 42
  women's role in, 149–50, 175, 178
  and youth, 178, 208–9
discipleship, 97–98
dissent, 102, 113, 152
Dominican Sisters, 210
Dowling, Kevin, 199
DRC. *See* Democratic Republic of Congo
Dulles, Avery, 84–87, 90–92, 98–99
Durkheim, Emile, 51

Eastern Africa, 164, 167
Eastern African, 137
ecclesial discernment, 11–12, 18–19, 93, 110–11, 117, 155, 172

ecclesia semper reformanda, 99
ecclesiogenesis, 91
education
   and dissent, 101
   theological, 101–2, 109, 214–15
   and women, 154, 164, 173, 176, 178–81
   and youth, 199, 205–6, 214
egalitarianism, 76, 151
enculturation, 132
Eswatini, 204, 216
ethics of synodality, 100–101, 104, 108, 118, 120
Eucharist, 48, 50, 81, 94, 106, 215–16
Evangelii gaudium, 90, 96
Evangelii nuntiandi, 41, 82
evangelization
   collaborative, 99
   digital, 213–15, 218
   role of laity, 34
   role of women in, 139, 164, 167, 177
   and synodality, 95, 107, 192
   and youth, 181
Eve, 28, 130

fellowship, 25, 51–52, 65–66, 74, 93, 95, 117, 179, 203
First Vatican Council. *See* Vatican I
formation
   and discernment, 12, 19
   women's role in, 167, 174, 176, 180–81
   and youth, 204–5, 208, 211–12, 214–15
Francis (Pope)
   on authority of clergy, 170–71
   on challenges to synodality, 36
   on clergy formation, 120
   and clericalism, 83–84, 92, 144
   on consultation, xvii
   on co-responsibility, 187, 191
   on evangelization, 95–97
   on Holy Spirit, 1–2, 16, 20, 88
   on importance of listening, 17, 35, 37, 45–47, 56–57, 90, 94, 102
   importance to history of synodality, ix–x, 2, 34–35, 119
   on laity, 36
   on need for inclusivity, 61, 63, 149
   on nonverbal communication, 59
   on technology, 215
   on youth, 201–3, 206–8, 218–19
Franks, Bernard, 91
Fratelli tutti, 137, 191, 222

gacaca, 39
Gadaa system, 151
Gaudium et spes, xii, 34, 57, 132, 190

Geldhof, Joris, 106
gender, 18, 46, 60, 103, 126, 148, 154, 177, 179, 203, 222
General Audience (2014), 83
Genesis, 52, 69–71
Ghana, 152
González, Gusto, 130
grassroots, 16, 132
Grech, Mario, 104
groupthink, 107
Gulu, 199

Habermas, Jürgen, 106
Harrington, S. J., 123
Healey, Joseph, 8
Hens-Piazza, Gina, 125–26
heresies, 130
hermeneutics, 61, 81, 124, 131–32, 137, 159, 164
Hill, Edmund, 103
Himes, Michael, 184, 186
HIV, 199
Holy Orders, 146
Holy Spirit
  and African religion, 8, 10
  central to synodality, 1–3, 7, 29, 31, 67–69
  and consultation, xvii
  in context of Trinity, 74–76
  and discernment, 12–13, 110
  and listening, xv, xvii, xix–xx, 11, 13, 105, 115
  and palaver, 14–18
  Pope Francis on, 1–2, 16, 20, 88
  and sensus fidei, 156
  and women, 129, 150, 172
Homily at Casa Santa Marta (2016), 84
Hood, Robert, 7
Humanae vitae, 104
humanization, 135–36
human rights, 41, 103, 195
human trafficking, 136, 140, 173

Igbo, 47, 49, 151
Ignatius of Antioch, 29, 188
Ignatius of Loyola, 111
IL. See *Instrumentum Laboris*
Ilo, Stan Chu, 107
illiteracy, 80
imago Dei, 13, 72–73
imago Trinitatis, 77
incarnation, 53, 68–69
inclusivity
  of laity, 36, 60, 88, 116, 149, 159–60, 163, 179
  and palaver, 16, 18
  radical, xviii, 98
  and women, 148–50, 168, 170, 178, 182
  and youth, 217, 223
inculturation, 8, 103, 124, 132–33
institutional persistence theory, 152
Instrumentum Laboris, 56, 100
Inter mirifica, 58
International Theological Commission, ix–x, xvii, 26, 90–91, 106, 197

International Union of Superiors General, 136
inyangamugayo, 37
Isaiah, 48
ITC. *See* International Theological Commission
Ivory Coast. *See* Côte d'Ivoire

John Chrysostom, 29
John Paul II, 70, 135, 175, 189
John the Baptist, 69
John XIII, 32
Jubilee Year, 202, 216–18
Judith, 126–27
Justice and Peace Commissions, 140

Kakuma refugee camp, 224
Kalilombe, Patrick, 199
Kenya, 140, 224
kerygma, ix
Kikuyu, 151
Kinshasa, 76
Kombo, J., 77
Küng, Hans, 87

LaCugna, Catherine, 87
laity
  access to theological education, 109
  in church hierarchy, 30, 118, 147
  and collegiality, 34
  and co-responsibility, xii, 40, 94–95, 116, 162, 182, 189, 198
  and evangelization, 34
  inclusion of, 36, 60, 88, 116, 149, 159–60, 163, 179
  in patronage-clientage systems, 113–14
  Pope Francis on, 36
  and Vatican II, xii, 34, 88, 189
Laudato si', 72
lectio divina, 81
Let Us Dream (Pope Francis), 16
LGBTQ+ community, 107, 154
liberation theology, 210
Lindbeck, George, 87
listening
  active, 55–57, 59, 80
  and dialogue, 57–59
  empathetic, 123, 138, 142
  and Holy Spirit, xv, xvii, xix–xx, 11, 13, 105, 115
  pedagogy of, 17, 159
Little Soldiers of Christ, 204
Lombardi, Federico, 130
Lord's Resistance Army (LRA), 199
luba, 151
Luciani, Rafael, 85, 89–90
Luis, Carlos, 107, 114
Lumen gentium, 2, 25, 33–35, 39, 41, 68–69, 76, 88, 95, 144–47, 157, 159, 183

Magesa, Laurenti, 6, 9
Magisterial Papalists, 103–4
Malawi, 199
male-female power relations, 154, 177. *See also* gender

Manja, 38
Mary Magdalene, 125
Mbuy-Beya, Bernadette, 124, 135
Mediterranean Meetings (2023), 207
mental health, 207, 212, 217
Middle Ages, 30–31, 43–44
Ministerial Collegialists, 103–4
missionaries, 6, 153, 214
missionary congregations, 167–68
Missionary Sisters of Charles de Foucauld, 224
Models of the Church, 98
Möhler, Johann Adam, 30–31
monarchies, 113, 146, 151
Montecel, Xavier, 106, 114
motherhood, 134–35
Mulieris dignitatem, 135
Muntu, 77
Mwoleka, Christopher, 75
mystical communion, 85–86, 93, 98

Nairobi, 6
National Associations of Sisters, 167
National Catholic Federation of Students, 211
natural resources, 7, 140
nepotism, 39, 76
Newman, John Henry, 30–31
Nganga wa kienyeji, 6
ngiga
  and communion, 48–49, 51
  defining, 47–48
  and dialogue, 60, 62–63
  lowering, 47–48, 63
  and palaver, 49–50, 54
  and ritual, 51–52, 63
Ngoinso, Chin, 131
Nigeria, 47, 55, 151
Nigerian Conference of Women Religious Against Human Trafficking, 140
Noceti, Serena, 85
Nolan, Albert, 210
nonverbal communication, 45, 58–59
Nostra aetate, 33
Nti bu ogaranya, 55
Ntu, 77
Nupe, 151
Nyumba Kumi Initiative, 140

Obirin meta, 77
Odama, John Baptist, 199
Oduyoye, Mercy Amba, 76
Ogbonnaya, Okechukwu, 75
Okure, Teresa, 134
O'Malley, John, 32
"On Dialogue with Unbelievers," 57
Openibo, Veronica, 178
orality, 4, 49, 80
Ordinary General Assembly (XV), 62
Ordinary General Assembly (XVI), 75, 115
ordination, 101, 118, 197

Oromo, 151
Oyeronke Oyewumi, 154

palaver
  and dialogue, 18–20, 49–52, 54
  and discernment, 15–17, 107–8, 223
  and Holy Spirit, 14–18
  and inclusivity, 16, 18
  and Ubuntu, 223
  as unbounded space, 17
palavra, 14, 49
Pan-African Catholic Theology and Pastoral Network, 214
pastoral care, 44, 84, 134, 197, 211, 213
patriarchal structures
  in African societies, 77, 103, 144, 154
  in church authority, 19, 60, 160
  in institutional model, 92
  and women, 76–77
patronage-clientage systems, 112–14
Paul (Apostle), 128, 130, 147, 185, 223
Paul VI, 31, 34
perichoresis, 222
Peter (Apostle), xiii, 104, 125, 146
pilgrim People, 32, 88
political anthropology, 143, 151
Pontifical Council for Culture, 181
Popper, Karl, 108–9

precolonial systems, 150–52
presbyters, 174, 188
pyramidal ecclesiology, 30–31, 33, 88, 90

Querida Amazonia, 35

Rahner, Karl, 23
Ratio Fundamentalis Institutionis Sacerdotalis, 118
rationalism, 108
Ratzinger, Joseph, 87. *See also* Benedict XVI
reciprocity, 70, 112, 141, 188
reconciliation, 17, 39, 140–41, 216, 222
redemption, 25, 68, 82, 128
reform, 30, 65, 89–90, 102, 105, 162, 170, 187, 198
Reformation, 44
Reid, Barbara, 127
Rejectionists, 103
relationality, xix–xx, 9, 13–14, 75, 99, 187
relativism, 87, 110
religious life, 136, 165–67, 172, 174, 179–81, 216
religious women, 121, 128–29, 131, 134, 136, 138–39, 141, 165, 182
resistance
  to change, 21, 42–43, 61
  civil, 177, 210
restorative justice, 39
roundtable approach, 45, 51, 59, 62

Ruth, 125–26
Rwanda, 37, 39, 151

SACBC. *See* Southern African Catholic Bishops Conference
Sacrosanctum concilium, 28, 34, 81
salvation, 41, 58, 67, 79, 82, 113, 185–86, 188, 192
SCCs. *See* Small Christian Communities
Schreiter, Robert, 21
Second Vatican Council. *See* Vatican II
sensus fidei, 19, 40, 89, 122, 129, 156–57, 221
servant-leadership model, 38, 74
Setiloane, Gabriel, 77
sexuality, 102–3, 115, 118, 135, 148. *See also* gender
Shema, 56, 80
silence, 1, 17, 159
Sinai covenant, 26
Sisters Leadership Development Initiative, 176
Small Christian Communities, 16, 76, 81, 121–22, 136–38, 140, 163–64, 193, 205, 212, 221, 223–24
social injustice, 96, 185, 203
social media, 61, 180–81
social teachings, 107, 180, 189, 221
Societies of Apostolic Life, 136, 169

solidarity, 14, 34, 37, 41, 99, 132–34, 137, 168, 205, 210, 212, 217, 222–23
South Africa, 39, 101, 199, 204, 209–11, 216
Southern African Catholic Bishops Conference, 204, 210
South Sudan, 139, 167, 199
Sudan, 139, 167
Swaziland, 151
Sybertz, Donald, 8
synaxis, 94, 107
synodality
  communal dimension, 5, 7, 19, 24, 63–64, 66, 93–94, 106, 157, 192–93
  constitutive dimension, xiv, xvi–xvii, 11, 173
  contributions of Pope Francis to, ix–x, 2, 34–35, 119
  and conversion, xi–xii, xvi, xxii, 1, 32, 42–44, 81, 158, 162
  and co-responsibility, xi, xix, 65, 91, 155–56, 185–86, 196–97
  and dialogue, xvi, 55–56, 62–63, 100–102, 106–9, 111, 114–15, 222
  and discernment, xvii, 11, 19–21, 93, 96, 99–101, 104, 106–7, 120, 221
  ethics of, 100–101, 104, 108, 118, 120

synodality *(continued)*
  and evangelization, 95, 107, 192
  goals of, xxi, 62
  importance of Holy Spirit in, 1–3, 7, 29, 31, 67–69
  and Ubuntu, 63, 221–22, 224
  Vatican II influence on, x–xii, 33, 44, 91–92
Synod Fathers, 81
Synod of Bishops, xi, xiv, 25, 31, 34, 75, 83, 95, 115, 149–50, 155, 161
Synod on Synodality, ix–xi, xx, 31, 39, 41, 46, 48, 51, 59, 62–63, 97–98, 149–50, 161–64, 171, 213
Synod on the Amazon (2019), 35
Synod on Youth (2018), 35
synodos, 94, 107

Talitha Kum project, 136
Tanzania, 139, 167
technology, 6, 62, 179–80, 213–15
Ten Houses Initiative. *See* Nyumba Kumi Initiative
Tertullian, 75
theopraxis, 25
Things Fall Apart (Achebe), 49
Tillich, Paul, 112
Tiv, 151
Towards an African Narrative Theology (Healey), 8

transparency, 116–17, 119, 160, 162, 176–77, 179, 182, 203
Trinity
  central to synodality, 24
  and communication, 47, 53–54, 66
  and communion, 54, 71, 74
  and community, 55, 68, 75–76, 79
  and co-responsibility, 183–84
  as egalitarian model, 76
  and relationality, 75
  and Ubuntu, 77–78, 222
  and Ujamaa, 75
Triune God, xix, 24, 39, 43, 66, 75–77, 79, 194
Tshitanini, 216
Tutu, Desmond, 221–22
typological approach, 87
Tzaneen Diocese, 216

Ubuntu
  and communion, 78, 222
  and community, 37, 107, 221–22
  and co-responsibility, 193
  and individualism, 108
  and palaver, 223
  and relationality, xx, 14
  and synodality, 63, 221–22, 224
  and Trinity, 77–78, 222
  and youth, 212
Uganda, 139, 151, 167, 199

Index

UISG. *See* International Union of Superiors General
Ujamaa, 63, 75
United Nations, 131, 148
Unsurpassed Great Spirit, 8
Urk-Coster, Eva van, 72
Uzukwu, Elochukwu, 38, 224

Vademecum, 100, 191, 194, 198
Vatican I, 103, 159, 161
Vatican II
  Ad gentes, 41
  and church authority, 32, 88, 103
  and collegiality, 161
  and communication, 46, 57
  and communion, 32–34, 86
  and co-responsibility, 189–90, 211
  on dialogue, 57
  Dignitatis humanae, 57
  and Dulles, 86
  Gaudium et spes, 57
  on Holy Spirit, 1
  influence on synodality, x–xii, 33, 44, 91–92
  and laity, xii, 34, 88, 189
  on liturgy, 81–82
  Lumen gentium, 35, 88
  and role of pope, 36
  on salvation, 69
  and Synod of Bishops, xiv, 25, 31
  on use of vernacular, 34
  and women, 172
Verbum domini, 66, 79, 81

vernacular languages, 34
Vita, Kimpa, 132
vows, 166–67, 172

Weber, Max, 144
West Cameroon, 153
woman, 22, 28
women, 17–19, 26–28, 40–42, 53–54, 61–62, 69–70, 101–2, 116–18, 121–40, 142, 147–50, 154, 158–60, 162–65, 168–71, 176–81, 197–98
  as cardinals, 130
  consecrated, 135, 139–40, 163–68, 170, 172–73, 175–77, 179–80, 182, 203
  and co-responsibility, 169–70, 182
  as deacons, 116
  and dialogue, 132–33, 162–63
  and dignity, 70–71, 129–31, 169, 171, 173, 177–78
  and discernment, 149–50, 175, 178
  and education, 154, 164, 173, 176, 178–81
  and evangelization, 139, 164, 167, 177
  and formation, 167, 174, 176, 180–81
  and Holy Spirit, 129, 150, 172
  inclusion of, 129, 148–50, 168, 170, 174, 178, 182

women *(continued)*
  and motherhood, 135
  and patriarchal structures, 76–77
  religious, 122–24, 127, 132, 141, 167, 175–76
  in scripture, 69–71, 126, 128–29
  theologians, 126, 131–33
  and Vatican II, 172
World Day of Social Communications, 56

Yoruba, 2, 77, 151
Young Christian Workers, 209
youth
  child-headed homes, 205
  consecrated women, 179–81
  and co-responsibility, 201
  demographics, 206, 217
  and discernment, 178, 208–9
  and education, 199, 205–6, 214
  empowering, 207–8, 210
  and evangelization, 181
  and formation, 204–5, 208, 211–12, 214–15
  inclusion of, 131, 148, 159, 217, 223
  and Jubilee Year, 216–18
  leadership programs, 211, 215
  Pope Francis and, 201–3, 206–8, 218–19
  and SCCs, 205–6
  and social media, 61–62, 181
  as transitional period, 179
  and Ubuntu, 212
  underprivileged, 212
  and women religious, 164, 179
youth groups, 210, 216–17
youth movements, 209–10, 212, 217, 223

Zambia, 139, 167
Zulu, 151